Old and New Generations in the 21st Century

The matter of simply living together, on both a global and a local scale, is complicated by the cultural, economic, religious, technological, and ecological challenges that we face in today's world. An educational–philosophical take on these complexities translates into reflections on, and attempts to answer, the questions that these challenges raise. How is the older generation to introduce a new generation into today's world and to 'prepare' it for the world to come? What sense can be given to such introduction and 'preparation'? Or in the more general terms of Friedrich Schleiermacher, 'What indeed does the older generation intend to do with the younger generation?'

The contributions in this book – originally presented during the 14th conference of the International Network of Philosophers of Education – address a broad range of philosophical issues related to the question of the educational relationship between generations today. The philosophical analysis offered by the authors in this volume creates openings, not only for other philosophers of education, but also for policy makers and practitioners. They serve as invitations, not only for further thinking but also for reconsidering educational practices; and most importantly, they generate new questions, for both today's and tomorrow's generations. This book was originally published as a special issue of *Ethics and Education*.

Stefan Ramaekers is an Associate Professor and the Head of the Laboratory for Education and Society (Research Group Education, Culture and Society), at KU Leuven, Belgium. His recent research has mainly focused on a critical investigation of the discourse of 'parenting' and the parent–child relationship, and on the 'pedagogical' significance of educational support. Recently, he has started collaborating with Dr. Naomi Hodgson on researching figurations of 'parenting' in cultural representations, such as film.

Old and New Generations in the 21st Century

Shifting Landscapes of Education

Edited by
Stefan Ramaekers

LONDON AND NEW YORK

First published 2017
by Routledge
2 Park Square, Milton Park, Abingdon, Oxon, OX14 4RN, UK

and by Routledge
711 Third Avenue, New York, NY 10017, USA

Routledge is an imprint of the Taylor & Francis Group, an informa business

© 2017 Taylor & Francis

All rights reserved. No part of this book may be reprinted or reproduced or utilised in any form or by any electronic, mechanical, or other means, now known or hereafter invented, including photocopying and recording, or in any information storage or retrieval system, without permission in writing from the publishers.

Trademark notice: Product or corporate names may be trademarks or registered trademarks, and are used only for identification and explanation without intent to infringe.

British Library Cataloguing in Publication Data
A catalogue record for this book is available from the British Library

ISBN 13: 978-1-138-24106-0

Typeset in Times
by diacriTech, Chennai

Publisher's Note
The publisher accepts responsibility for any inconsistencies that may have arisen during the conversion of this book from journal articles to book chapters, namely the possible inclusion of journal terminology.

Disclaimer
Every effort has been made to contact copyright holders for their permission to reprint material in this book. The publishers would be grateful to hear from any copyright holder who is not here acknowledged and will undertake to rectify any errors or omissions in future editions of this book.

Contents

Citation Information vii
Notes on Contributors ix

Introduction: Old and new generations in the 21st century:
shifting landscapes of education 1
Stefan Ramaekers

1. The authority of *Bildung*: educational practices in early childhood education 3
   Christiane Thompson

2. On (philosophical) suffering and not knowing one's way about (yet)
   in educational philosophy. Reply to Christiane Thompson 17
   Stefan Ramaekers

3. Postliberal education 23
   Robert A. Davis

4. Transition to parenthood and intergenerational relationships:
   the ethical value of family memory 36
   Monica Amadini

5. Exhausting the fatigue university: in search of a biopolitics of research 49
   Florelle D'Hoest and Tyson E. Lewis

6. Epistemic empathy in childrearing and education 61
   Kai Horsthemke

7. For the sake of peace: maintaining the resonance of peace and education 73
   Kanako Ide

8. Education in times of fast learning: the future of the school 84
   Jan Masschelein and Maarten Simons

9. Taking a chance: education for aesthetic judgment and the criticism of culture 96
   Naoko Saito

CONTENTS

10. Character education and the disappearance of the political 105
    Judith Suissa

11. Formal criteria for the concept of human flourishing: the first step in defending flourishing as an ideal aim of education 118
    Lynne S. Wolbert, Doret J. de Ruyter and Anders Schinkel

    Index 131

Citation Information

The chapters in this book were originally published in *Ethics and Education*, volume 10, issue 1 (March 2015). When citing this material, please use the original page numbering for each article, as follows:

Introduction
Old and new generations in the 21st century: shifting landscapes of education
Stefan Ramaekers
Ethics and Education, volume 10, issue 1 (March 2015) pp. 1–2

Chapter 1
The authority of Bildung: educational practices in early childhood education
Christiane Thompson
Ethics and Education, volume 10, issue 1 (March 2015) pp. 3–16

Chapter 2
On (philosophical) suffering and not knowing one's way about (yet) in educational philosophy. Reply to Christiane Thompson
Stefan Ramaekers
Ethics and Education, volume 10, issue 1 (March 2015) pp. 17–22

Chapter 3
Postliberal education
Robert A. Davis
Ethics and Education, volume 10, issue 1 (March 2015) pp. 23–35

Chapter 4
Transition to parenthood and intergenerational relationships: the ethical value of family memory
Monica Amadini
Ethics and Education, volume 10, issue 1 (March 2015) pp. 36–48

Chapter 5
Exhausting the fatigue university: in search of a biopolitics of research
Florelle D'Hoest and Tyson E. Lewis
Ethics and Education, volume 10, issue 1 (March 2015) pp. 49–60

CITATION INFORMATION

Chapter 6
Epistemic empathy in childrearing and education
Kai Horsthemke
Ethics and Education, volume 10, issue 1 (March 2015) pp. 61–72

Chapter 7
For the sake of peace: maintaining the resonance of peace and education
Kanako Ide
Ethics and Education, volume 10, issue 1 (March 2015) pp. 73–83

Chapter 8
Education in times of fast learning: the future of the school
Jan Masschelein and Maarten Simons
Ethics and Education, volume 10, issue 1 (March 2015) pp. 84–95

Chapter 9
Taking a chance: education for aesthetic judgment and the criticism of culture
Naoko Saito
Ethics and Education, volume 10, issue 1 (March 2015) pp. 96–104

Chapter 10
Character education and the disappearance of the political
Judith Suissa
Ethics and Education, volume 10, issue 1 (March 2015) pp. 105–117

Chapter 11
Formal criteria for the concept of human flourishing: the first step in defending flourishing as an ideal aim of education
Lynne S. Wolbert, Doret J. de Ruyter and Anders Schinkel
Ethics and Education, volume 10, issue 1 (March 2015) pp. 118–129

For any permission-related enquiries please visit:
http://www.tandfonline.com/page/help/permissions

Notes on Contributors

Monica Amadini is an Associate Professor in the Department of Pedagogy at the Università Cattolica del Sacro Cuore, Brescia, Italy. She researches and teaches on education for sustainability, social and intercultural education, and communication education. She is also an Advisor to the Table for Education for the city of Orzinuovi.

Robert A. Davis is a Professor of Religious and Cultural Education at the University of Glasgow, UK. His current research engages with the effectiveness of religious education, the cultural history of early childhood, and Scottish children's literature. Teacher education remains central to his interests, encouraging a wider exploration of professional values and professional formation more generally.

Doret J. de Ruyter is a Professor and Head of the Department of Research and Theory in Education at the Vrije Universiteit Amsterdam, The Netherlands. Her research interests include ethics and education, human flourishing, parental responsibility, professional ideals, and children's rights. She is an Assistant Editor of *Journal of Philosophy of Education*.

Florelle D'Hoest completed her PhD in 2016, awarded by the Department of Theory and History of Education at the Complutense University of Madrid, Spain. Researching pedagogical philosophy, her doctoral thesis was titled Apprenticeship: from Sign to Fiction. She is now a research fellow based in the same department.

Kai Horsthemke is an Associate Professor and holds the Chair for Philosophy and Systematic Pedagogics at the Katholische Universität Eichstätt-Ingolstadt, Germany. Apart from animal rights, his research interests include African philosophy, indigenous knowledge (indigenous science, ethnomathematics, ethnomusicology), and humane and environmental education.

Kanako Ide is an Associate Professor in the Faculty of Education at Soka University, Tokyo, Japan. Her research, focused on the modern educational philosophy of the USA, looks at democratic education, peace education, aesthetic education, social justice issues from a philosophical perspective, and questions of patriotism examined through a philosophical lens.

Tyson E. Lewis is an Associate Professor of Art Education, and Art Education Program Coordinator/Visual Art Studies, at the University of North Texas, Denton, TX, USA. His scholarship focuses on the intersections between a phenomenology of perception, biopolitics (as the politics of the body), and art education/aesthetic appreciation.

NOTES ON CONTRIBUTORS

Jan Masschelein is a Professor of Philosophy of Education at the Laboratory for Education and Society (Research Group Education, Culture and Society), at KU Leuven, Belgium. His research can be situated in the broad domain of the formation of educational theory, critical theory, social philosophy, and governmentality studies.

Stefan Ramaekers is an Associate Professor and the Head of the Laboratory for Education and Society (Research Group Education, Culture and Society), at KU Leuven, Belgium. His recent research has mainly focused on a critical investigation of the discourse of 'parenting' and the parent–child relationship, and on the 'pedagogical' significance of educational support. Recently, he has started collaborating with Dr. Naomi Hodgson on researching figurations of 'parenting' in cultural representations, such as film.

Naoko Saito is an Associate Professor in the Graduate School of Education at the University of Kyoto, Japan. Her area of research is American philosophy and pragmatism, and its implications for education. She has been working as a mediator in cross-cultural settings, especially between Japan and Anglo-American cultures, and more recently European cultures.

Anders Schinkel is an Assistant Professor of Philosophy of Education in the Department of Research and Theory in Education at the Vrije Universiteit Amsterdam, The Netherlands. His research interests include the aims of education; meaning in life, and the meaning of life; moral education; ethical theory; and the process philosophy of Alfred North Whitehead.

Maarten Simons is a Professor of education and educational policy at the Laboratory for Education and Society (Research Group Education, Culture and Society), at KU Leuven, Belgium. His research interests are educational policy and political philosophy, new forms of government(ality) in education, the public role of (higher) education, and current transformations of the university.

Judith Suissa is a Professor in the Philosophy of Education at the Institute of Education, University College London, UK. Her interests are in political and moral philosophy, with a particular focus on questions to do with the control of education, social justice, libertarian and anarchist theory, the role of the state, political education, and the parent–child relationship.

Christiane Thompson is a Professor in the Faculty of Educational Sciences, at the Department of Theory and History of Education at Goethe University, Frankfurt-am-Main, Germany. Her research looks at educational theory, cultural studies and education research, and how education intersects with power, culture, and language. She is also researching scepticism as educational and cultural practice.

Lynne S. Wolbert is a PhD student in the Department of Research and Theory in Education at the Vrije Universiteit Amsterdam, The Netherlands. The central focus of her research is on education for human flourishing, with attention to both the aims and the means of education and upbringing.

INTRODUCTION

Old and new generations in the 21st century: shifting landscapes of education

'No problem'. When Sharon Todd began her own INPE Conference Special Issue editorial (Todd 2014) with this Amharic idiom, she recalled the attitude of calm, generosity, hospitality, graciousness even, of our Ethiopian colleagues who hosted the 2012 INPE conference in Addis Ababa. In doing so, she also appealed to an experience shared by all participants. It seems particularly apt to recall these words here. 'No problem' was a phrase heard frequently during INPE's 14th Biennial Conference, held in Cosenza, Italy, from 20 to 23 August 2014. I feel quite confident when I say that I am gesturing at a shared experience among participants when I recall the sense of calmness, generosity, hospitality and graciousness shown by our Italian colleagues and hosts during the entire conference, whether confronted with problems that needed to be solved quickly or with changes in the programme that needed to be accommodated. This is of course not to level out cultural differences, different ways of doing things, varieties of 'styles' perhaps, which there obviously are, and for which I am glad that Wittgenstein gave us the concept of 'family resemblances'.

The theme of the conference, 'Old and new generations in the 21st century: shifting landscapes of education', was intended as an invitation to participants to bring philosophical discussion of education (broadly conceived) to bear on the (undeniably hard to tackle, let alone solve) issue of the relationship between generations in today's world, with all its complexities – economic, (inter-, cross-, trans-)cultural, religious, technological, ecological, etc. Complexities I would like to express in terms of the following questions: *How is an old generation to introduce a new generation into today's world and to 'prepare' it for the world to come? What sense can be given to such introduction and 'preparation'?* The subthemes of the conference theme indicate the many aspects addressed in relation to these questions: authority and responsibility in teacher–student/parent–child relationships today; the twenty-first century school and university as sites for democracy; the impact of new technologies for teaching and learning; changing conceptions of youth and adulthood; the neuro-scientific turn in education and childrearing; shifting boundaries between public and private dimensions of education and childrearing; education, childrearing and the search for a common world.

As these subthemes suggest, it was also my intention to open up other areas of education, broadly conceived, to (further) philosophical discussion, namely, the areas of childrearing and parenting. Discussions in philosophy of education – predominantly in the Anglo-Saxon tradition but also recently in its Continental counterpart – have tended to focus on education as formal education (in schools, universities, colleges) and hence on issues and topics such as teaching and learning, the curriculum, the teacher-student relationship, etc. Issues of raising children in families ('upbringing') have been left to other disciplines, such as developmental psychology, sociology and the like. I am glad to say that a good proportion of the papers presented at the conference explicitly, some exclusively, focused on aspects of the parent-child relationship and the general concept of childrearing.

The Conference Programme comprised 3 Keynote Addresses, 30 Concurrent Papers, 52 Working Papers and 9 Round Tables, and around 140 scholars participated. The Conference Programme can be accessed via the INPE website. The INPE Conference Special Issue is usually formed of the Keynote Papers and selected Concurrent Papers. Here you will find the Keynote Address by Christiane Thompson (Goethe-Universität, Frankfurt) and the Terence McLaughlin Memorial Lecture presented by Bob Davis (University of Glasgow). The third keynote speaker, Franco Cambi (University of Florence), decided not to have his paper included. The final decision on which Concurrent Papers to include here lied with me. All full papers submitted for the conference were subjected to a double-blind review by the members of the Programme Committee. I selected the papers included here on the basis of the comments and suggestions generated by the blind review process and of further comments and feedback solicited from the members of the Programme Committee after the conference. The selection of papers is a reflection of the diversity of topics addressed in relation to this year's conference theme and, though to a lesser degree, of the diversity of nationalities present at this conference. Most of all, however, I hope that this selection of articles will generate further discussions about the issues addressed by my fellow philosophers of education here. As the authors demonstrate, the complexities and intricacies of the educational aspects of the relation between old and new generations deserve careful theoretical and philosophical analysis. And – if I am permitted to speak in their name – they will concur, perhaps, with the appraisal that such analyses create openings (not just for other philosophers of education but also for policy makers and practitioners), function as invitations (not just for further thinking but also for reconsidering educational practices) and, clearly, also generate new sets of questions (for both today's and tomorrow's generations).

Stefan Ramaekers
Programme Chair INPE 2014, Belgium

Reference

Todd, S. 2014. "Introduction to INPE Special Issue: Passion, Commitment and Justice in Education." *Ethics and Education* 9 (1): 39–41.

The authority of *Bildung*: educational practices in early childhood education

Christiane Thompson

> This paper is concerned with the transformation of the field of early education in Germany. It poses the question whether these changes can be generally related to the German concept of *Bildung* – as denoting the children's autonomous activity of engaging themselves and the world. Investigating film material on practices of documentation in early education the paper seeks to clarify the impacts that *Bildung* has for the constitution of children's subjectivity. Does *Bildung* bring about a regime of individualization that obfuscates modes of sociality and being with? Are there alternative ways to interpret the modes of subjection in observation?

> The educator recounts that the boy had finished a picture, in her view, a very beautiful one. The other children also had finished drawing, the time of the pedagogical exercise was quite advanced. When getting started with cleaning up – the supervisor already had started to take pictures – the boy suddenly began to paint over his drawing with blue color. The educator recounts that she shortly felt the impulse to stop the boy, but then noticed that the boy had something else in mind. At the end, the houses were gone and only blue paint left. The educator approached the boy and soon it was clear that the boy had drawn the high water [last year the entire region around was set under water, C.T.]. The educator concludes that she would have hindered the boy in former times to paint over the houses [. . .].

This short sequence stems from field notes[1] from an early education setting. To be more exact: they are from the closing event of a supervision and training. The educator in the scene relates the story of a boy who paints over a beautiful picture with houses using plain blue color. The theme of the educator's reflection, here, is her urge to prevent the boy from doing so, and she recounts that in earlier times she would have definitely kept the boy from destroying the former drawing. However, the educational framework of early education has changed. The educator today has moved into a position of observation and later engages with the boy in order to find out about the blue color. The boy had 'processed' his experience of the flood, as the educator describes this.

 In this short sequence, the educator is picking up on a fundamental change that has been going on for the past 10–15 years in the field of early education in Germany. There has been a fundamental reformation and expansion of the field with initiatives in the context of professionalization and organizational development (see, e.g. Thole et al.

2008). However, the changes are also related to the understanding of education: the idea of *'Bildung'* has made its way into early education (see, e.g. Schäfer 2011). *'Bildung'*, this term with its very specific German social and political history (Bollenbeck 1994), is used to describe and emphasize the children's individual engagement with the world in an early education setting. Accordingly, in the field notes quoted above, the educator assumes that the child's activity to paint over the houses is in and of itself meaningful even though it implies the destruction of the already finished picture. This 'meaning bearing activity', however, requires the educator to reflect on her own comportment toward the child.

Let me now present a few thoughts on *Bildung* – since this concept marks a German singularity and is the educational–philosophical leading clue here. As Adorno has pointed out once in a very straightforward way: *'Bildung'* signifies a process that at once is to bring about cultivation or civilization (in the sense of refinement or adjustment) *and* criticism of the existing social order (Adorno 2004). *'Bildung'* thus stands for the promise of a good social order. Now, what runs as leading thread through the tradition of educational thought in the modern era is precisely the question of how to describe and conceive of this notion of *Bildung*.

Friedrich Nietzsche has, in his lectures 'On the Future of our Institutions of *Bildung*' during the beginning of the 1870s, also brought up this question: how to speak about the notion or the philosophy of *Bildung*? Nietzsche actually mentions that his audience will probably expect tables and available conclusions – and that he fears that he will not be able to provide them and thus leaving the audience most likely dissatisfied (Nietzsche 1988, KSA 1). He then suggests that what would be necessary would be a movement that follows the allegory of the cave: you start down there in the cave in the dark and limited space of that which appears to you. But then you have to make a painful way out in the realm of conceptualization and eventually return back down into the cave.

Even though I will not cling to the Platonic epistemology here, I think that Nietzsche's indirect reference to Plato, while contemplating on how to speak about the notion of *Bildung*, is helpful. An important aim of this paper is indeed to provide a setting for this question: how may one speak about the notion of *Bildung*? And I follow a Deleuzian intuition according to which the philosophical is to be affected by the non-philosophical (Thompson Forthcoming). In the following, the task to be performed will be the interplay between the philosophical and the non-philosophical in the context of *Bildung*. I will engage with the field of early education and simultaneously engage with questions of philosophical conceptualization.

In the first part of the paper, I will take a closer look at the constitution of educational reality in and through social practices – by referring to the works of Judith Butler and Theodore R. Schatzki. Here my aim is to set up a conceptual framework that allows me to analyze social practices in early education. In the second part of the paper, I will turn toward a camera-ethnographic study that has been undertaken in an early education institution (Mohn and Hebenstreit-Müller 2007). This study shows newly instituted practices of 'observation' by the educators. I will take a closer look at these practices and describe how they 'configure' the educational realm, including educational relations, in a particular way. In the third part of the paper, I will compare this analysis to recent works on the transformation of education. Primarily I will take up Jan Masschelein's and Norbert Ricken's criticism of *Bildung* (Masschelein and Ricken 2003). In the fourth and final part of the paper, I will suggest an alternative route to think about *Bildung*.

OLD AND NEW GENERATIONS IN THE 21ST CENTURY

1. The constitution of education in and through practices

The notion of 'social practices' has strongly shaped the ways of approaching and understanding the ways we look at the 'educational world'. The bundle of theories under the headline 'practice theories' has in common that they view social reality not as the effect of the subject's rationally calculated intentions. Rather these theories, uniting very different figures such as Dewey, Heidegger, the later Wittgenstein, focus on situated corporality and pre-reflective activities in which we take part (Schatzki, Knorr Cetina, and von Savigny 2001). Correspondingly, the 'educational world' is captured in and through this 'participation'. It is, according to Theodore R. Schatzki, the 'sets of sayings and doings' that disclose the making of the educational world – and not the subject's conceptual or philosophical orientation.

In his works of practice theory, Theodore R. Schatzki has described the constitution of social order as arrangement of people and artifacts in practices (Schatzki 2001, 53). The idea, here, is that meaning and identity result from the relational situatedness of all participants within the practices. This is to say that people and artifacts gain their identity and meaning *within* the arrangement in and of practices. For Schatzki, this identity constitution includes the realm of normativity: norms and values do not spring from convictions and beliefs; instead they are formed within practices. There are 'teleoaffectice structures' (as Schatzki notes combining Heideggerian and Aristotelian intuitions) that are to be considered as one aspect of the activities and arrangement in social practices:

> Implicit in my discussion in the previous section is the fact that when people participate in a particular practice their actions express understandings, rules, teleologies, and affectivities that number among those organizing the practice. This means that what makes sense to them to do is determined – at least in part – by these phenomena. [...] In any event, when people carry on a practice, the organization of the practice is partly responsible for what they do and, thus, for the orders they effect. (Schatzki 2001, 54)

Theories of practice describe the educational realm as enactment in and through practices. Included in this enactment are norms and attachments, values and objectives. Something like 'educational responsibility' is then associated with the practices and their teleoaffective embeddedness, e.g. in relation to the modes of interaction, such as 'care' in early education. Certainly, this does not negate the existence of convictions, values, and the like. However, practice theories criticize 'worldless subjectivity' and the idea of the subject as the foundation of knowledge – as Descartes had famously proposed.

In our research group we have followed Butler (1997) and her theory of subjection in order to disclose the normative dimension of the educational world as it is continuously re-instituted in practices. According to Butler we become subjects by being called into a situation and activity. By way of this 'interpellation', Butler argues following Althusser and Foucault in 'The psychic life of power', the subject and power relations are generated, disclosing possibilities of becoming and action. In the midst of this effect of subject and power, *norms of recognition* are constituted or (re-)instituted. Butler describes these norms in terms of categories and names that are not of the subject's own making (Butler 1997, 20). In other words, the subject is bound to striving to its existence via these other norms.

By looking at practices in such a way, we are put on the verge of the coming to being of the social. In other words, my practice-theoretical view (following Schatzki and Butler) shapes my empirical gaze in what is to come in this discussion. At the same time it captures – in a programmatic fashion – the drifting thrust between the philosophical and the non-philosophical: practices have to be made intelligible, they have to be re-constituted, also in order to open them up to elaboration. As a consequence, the range of *'Bildung'* in early education has to be disclosed via the *practices* in the field of study rather than by conceptual ideas or theoretical coherence. Furthermore, the analysis gains its richness and quality by studying concrete practices of the field. In the following I will engage with practices of observation. For various reasons, they represent an interesting and substantial focus in this regard.

First of all, today 'observation' is conceived as one of the most important activities for educators in the area of early education. This can be concluded from the uncountable number of training programs that are currently offered in the field.[2] 'Observation' has also been described a crucial activity in the so-called *'Bildungspläne'*, the programs of *Bildung*, which have been instituted obligingly in all the German states within the past 15 years. These programs[3] emphasize the importance of observation as well as documentation with regard to an ever-active child who engages independently with its surrounding.

In our research we have found that practices of observation include an all-encompassing technology to shape, organize, and authorize educational subjectivity[4]: A closer look at 'observation manuals' for educators,[5] for example, shows that observation is not adequately described by a set of rules supposedly providing an *objective* account of what the child is doing. These manuals on observation, on the contrary, include normative and affective dimensions of education – or put more precisely – educational aims and purposes, ideals of educational relations and so forth. Consequently, it makes sense to draw attention to 'observation' in order to clarify the constitution of the 'educational world' in this field. This brings me to another interesting point.

The notion of observation, as it is currently present in early education, forms somewhat a contrast to the competence orientation. As you know, many educational settings or fields currently undergo multiple forms of standardization or canonization. It is remarkable that alongside the rigorous diagnostic gaze of competence, there are strong claims for observation to be found as essentially *open procedure*. This is to say that children may not be observed using pre-given measures or standards: Observation, here, requires open and unprejudiced encounters. It is not clear beforehand what there is to be seen or what should be seen. In view of this indeterminacy, it is quite interesting to take a look at *what educators eventually see* and how this differs to competence-oriented procedures.

There is a third reason why I am engaging with observation – and that is: observation is itself very laden from a philosophical point of view. Think about the etymology of *theorein*, *theoria*, and thus the strong directedness of Western philosophy to build itself around modes of vision, of perspective, of bringing into view. With the observation of observational practices, we are in the middle of a complex realm of knowledge production[6] and reflection – with the camera-ethnographic[7] material.

Let me for now pose some guiding questions for the following analysis. I will investigate the camera-ethnographic material focusing on: how does the practice of observation form the educational subject? What is reasonable, meaningful, and significant when observing the child's activity? What are the limits of this activity? How is education or *Bildung* conceived in this context?

I have chosen an ethnographic research study, a camera-ethnography, conducted by Bina Elisabeth Mohn and Sabine Hebenstreit-Müller (Mohn and Hebenstreit-Müller 2007). This study fits the purpose very well because it is itself indebted to reflect on the educational gaze.[8] The camera-ethnographic video-DVD is entitled 'Kindern auf der

Spur', which literally means 'Following the path of children'. The camera-ethnography makes 'observation' very accessible in its sayings and doings. Following Geertz' question 'What the hell is going on here?!' (Geertz 1983), the camera-ethnography captures the situatedness of educational practices. The camera participates on the scene, it provides viewpoints on the border of the field, an 'attending gaze'. The camera-ethnographic research by Bina Mohn presents subjects in their relatedness to other subjects, in their involvement with others, including the camera.[9]

2. *'Bildung'* – in and under observation

So far I have argued that it is necessary to investigate the social practices if one wants to clarify the education and its boundaries in a particular field (here early education). From the viewpoint of social practices, the formation of educational subjectivity is related to the norms of recognition within these practices. For the field of early education, practices of observation form a substantial and thought-provoking object of study because the technology of observation entails an *educational initiation* – i.e. ideas how to constitute at all a pedagogical view or attitude. The camera-ethnography 'Following the path of children' is used to recapitulate this process. The following video sequence has the title 'The educator as observer'.

The sequence shows several scenes from an early education center, mainly outside scenes with children 'being active'. The camera focuses on the children and their activities. However, it also focuses on the educators on the scene who are busy with observing and documenting the children's activities. I will present a few stills in order to highlight the correlative logic of children's activity and educators' observational practice.

The film still shown in Figure 1 is somewhat paradigmatic for the entire sequence: there are two children present in the scene being involved with some activity, here: the swings. One child is sitting on the swing, not swinging, but exploring the chain while sitting on the swing and talking to the other child. The other child is approaching the second swing. The educator is present in the scene but not taking part in the activity itself. Instead, he remains literally at the border of the swinging area, observing the children and taking notes. The observing camera is *providing a frame* of this scene with the children at the center and the educator being placed at the side of the scene. Put differently, the camera as second-order observer emphasizes the activity of observation and confirms that there is something to see. What is there to see here?

Figure 1. The practice of observation (Mohn, in: Mohn and Hebenstreit-Müller 2007, Chap. 9, 1'40"). Reproduced with permission of Bina Elisabeth Mohn.

Figure 2. What is there to see here? (Mohn, in: Mohn and Hebenstreit-Müller 2007, Chap. 9, 0′24″). Reproduced with permission of Bina Elisabeth Mohn.

The sequence precisely suggests this question at the beginning (Figure 2): 'What is there to see here?' As one can see (again), there are several children present in the scene – involved in their own activities. In the foreground, on the left-hand side, there are two children engaged with a mono-swinger. In the back of the frame there is a group with at least 16 adults standing behind a tree and thus somewhat separated from the scene (unlike the camera). Some of the adults are looking into the playing area. From the sequence it becomes clear that they are visitors who want to observe the children. *They come to see what there is to see in the early education center.*

When one of the educators is interviewed later on, the camera will precisely pick up on this visiting observation. The young man who is asked about observation describes what it means to observe the children. His main point is the distinction between observation and interpretation. Observation is supposed to remain close to neutral and action-oriented description, i.e. without judging the children's activities. When making this point, the camera suddenly goes over to the very example that the interviewed observer is giving. So the viewer of the film is transformed into an observer by (1) receiving instructions on observation and (2) by witnessing the children's activities. The camera suggests a point of view from which the adults are observed. Having been interviewed, the educator makes this point of view explicit – he *proposes* observation.

What is there to see here? This question can only be treated or answered when taking up the standpoint of observation. The standpoint of observation, however, requires the adult to consider themselves as *separate* from the scene. In a way, the adults from the video sequence are in a very general way 'visitors'. They enter into a scene that is already taking place: the children's activity (which is just to be described, not interpreted). The children appear as engaged in their own activity – this is where the idea of self-directed *Bildung* comes into play.

Figure 3 shows a picture that has become very common in early education institutions: There are folders with collections of documented observations. As you can see here, the folders carry the names and the pictures of the individual children. As Sandra Koch and Gesine Nebe have shown with respect to the so-called learning stories,[10] these folders can be regarded as inscriptions (Latour) of *Bildung* (K. Koch and Nebe 2013); for in these practices of documentation the written material becomes the sign of the individual's *Bildung*. The documentation is about the production of educationally relevant and individual knowledge, a knowledge that transgresses the situation of its origin.[11] In

OLD AND NEW GENERATIONS IN THE 21ST CENTURY

Figure 3. Documentation folders (Mohn, in: Mohn and Hebenstreit-Müller 2007, Chap. 9, 2'33"). Reproduced with permission of Bina Elisabeth Mohn.

conclusion, observation and documentation constitute practices in which the educators become *mediators* of the children's processes of *Bildung*. This means that the educators' attention remains centered around the children's activity (being a 'visitor' on the scene).

Over the course of the stills, it becomes more and more evident that the children's ongoing activity forms the center of the attention. The educators are 'visitors' on the scene – literally but also figuratively. This resonates very much with how *Bildung* is presented in the state programs. In the state of Thuringia, e.g. children are presented as building 'their own hypotheses and theories of the world'.[12] Their activity has its own dignity which is also expressed in the vocabulary.

In the video sequence, the educators appear as 'set back' from the scene. The children's activity lies uncompromised in the center. It requires all the attention of the educator who is generally not interfering or engaging in the activity. The educators remain at a distance, at the border of the scene. The educators' relation to the children is mediated through observation, i.e. the observation is the medium of the educational relation. Put differently, the educator does not play an *explicit* role in the children's activity. The implicit role of the educator is, in turn, to make the children visible as '*bildsam*', as 'subjects of *Bildung*'.

This is where the practice of filming can itself be read as a *pedagogization* of the scene: The beginning phrase 'What is there to see here?' is itself provoked by the camera angle. The view of the camera is not something simple or natural but a particular view suggested to the adults. The subtitle of the video is 'the school of gaze', i.e. the camera-ethnographic material presents itself as an opportunity to school one's own researching gaze. I am particularly interested in the position of observation as the medium of *Bildung*. The educator's responsibility is fulfilled with the observation and documentation of the individual's engagement with the world. It appears as if the camera had been looking for instances of *individual and unforeseeable encounters*: the swing not used for swinging (Figure 1) or the mono-swinger that is moving a tub of blue plastic (Figure 2). The educators are placed in the scene in order to witness these unique situations. It has been mentioned before that this has become the educators' true responsibility – or, put differently, the authority of educational practice resides within the children's self-directed activity or *Bildung* – like in the picture painted blue mentioned earlier.

How do these observational practices shape educational relations? One can already infer from the video sequence that practices of observation assign the educators the position of attending as well attentive inactivity. The adults' and children's presence differs even though there is a strong attention toward the children's doings. Are we witnessing, here, *Bildung* as a regime of individualization and coming along with this: an increasing decomposition of educational relations?

3. *Bildung* as regime of individualization?

In a paper from 2003, Jan Masschelein and Norbert Ricken have posed the question: 'Do we still need the concept of Bildung?' (Masschelein and Ricken 2003). In this paper the authors suggest that *Bildung* is to be viewed as part of a particular power-apparatus (following Foucault). To be more precise, they view '*Bildung*' as a particular crossing point of power relations in which the individuals start to consider their lives as dynamic enterprises, as individual enterprises that are to be carried out in an autonomous fashion:

> The establishment of the idea of *Bildung* can inform an analysis of the construction and establishment of a "government of individualization" or of an "apparatus of individuality" as a power mechanism which still operates. Foucault's concept of "apparatus" ("*dispositive*") attempts to embrace different domains which are not separated methodologically and by discipline, but are jointly encompassed as theoretical and practical conditions. (Masschelein and Ricken 2003, 147)

Referring to Foucault, Masschelein and Ricken direct their attention to how human subjectivity is formed in the light of the humanist notion of '*Bildung*'. In their view '*Bildung*' goes hand in hand with specific networks or relations of power. These relations provoke subject formations in terms of individuality or individual becoming. The authors discuss a governance of individualization or an apparatus of individuality.

This view of *Bildung* seems to be quite translatable to the field of early education (as presented here). It has been precisely shown above that *Bildung* appears as a kind of crossing point for theoretical and practical aspects, i.e. the theoretical description of observation that is distinguished from interpretation. I have also mentioned practices of gaze and practices of how to represent these practices, e.g. in camera-ethnography. Certainly, there are far more aspects to be taken into consideration. Sandra Koch and Gesine Nebe have, e.g. discussed the increasing significance of social research methodology in practices of observation (S. Koch and Nebe 2013). As you can see the 'will to truth' brings forth 'new technologies' of 'making sense of a situation'.

In the text mentioned above as well as in other publications, Masschelein and Ricken emphasize the 'immunizing' side of *Bildung* and its regime of individualization. According to the authors, this regime obfuscates certain modes of human existence: being-togetherness or sociality (Masschelein and Ricken 2003, 150). Bringing into view one last time the film sequence it is interesting to see that – while the observed scenes often show more than one child in action – the folders are folders for one/each individual. Thus, despite the complex sociality and mediatedness, the documentation ultimately relates to the *Bildung* or *self-directed and individual activity of the single child*. In this regard, one could indeed ask whether the prominence of '*Bildung*' in early education obfuscates forms of sociality and togetherness. It is '*Bildung*' that appears as the natural ground for the individual's experience and this is also why it is the major task or responsibility of the educator to observe and document it.

However, what speaks against the interpretation of early education or *Bildung* in the light of Masschelein's and Ricken's critique is the complex relational constellation within the early educational practice of observation. Masschelein and Ricken have argued that *Bildung* marks a governance of individualization because it perpetually requires the individual to engage anew with the world. However, the matter is different here: '*Bildung*' appears as something that is always already taking place in the children's activities. Here, the natural quality imposes a 'claim'[13] on the side of the educator: to authenticate *Bildung*, to witness the unique process, and to give it presence within the institution of early education. In this regard, there is a shift in the power constellation: the authority of *Bildung* does not require the individual to govern itself in the light of future possibilities. Rather, the educator is called into the relation toward the children's authoritative and self-evident processes of *Bildung*.

The position of observation entails an indissoluble double paradox: there is the paradox of non-interference versus representation *and* the paradox of confirmation and uncertainty. The *first paradox* refers to the educator's particular presence on the scene. S/he serves as the 'representative' of *Bildung*; s/he is writing down *what is there to see* (this is the purpose of description). At the same time, the educator is not to affect the situation to be documented: neither on the level of activity (engagement) nor at the level of documentation (interpretation). The *second paradox* refers to the continuous call to re-assure the observer's viewpoint. There are always new activities to be expected from the children. This is why the self-confidence of observation simultaneously requires openness.

The double paradox brings about a powerful constitution of the educational subject: the totality of educational responsibility constitutes a continuous field of tension with regard to the self-directedness and dignity of the children's activity.[14] To summarize the authority of *Bildung* brings about a very particular form of educational relation. It is a relation that has *Bildung* at its center or point of reference (and not, e.g. the experience that one makes with the other). In this context the educator becomes the (dependent) 'origin' of educational knowledge which is collected and validated in and through observation (see Jergus, Koch, and Thompson 2013, 754). In the self-description of the field of early education, this orientation toward the child of *Bildung* is presented as the path of professional development, the path of resource orientation and educational confidence.

Certainly, it would be interesting to investigate in how far the development that has been sketched out here is related to the debates surrounding the childhood studies and sociologies of childhood (Alanen 2001): there has been a considerable criticism in this area of research concerning the idea of *generation*. The main point of this criticism refers to the dependency and deficiency of childhood when looking at it from the point of view of a 'new generation'. To consider children as 'not yet being able' overlooks their *original agency*. I cannot expand on this discussion here, but it seems that the reference to *Bildung* has certainly promoted the idea of 'original agency'.[15]

4. Alterity and the withdrawal of *Bildung*

How are we to judge the development in the field of early education? Is this not exactly what thinkers such as Wilhelm von Humboldt and Friedrich Schiller were having in mind when talking about *Bildung* as world disclosure, *Welteröffnung*? Humboldt described *Bildung* as the most unhindered, free, and general interaction between ego and world – and as a matter of fact, he was very explicit that this interaction should not be compromised by social regulations and expectations. Even Adorno picks up on this view in his 'Theory of *Halbbildung*' in 1959, even though the criticism of *Bildung* is presented as a fundamental problem or question (Adorno 2004, 103). One could argue that the practices of observation as presented and analyzed in this paper somewhat pick up on the classical concept of *Bildung*: observation is presented in terms of witnessing the singular presence when children interact with the world.

Or is it more appropriate to follow the line of argumentation provided by Jan Masschelein and Norbert Ricken? They have pointed out the regime of individualization. In their view, *Bildung* itself suggests a very particular subject formation, a subject formation that neglects or obfuscates certain forms of sociality. Here, the individual is required to have his or her own development in mind, a development that has to be organized as a 'story of *Bildung*'. In relation to observational practice, one could indeed present the observing educators as *placeholders for individuality*: observation produces an *aura* surrounding the children's activity. It requires the educator to become the discoverer of the children's individuality.

However, even though both interpretations sound reasonable and justifiable, I would like to take a different route at the end of this paper. In doing so, it is necessary to return to the notion of social practices and their continuous reshaping[16] of social orders in these practices as thinkers such as Butler or Laclau and Mouffe have pointed out:

> The multiformity of the social cannot be apprehended through a system of mediations, nor the "social order" understood as an underlying principle. There is no sutured space peculiar to "society", since the social itself has no essence. (Laclau and Mouffe 1985, 96)

This quote denotes the non-identical side of practices and social reality. This, however, brings me back to the role and necessity of philosophy or educational philosophy. The analysis of social practices ought to be complemented by that which escapes the intelligibility of practices, the impossibility of fulfilling representation. Embarking once again with the camera-ethnography, I would like to suggest that *Bildung* and the significance of educational philosophy have something in common: namely, to warrant difference and alterity.

Figure 4 shows a still from the video sequence in which an observer and a child are both sitting on a wall, turned toward the same side. The educator is busy with making notes. The child comes to sit next to the observer. She is mostly staring in one direction, once in a while dangling her feet, generally though looking absent-minded and unimpressed by the surrounding scene. How should we describe what is going on here? Should we consider this scene as an interruption of observation or as a refiguration of the scene by boredom?

Figure 4. Limits of observation? (Mohn, in: Mohn and Hebenstreit-Müller 2007, Chap. 9, 0′41″). Reproduced with permission of Bina Elisabeth Mohn.

Does this scene 'displace' the notion of the 'child' as active individual? This scene offers a possibility of viewing observation differently – the standstill of disclosure, the openness of discernment, the impossibility of identification. Instead of assuming a judgmental stance toward '*Bildung*' and the practice of 'observation', it is crucial to complement the analysis of practices by *the possibilities of how things offer themselves for a different view.*[17]

The notion of *Bildung* becomes prominent, here, in the systematic void in world disclosure separating the subject from the fulfillment of experience, of its gaze. This provokes a different view of observational practice – by the educator and also by the camera (i.e. the spectator's and the researcher's view). Is it possible to leave the following questions partly open or unanswered: 'What there is to see?' What are the modes of not-answering that we can think of? Are there any limits to the confidence of 'observation' in early education? What are the modes and strategies that turn educational practices in something definite and finite? Are we to characterize the educational(–philosophical) gaze as a point of view that leaves alterity in play? How would such a gaze alter the figure drawn above concerning the educational relation?

I have argued here not to place *Bildung* in an identificatory construction, as a title for a certain type of behavior, knowledge, etc. (Thompson 2009). Rather the limits of identification and thus the limits of our experience are seen as an important reference point to shift the views and positions suggested in the social realm. In my view, this is the significance of educational–philosophical endeavor. To be sure, this endeavor might bring about challenges. Following Butler, the work on these limits can imply shifts within the norms of recognition and thus the possibilities of de-identification. Concluding this paper, I suggest that what is characteristic for the realm of *Bildung* and for educational relations is the emergence of new situations that *outgrow* former situations or go beyond them, e.g. go beyond the view of the child as continuous origin of individual activity. This might slow down or liberate our gaze, bring forth a different stance toward the situation at hand, and thus toward the claims posed on us.

Acknowledgments

This text has been presented as a *keynote* at the 2014 INPE Conference in Cosenza, Italy. I express my gratitude to Stefan Ramaekers for helpful comments and lively debates. The text has been complemented by some references and shortened cautiously in order to preserve the style of the presentation.

Disclosure statement

No potential conflict of interest was reported by the author.

Notes

1. These field notes stem from the research project 'Authorizing the Educational Subject' that I carry out together with Dr Kerstin Jergus, funded by the *German Research Foundation* (DFG). The field notes were written by Sandra Koch. Over the course of the paper I draw continuously on this research. The members of this research group are: Kerstin Jergus, Sandra Koch, Sabrina Schröder, Pauline Starke, and myself. In my view, it is this community that fosters research, makes it productive. I am indebted to this community in terms of the path of thinking developed here.
2. There are a number of early childhood centers that require their personnel to having participated in such a training, to being able to execute a high quality 'observation'.

At this stage several observation programs and conceptions are available. Cloos and Schulz (2011) have issued one of the first book editions in Germany to discuss the different procedures of observing children. An historical account of child observation has been given by Tervooren (2008) who shows the relation to the idea of development and to normalization.

3. I use the term 'program' rather than 'curriculum' because these programs are not so much about what is to be the object of learning or *Bildung* but rather about *how to see* children in their learning activities.
4. Koch and Schulz speak about a 'style of knowledge production' and discuss the educational theory–practice relationship from here (Koch and Schulz 2014).
5. See Jergus, Koch, and Thompson (2013).
6. This has been brought up in a recent book that combines observation and reflection: see de Boer and Reh (2012).
7. The camera-ethnographer Bina Elisabeth Mohn has precisely elaborated on these practices of view (Mohn 2013).
8. It should be emphasized that the analysis here is not about a professional critique of the educators in the material nor of the camera-ethnography. Rather, the ethnographical gaze is 'extended', as it were, in order to analyze how viewing is constituted.
9. This notion of research certainly contradicts the claims of standardization that precisely attempts to cut the subject's relation to the 'object of research' (see Mohn 2010b, 2013). Furthermore, Sabine Reh has shown how the reactions to the camera in the field are productive for the research (Reh 2014).
10. The learning stories are narratives by educators in the form of a story on children. The story is essentially addressed to the child as well as the parents. Most recently the conception of learning stories, originally deriving from New Zealand, has been extended to an all-encompassing pedagogical approach.
11. K. Koch and Nebe (2013) refer to Latour's concept of 'cascades' in order to describe the re-formations and re-arrangements of this knowledge.
12. This quote comes from the program of *Bildung* in Thuringia. Compare also the interpretation by Kerstin Jergus and myself (Jergus and Thompson 2011).
13. S. Ramaekers and J. Suissa have explicated the various meanings of 'claims' in their book on parenting (Ramaekers and Suissa 2012).
14. In the ethnographic fieldwork within the project 'Authorizing the Educational Subject' we have witnessed in seminars for training educators this power-productive double paradox. Educators are supposed to manage *every* task of observation and at the same time they can *never* be sure to have mastered it.
15. What does that mean for the relation of the generations? This question has been of major interest to the INPE conference. I guess it will refer us to the concept of 'generation' to give it more educational–philosophical attention.
16. Some practice theorists such as Bourdieu emphasize more strongly the hysteretic logic of social practices. For a comparison of Butler and Bourdieu in this regard, see Jergus, Schumann, and Thompson (2012).
17. This route is precisely taken up by Bina Mohn, the maker of the camera-ethnography, who describes camera-ethnography in the context of '*bildendes Forschen*' ('visual research'; Mohn 2010a, 154).

References

Adorno, Th. W. 2004. "Theorie der Halbbildung [Theory of Halbbildung]." In *Soziologische Schriften I*, edited by Th. W. Adorno, 93–121. Frankfurt/Main: Suhrkamp.
Alanen, L. 2001. "Explorations in Generational Analysis." In *Conceptualizing Child–Adult-Relations*, edited by L. Alanen and B. Mayall, 11–22. London: Routledge.
Bollenbeck, G. 1994. *Bildung und Kultur: Glanz und Elend eines deuschen Deutungsmusters*. Frankfurt/Main: Insel.
Butler, J. 1997. *The Psychic Life of Power*. Stanford, CA: Stanford University Press.

Cloos, P., and M. Schulz, eds. 2011. *Kindliches Tun beobachten und dokumentieren*. Weinheim: Beltz & Juventa.

de Boer, H., and Sabine Reh, eds. 2012. *Beobachtung in der Schule. Beobachten lernen*. Wiesbaden: Springer VS.

Geertz, C. 1983. *Dichte Beschreibung. Beiträge zum Verstehen kultureller Systeme*. Frankfurt/Main: Suhrkamp.

Jergus, K., S. Koch, and C. Thompson. 2013. "Darf ich dich beobachten? Zur 'pädagogischen Stellung' von Beobachtung in der Frühpädagogik." *Zeitschrift für Pädagogik* 59 (5): 743–761.

Jergus, K., I. Schumann, and C. Thompson. 2012. "Autorität und Autorisierung." In *Judith Butler: Pädagogische Lektüren*, edited by N. Ricken and N. Balzer, 207–224. Wiesbaden: Springer VS.

Jergus, K., and C. Thompson. 2011. "Eine theoretische und empirische Analyse." In *Erkenntnispolitik und die Konstruktion pädagogischer Wirklichkeiten*, edited by R. Reichenbach, N. Ricken, and H.-Ch Koller, 103–122. Paderborn: Schöningh.

Koch, S., and G. Nebe. 2013. "Beobachtung – Dokumentieren – Bildung entdecken?" Conference paper presented at the "Multipluritrans 2013", University of Luxemburg, unpublished manuscript.

Koch, K., and G. Nebe. 2013. "Wie das Kind geschrieben wird. Lerngeschichten als Inszenierungspraxis in Kindertageseinrichtungen." In *Inszenierung und Optimierung des Selbst. Zur Analyse gegenwärtiger Selbsttechnologien*, edited by R. Mayer, C. Thompson, and M. Wimmer, 111–136. Wiesbaden: Springer VS.

Koch, S., and M. Schulz. 2014. "Im Erkenntnisstil des Okularen." . Paper presented at the conference Von der 'Erziehungswirklichkeit' zur Empirie des Pädagogischen, Göttingen, September 30–Oktober 1.

Laclau, E., and Ch. Mouffe. 1985. *Hegemony and Socialist Strategy*. London: Verso.

Masschelein, J., and N. Ricken. 2003. "Do We Still need the Concept of Bildung?" *Educational Philosophy and Theory* 35 (2): 139–154.

Mohn, B. E. 2010a. "Dichtes Zeigen beginnt beim Drehen. Durch Kameraführung und Videoschnitt ethnographische Blicke auf Unterrichtssituationen und Bildungsprozesse entwerfen." In *"Auf unsicherem Terrain". Ethnographische Forschung im Kontext des Bildungs- und Sozialwesens*, edited by F. Heinzel, W. Thole, P. Cloos, and S. Köngeter, 153–169. Wiesbaden: Springer VS.

Mohn, B. E. 2010b. "Zwischen Blicken und Worten: Kamera-ethnographische Studien." In *Frühkindliche Lernprozesse verstehen: Ethnographische und phänomenologische Beiträge zur Bildungsforschung*, edited by G. Schäfer and R. Staege, 207–231. Weinheim: Juventa.

Mohn, B. E. 2013. "Differenzen zeigender Ethnographie. Blickschneisen und Schnittstellen der Kamera-Ethnographie." In *Soziale Welt. Themenheft Visuelle Soziologie*, edited by B. Schnettler and A. Baer. Vol. 1–2, 171–189.

Mohn, B. E., and S. Hebenstreit-Müller. 2007. *Kindern auf der Spur. Kita-Pädagogik als Blickschule*. Kamera-Ethnographische Studien des Pestalozzi-Fröbel-Hauses Berlin I. DVD. Göttingen: IVE.

Nietzsche, F. 1988. "Die Geburt der Tragödie." In *Kritische Studienausgabe Band 1*, edited by Giorgio Colli, Mazzino Montinari. Munich: dtv (cit. KSA).

Ramaekers, R., and J. Suissa. 2012. *The Claims of Parenting*. London: Springer.

Reh, S. 2014. "Die Kamera und der Dritte. Videographie als Methode kulturwissenschaftlich orientierter Bildungsforschung." In *Interferenzen. Perspektiven kulturwissenschaftlicher Bildungsforschung*, edited by C. Thompson, K. Jergus, and G. Breidenstein, 30–50. Weilerswist: Velbrück.

Schäfer, G. E. 2011. *Bildungsprozesse im Kindesalter: Selbstbildung, Erfahrung und Lernen in der frühen Kindheit*. Weinheim: Beltz & Juventa.

Schatzki, T. R. 2001. "Practice Minded Orders." In *The Practice Turn in Contemporary Theory*, edited by Th. R. Schatzki, K. Knorr Cetina, and E. von Savigny, 50–63. London: Routledge.

Schatzki, Th. R., K. Knorr Cetina, and E. von Savigny. 2001. *The Practice Turn in Contemporary Theory*. London: Routledge.

Tervooren, A. 2008. "'Auswickeln', Entwickeln und Vergleichen: Kinder unter Beobachtung." In *Ganz normale Kinder. Heterogenität und Standardisierung kindlicher Entwicklung*, edited by H. Kelle and A. Tervooren, 41–58. Weinheim: Juventa.

Thole, W., H. Rossbach, M. Fölling-Albers, and R. Tippelt. 2008. *Bildung und Kindheit. Pädagogik der Frühen Kindheit in Wissenschaft und Lehre*. Opladen: Budrich.

Thompson, C. 2009. *Bildung und die Grenzen der Erfahrung. Randgänge der Bildungsphilosophie*. Paderborn: Schöningh.

Thompson, C. Forthcoming. "The Philosophy of Education as the Economy and Ecology of Pedagogical Knowledge." *Studies in Philosophy and Education*.

REPLY

On (philosophical) suffering and not knowing one's way about (yet) in educational philosophy. Reply to Christiane Thompson

Stefan Ramaekers

Philosophers suffer (Cf. Cerbone 1994, 163). At least, according to a particular conception of doing philosophy. In his work on Wittgenstein's later philosophy, Stanley Cavell draws attention to a certain relationship between (doing) philosophy and an idea of struggling and suffering. Most commonly this is attributed to Wittgenstein's understanding philosophy as "a scene of captivity, bewitchment, dissatisfaction, torment, and illusion" (Cerbone 1994, 163). Wittgenstein famously described philosophy as "a battle against the bewitchment of our intelligence by means of language" (Wittgenstein 1953, I, 109); he saw "philosophical problems aris[ing] when language goes on holiday" (38). And thus we struggle, we have to, in order "to bring words back from their metaphysical to their everyday use" (116) and to have "a clear view of the use of our words" (121). This may sound a familiar and, to some, a relatively simple take on philosophy. But Cavell draws out further layers to this. He perceptively alludes for example to an ambivalence of the "by" in Wittgenstein's familiar bewitchment passage. When Wittgenstein says that "Philosophy is a battle against the bewitchment of our intelligence by means of language", the "by" may mean not only to "[name] language simply (perhaps not at all) as the efficient cause of philosophical grief", Cavell says (1996, 337). But also it refers to language "as the medium of its dispelling" (Ibid.). So the (supposed) cause of philosophical troubles is at the same time the means by which we try to deal with them. Furthermore, in Cavell's reading of his work, it is not clear that Wittgenstein is necessarily saying that it is a bad thing when we use words outside what is ordinarily thought to be their "original home" (Wittgenstein 1953, I, 116). Experientially this is, I suppose, something we encounter when someone is stretching the boundaries of a concept. This gives a wholly different take on what it means to command a clear view of the use of one's words. At least, it suggests that achieving such a clear view is far from the easy task it is sometimes imagined to be. So when Wittgenstein further describes a philosophical problem in terms of "I don't know my way about" (123) (in German, "Ich kenne mich nicht aus"), then there is no definite set of criteria with reference to which I can safely claim that I do know my way about.

I find a great deal of struggling, and perhaps also suffering, in Christiane Thompson's text (Thompson 2015). The struggling is there, I find, in the tentative or exploratory nature with which she describes her analysis of the videographic material. It is there in her attempt to bring together different registers of methodological jargon, to force rapprochement between ways of researching the educational world which are not naturally inclined to seek rapprochement. To me all this reads as a search for the right words with which to express what she herself is doing, even as a testing of words to find out what then becomes possible – seeking for words in order to find out what one is in fact doing. So this also, then, reads to me as an attempt to show what is at stake, what claims can legitimately be made about early childhood education. And the many questions she raises – as well as the suggestion regarding "the significance of educational philosophy" – I take as implying "Ich kenne mich *noch* nicht aus" ("I don't know my way about *yet*.").

Despite all this, I would like to ask her for an even clearer view of the use of some of her words; or at least, I would like to ask her to give some criteria for determining what a clear use of words could be in the cases I am interested in. But let me first say this. I find that Thompson's paper expresses a real concern for the kind of work we do as educational philosophers. In a general sense, it is clear to me that it is an attempt to redefine, or even renew what we do, in view of recent shifts in the theoretical landscape, which I attribute to something broadly subsumed under the heading "post-humanism". Thompson does not explicitly mention post-humanism, but with references to Schatzki and Latour it is clear what the background of her discussion is. In a sense, her text strikes me as a struggle to find a place or a role for philosophy of education, or for "educational philosophy". That she does not use "philosophy of education" in her paper, but rather consistently speaks of "educational philosophy", I take to be in itself a mark of a search for its place.

I am particularly intrigued by the use of words such as "disclose", "study", "concrete practices", "complement", and the expression "what is there to see". Let's take the following instance (Thompson 2015, 6):

> The range of '*Bildung*' in early education has to be disclosed via the *practices* in the field of study rather than by conceptual ideas or theoretical coherence. Furthermore, the analysis gains it richness and quality by studying concrete practices of the field.

What does this imply for the way Thompson as an educational philosopher relates to the videographic material she is using? What is this "study" that she has in mind here? And what bearing does the use of "to disclose" have here? The suggestion seems to be that, for her purposes, a philosophical account of educational practices does not fully exhaust what "studying" means here. Perhaps the suggestion also is that, for her purposes, a philosophical study is somehow insufficient, or lacking, and that it needs to be complemented by an analytical approach of a different (perhaps more empirical?) nature. ("But what are there purposes?" I am then inclined to ask.) There even seems to be a suggestion that a philosophical study of education does not deal with concrete educational practices, or at least not with these practices in a concrete form, or in a form that is concrete enough, but instead deals with it only in some abstract way. What is it that she hopes can be disclosed by such a "study" that is different from the kind of disclosing that educational–philosophical analysis can achieve, or cannot perhaps be disclosed by educational–philosophical analysis at all? (And, clearly, I do not mean to evoke here the ordinary distinction between empirical questions and philosophical questions. My guess is that she is hinting at something beyond this distinction.)

Toward the end of the paper, however, things seem to be somewhat different. I was quite surprised to suddenly see "the significance of educational philosophy" being mentioned toward the end of the paper. To be clear, I am not referring to the *specifics* of the role Thompson assigns to it, i.e. what she says it has in common with *Bildung*, "to warrant difference and alterity" (Thompson 2015, 12); I have no quarrel with that. I also do not mean that I was surprised to see this mentioned *only* toward the end of the paper. I mean to say that I was surprised to see it being introduced *at all*. For the questions that immediately came to mind were: "But what has she been doing then in the preceding pages of the paper?" "Doesn't that constitute some version of educational philosophy?" I was particularly struck by the use of the word "to complement": (Thompson 2015, 12) "the analysis of social practices ought to be complemented by [such and such]" and (Thompson 2015, 13) "it is crucial to complement the analysis of practices by [such and such]" – where what this analysis has to be complemented with is something that should be provided by educational philosophy. Moreover, Thompson grounds this in an ontological claim about the continual flux of reality, i.e. when she brings in (Thompson 2015, 12) the idea of the "continuous *reshaping* of social orders in [social] practices" (my emphasis). This suggests to me that we can only do justice to what is really going on by means of doing (or perhaps adding a dose of) educational philosophy rather than by doing an analysis of some other kind.

In the paper, Thompson seems to be pulling simultaneously at the two opposite ends of a rope. And so she seems to be caught between on the one hand the necessity for "studying concrete practices" combined with a sense that educational philosophy cannot entirely do the job here, and on the other hand the necessity for warranting difference and alterity combined with a sense that educational philosophy is absolutely indispensable.

Another tension that is related to this comes out in the complicated ways the expression "what is there to see" works in Thompson's paper. On the one hand, there is the way this expression appears in the footage showed.[1] Thompson perceptively draws attention to how this contributes to a certain configuration or arrangement of the educational practice at hand. As an aside, and specifically in relation to what the educator is saying in the video-sequence Thompson uses for her paper, allow me to add that I find what this educator is saying about "observing" and "interpreting" is highly problematical. He says that it is important to "write down what we can see without interpreting", and gives an illustration of what that means. The distinction he drives between observation and interpretation is, I find, untenable; much more should be said about that distinction, not in the least about the way his own observation always is informed by presuppositions of diverse kinds, and about the symbolic violence inherent in his notion of observation. "Was gibt es hier zu sehen?" the question is. Well, when viewing the particular scene he was referring to I saw colorful hats/bonnets and colorful coats. At some point he says, referring to a particular child: "macht das Gleiche nochmal" ("does the same thing again"), but, if I may be so boring to point this out: when is something the same? Isn't there at least some form of interpretation involved here? What concept of observation, what concept of seeing is he using here? The educator's entire attitude reminds me of Nietzsche's rather cynical description of the figure of the scholar in terms of a so-called "objective man", in which he criticizes this figure's attitude of abstinence:

> the objective man is in fact a mirror: accustomed to submitting to whatever wants to be known, lacking any other pleasure than that provided by knowledge, by "mirroring" – he waits until something comes along and then gently spreads himself out, so that not even the lightest footsteps and the fluttering of ghostly beings shall be lost on his surface and skin. Whatever still remains of his "own person" seems to him accidental, often capricious, more

often disturbing: so completely has he become a passage and reflection of forms and events not his own. (Nietzsche 1973, 207)

What is at stake here is an investment of the self that I wish to phrase in terms of a willingness to relate to the world, to be interested in the world; Nietzsche's critique here is a critique of a willingness to empty out one's self, a critique of a movement of un-selfing. Human-all-too-human as this may be, it nevertheless is an attitude of dis-interest-edness: not wanting to be connected with, or involved in, the world. Cavell has a brilliant way of putting this attitude when he says: "It is as though we try to get the world to provide answers in a way which is independent of our responsibility for *claiming* something to be so [...]" (1979, 216). More is to be said about this, but this doesn't seem to me to be an attitude worthy of someone calling himself an educator.

On the other hand, and apart from whatever it is we think this educator is doing, I am wondering what registers of the expression "what is there to see" Thompson herself wants to allow in her own work, for some sense of it is operative in her paper as well. This is seen toward the end of paper where she explicitly opens up the discussion on the observational practice of the *researcher* (and not just of the educators) by asking to leave this question partly unanswered and to consider "modes of not-answering that we can think of" (Thompson 2015, 13). But it is there in the rest of the paper as well. Take, e.g. on page 4 where she slips in the notion of having a "closer look" (Thompson 2015). More generally, it is there in the duplication of the investigative gaze: the entire setup is one in which she is observing educators who are observing children; she is "witnessing" educators "witnessing" children's activities. At places in the paper, the register of "what is there to see" seems to be one of a registration of an objective world out there, suggesting the researcher takes a distanced and dis-interested stance: for example, when she says that "The camera-ethnography 'Following the path of children' is used to *recapitulate* [the constitution process of an educational subject]" (Thompson 2015, 7, my emphasis); or, more clearly, when she uses the idea of "how things *offer themselves* for a different view" (Thompson 2015, 13, my emphasis). But this seems to be in contrast to her interest in warranting difference and alterity, something which, indeed, requires an interested relation to the world.

What kind of seeing, observing, witnessing is Thompson working with in her paper? And, in relation to the suggestion to warrant difference and alterity, I would like to ask: what kind of invitation is this? To what kind of seeing are we invited here? I am inclined to say: what is this if not an invitation for further *thinking* and not looking? (Cf. Cerbone 1994) Many today seem to be fascinated by words such as "registration", "observation", "mapping", etc. – a fascination induced, I would like to think, by the recent post-humanist surprise attack on the humanities. But as we all know, and perhaps are familiar with, being fascinated by something sometimes is a modus of, or borders on, being bewitched by something.

Incidentally, I do not think Thompson's analysis differs all that much from an analysis such as the one by Masschelein and Ricken. In brief, here is my understanding of what Thompson does in Sections 2 and 3. She is using videographic material (and thus drawing on observations) to say something about practices of observation and about how these observations (by the educators) are part of a particular configuration of the educational field. Now, I assume that the educators make claims about reality; that is, they think that what they observe and document and what they communicate about is really the case, that children *are* "bildsam" and that the children's activities *are* part of a journey of self-directed *Bildung*. So there's a claim to reality here, a claim to the existence of self-directed *Bildung*.

Thompson, by observing this material, is observing educators observing children. And she is also making a claim to reality – i.e. that what is really going on can only be grasped by seeing the setting in terms of (or as) a social practice; that is, as an arrangement of some sort from which people and artifacts get their meaning and identity. The claim, then, is that children are not really *bildsam* in the way these educators think they are, but that they are made visible as subjects of *Bildung*. Note that her claim (the researcher's claim) as to what is going on trumps the educator's claim to what is going on. The educator's claim is "exposed" as being a non-claim. Note also that her claim is based on a presupposition of "seeing more"; the educator positions himself on the border and may experience himself as sitting on the border, but he does not see himself sitting on the border and does not see what this is contributing to the arrangement of the situation; he is lacking the "proper" distance to see this; so Thompson's seeing is a seeing of the entire situation, or more modestly, seeing more of the entire situation; it is a about the "entirety" of the situation.

But how different is this from an analysis such as the one by Masschelein and Ricken? Whereas their analysis draws out the workings of a regime of individualization and the effects thereof, Thompson's analysis draws attention to "the complex relational constellation within the educational practice of observation" (Thompson 2015, 10–11) and more particularly to how deeply implicated the educator is, in and through her practices of observation, in the staging of early childhood education. Whereas Masschelein and Ricken's analysis focuses on an individual child and its self-governance, Thompson's analysis adds an extra something to that, i.e. it focuses on how the educator brings forth this process of self-directed *Bildung*. But in both cases the process is one of exposing what is going on. In both cases, it is – to use a very laden word – a form of critique on the way the concept "educational" is being used, claiming that what is educational can also be understood in different ways. In both cases, to put this rather bluntly, a superior kind of educational knowledge is provided (or at least promised), one that is more superior than the superior kind of educational knowledge the educators think they are providing. (But, perhaps, isn't that what academics always seem to think, i.e. that what they are providing (or are expected to provide) is "superior" knowledge, that is, knowledge that is not readily accessible to non-academics?).

A final word, going back to how I started my reply to Thompson, bringing to mind a relation between doing philosophy and struggling and suffering. My questions and expressions of puzzlement should not be taken to imply that I think (or even hope) that at some point definitive clarity about the use of our words can be achieved – that philosophical problems could be solved once and for all, which in this particular case would mean that we could be clear about what constitutes doing educational philosophy (what it is, how to do it, etc.). And, perhaps, it is not all together that bad that, upon noticing that language goes on holiday, we let it do so for a while. For, stretching Wittgenstein's metaphor a little, doesn't home, sometimes, seem to be more interesting after having been on holiday? As if it (re)gained a certain newness, as if we notice some things we have somehow forgotten were there, or have never seen before.

Disclosure statement

No potential conflict of interest was reported by the author.

Note

1. During the presentation at the INPE-conference in Cosenza. See also the stills in Thompson's paper.

References

Cavell, Stanley. 1979. *The claim of reason. Wittgenstein, skepticism, morality, and tragedy.* New York: Oxford University Press.
Cavell, Stanley. 1996. "Declining decline." In *The Cavell reader*, edited by Stephen Mulhall, 321–352. Oxford: Blackwell Publishers Ltd.
Cerbone, David R. 1994. "Don't look but think: Imaginary scenarios in Wittgenstein's later philosophy." *Inquiry* 37 (2): 159–183.
Nietzsche, Friedrich. 1973. *Beyond good and evil. A prelude to a philosophy of the future.* Translated and edited by R.J. Hollingdale. London: Penguin Books.
Thompson, C. 2015. "The Authority of Bildung: Educational Practices in Early Childhood Education." *Ethics and Education* 10 (1): 3–16.
Wittgenstein, Ludwig. 1953. *Philosophical Investigations.* Translated and edited by Mary Anscombe. Oxford: Basil Blackwell.

Postliberal education

Robert A. Davis

> The 2014 INPE McLaughlin Lecture explores the emergent concept of the 'postliberal' and the increasing frequency of its formal and informal uses in the languages of educational theory and practice. It traces the origins of the term 'postliberal' to certain strains of modern Christian theology, maps its migration into liberal democratic theory and examines its important role in the discussion of religious schooling as led for a time by Terry McLaughlin himself. Acknowledging the looseness of the concepts 'liberal' and 'postliberal' in much current educational polemic, the article nonetheless argues that recurrent adoption of the term 'postliberal' in Britain especially signifies a change in attitude towards 'progressive' versions of liberal education with which philosophers and theorists must engage.

Introduction

In the last 30 years the term 'postliberal' has borne several, often highly divergent meanings. It has been suggested by figures such as Zygmunt Bauman that in this range of repeated and sometimes wildly varying iterations, we can see the unfolding of a 'crisis of liberalism' (Bauman and Donskis 2013, 49–54) akin to the crisis which induced the collapse of the intellectual order of the *ancien regime* itself and which prompted political philosophers and early social theorists, from Hegel to Bentham, to seek out a new vocabulary for interpreting the shifting 'post-mercantile' (to use Sophus A. Reinhert's term) cultural and epistemic realities around them (Reinhert 2011).

I reserve judgement for the moment on the legitimacy of the often over-used 'crisis' as an epithet for the current predicaments of liberalism and liberal education. Instead, in this essay I intend more modestly to disentangle several different strands of thought associated with the terms 'postliberal' and 'postliberal education', to identify the genealogies associated with a number of these strands that I consider to be significant and to suggest that what I take to be the most recent of them – a development within political and philosophical 'postliberalism' of the last 10–15 years – has begun to adumbrate a vernacular view of popular education, liberal education and indeed classroom educational practice (most especially in the terms of mass schooling central to the historic experience of the UK), which poses a particular (and peculiar) challenge to the philosophy of education in 2014 – albeit from mostly unfamiliar quarters. Let me stress, however, that it is not only in relation to the latest expression that I perceive a lasting or living educational question crystallized by the messy discourses of postliberalism. The exercise I am conducting is not at any stage merely forensic or archival. The goal of our intellectual endeavours should not be merely to mirror reality accurately or describe it curatorially, but, as Dewey argued in 1917 in 'The Need for a Recovery of Philosophy', 'to free experience from routine and caprice.' 'Unless professional philosophy can mobilise itself sufficiently to assist in this clarification and redirection of men's thoughts,' Dewey went on, 'it is likely to get more and more sidetracked from the currents of contemporary life' (Dewey 1973, 59). All of the major versions of postliberalism are, I believe, visible in the currents of contemporary educational life, even if it is to the most immediate of them that active educational enquiry – in an inevitably inchoate, unfinished and possibly even *prephilosophical*' style – is presently and confusingly attending.

I also preface my overall task today with one significant disavowal. I am keenly aware as I examine these debates and interactions, that the term 'postliberal' may not in fact be an altogether accurate or convincing label to attach to some of the movements of thought on which I will touch at all. Indeed, it ought to be apparent that 'postliberal' and 'postliberalism' are highly contested and in certain respects doubtful banners to place over the protean clusters of ideas and argument with which I shall connect. Postliberalism may be little more than a flag of convenience for certain polemical interests and alignments, either in essence opposed to the liberal educational project *tout court* or indeed in their advocacy agitating within the established, if historically flexible, parameters of liberalism and liberal educational values quite simply for the enlargement of their moral or epistemological compass. This problem – of the extent to which 'postliberal education' is in many of its manifestations merely liberal education 'remastered' (to use a musical metaphor) in order to emphasize certain themes within its multiple harmonics and to suppress others – remains deliberately unresolved in my exposition – although I hope it might inform future reflection and discussion. Recall, for example, the dismay with which E.D. Hirsch has met the repeated criticism from constructivists that his prescriptive approach to curriculum planning is in key aspects 'illiberal' and his rejoinder that he considers Core Knowledge to be the last best defence of Liberal Education (Noddings 2013, 30–34). I remain absorbed, nevertheless, in searching out and understanding the need that these movements or programmes with which I am occupied have felt in specific academic and historical contexts to appropriate the term 'postliberal' even if only as a campaigning slogan, a think-tank brand-name or a social media rallying call. Philosophers of education, I contend, perhaps Dewey-style, ought to be interested in all three of these possible motivations – and more.

The postliberal

'[T]he prefix "post",' remarks Brown,

> Signifies a formation that is *temporally after but not over* that to which it is affixed. 'Post' indicates a very particular condition of afterness in which what is past is not left behind, but, on the contrary, relentlessly conditions, even dominates a present that nevertheless also breaks in some way with this past. In other words, we use the term 'post' only for a present whose past continues to capture and structure it. (2010, 21)

The concept 'postliberal' first gained serious educational traction in a perhaps quite unexpected domain, but with subsequently important resonances for, and within, the successive rebrandings of the term. *Postliberal theology* arose in the 1970s in American and German divinity schools as a concentrated doctrinal and pastoral dissatisfaction with the philosophical and scriptural settlement that had come to be known as 'Liberal Theology' and which represented, as many now recognize, a prevailing nineteenth- and early twentieth-century-educated accommodation between mainstream Christianity and the Enlightenment – most specifically with the avalanche of discoveries of historical and textual criticism, the monumental advances in the natural and life sciences and the rise of comparative and analytic philosophical methods gaining prestige across this broad modernizing canvas (DeHart 2006). Largely abandoning the props of a biblical or ecclesial magisterium, Liberal Theology accepted all of the major claims of the Enlightenment for the priority of reason and the practice of sceptical enquiry and in turn strove to develop a refreshed theological language equipped to reformulate the classical doctrinal truth claims of the historic Christian creeds in terms compatible with the rational and scientific spirit of the age. The strongholds of Liberal Theology were the universities and seminaries of the major Protestant congregations in Europe and America and their programmes of ministerial and pastoral training saw the movement impact on the work of these Churches in parishes, voluntary associations and even schools all over the world (Cathey 2009).

Post-liberal theology of the 1970s and 1980s originated as a serious reaction against this settlement, perhaps best characterized by the leadership of the philosopher and theologian Stanley Hauerwas. The primary focus of Hauerwas' work was the systematic promotion of a counter-cultural social and educational ethic protesting the hypocrisies of enlightened 'modernity' and critiquing the impoverished notions of autonomy and spirituality behind which, he alleged, it disguised structures of systematic violence, exploitation and anomie. Set against this pervasive consumer nihilism and cynicism of modern culture, Hauerwas and his followers daringly recommissioned more ancient and abiding forms of individual and communal formation, contemplation and discipline – dedicated to a resumption of the pursuit of theological truth and the affirmation of scriptural revelation within coherent and confident habits of philosophical dialectics (Hauerwas 1997).

Echoing wider misgivings of the period articulated by secular thinkers such as Fish (1997), Hauerwas critiqued what he called the 'self-promotion' of the liberal temper. While classical liberalism represented itself as a place of neutrality outside the partisan struggles that mark the contest of religious and other non-conditional convictions, it was in fact an undeclared participant in these struggles, aggressively advancing its own values, which it masked as universal – values such as autonomy, individual freedom and reasonableness – and circumscribing the concept of religion as private and personal in order better to police its subversive demands through the unacknowledged coercion of the liberal state (Gaus 2003). Liberalism – while affecting preservation of the neutrality and tolerance of its early modern Lockean origins – must then be seen by this light not as the impartial arbiter but as the temporary victor in an ongoing battle for the maintenance of what William Cavanaugh, following Nietzsche rather than Rudolph Bultmann, subsequently defined as its three 'religious' myths: the myth of the violent state as the rescue from violence; the myth of collusive civil society as free space; and the myth of dehumanizing economic globalization as authentic, achieved catholicity (Cavanaugh 2002).

Hauerwas and the champions of postliberal theology may have been heard at the time and since as voices of an exotic coterie specialism, residually present within the academy and school, perhaps, but firmly outwith the boundaries of mainstream majority educational study. Yet postliberal theology did refract certain important educational themes of the age, as the so-called 'return of religion' began to impact upon the politics of multiculturalism, religious education and the longstanding controversies of faith-based schooling. We can indeed see in some of Terry McLaughlin's important work of the 1990s on religion in the common school and the place of Catholic schools in the democratic polity an intervention possibly even more prescient than his parallel writings on philosophy and educational policy. The sometimes overcharged rhetoric of 'postliberalism' or 'postliberal theology' would certainly have provoked that rare yet characteristic capacity of Terry's to be indulgent towards his earnest interlocutors without appearing patronizing, quizzical without being scornful (accompanied no doubt with one of his pithy self-mocking asides). There remains nevertheless a concern in these aspects of Terry McLaughlin's *oeuvre* with what we might call the limits of liberalism – or, better, with the self-imposed limits of certain prevailing or attenuated versions of liberalism which are then tested by the moral and epistemic demands of an increasingly plural and variegated polity:

> A powerful argument for the involvement of the common school with the non-public domain arises from the need for the development in pupils of imaginative engagement, understanding and sympathy with views with which they disagree. Silence about the 'non-public' domain is not neutral in effect and is also likely to disfavour cultural minorities, whose own distinctive moral perspectives may therefore fail to receive attention. Indeed, such silence might itself constitute, in effect if not in intention, a form of repression. The aim of helping pupils to become 'morally bilingual' also requires connections to be made between 'public' moral language and the 'non-public' moral language of pupils if they are not to become schizophrenic. Further, the absence from the common school of wide-ranging substantial moral debate could scarcely be a good preparation for democracy. (McLaughlin 1995a, 250)

For McLaughlin, of course, this 'bilingualism' (or maybe what we might call today 'intercultural multilingualism') was something conferred by the interactive and collegial processes of being educated in difference in the first place. It applied regardless of whether this was the difference resultant from actual proximity to others (or 'the Other'), or simply the effect of an engagement with the diverse cultural repositories of civilization in a vibrant humanist curriculum hospitable to forms of thinking, feeling, remembering and experiencing upon which the claims of 'Liberal Rationalism' would impose no inappropriately universalizing educational contrivances. It seems entirely clear that even in his return to Wittgenstein as the ground for a replenished recognition of the religious encounter that might actually also work as a pedagogy and (in outline at least) even a possible high school syllabus, McLaughlin believed himself to be serving and strengthening liberal practice rather than merely rebuking or abandoning it:

> Wittgenstein's general approach clearly calls into question a number of the major features and philosophical underpinnings of the Liberal Rational conception. From a Wittgensteinian perspective, it is no longer possible (for example) to maintain a sharp distinction for educational purposes between fostering religious belief and practice and developing religious understanding; the presentation of religion as uncertain and requiring rational assessment, decision and commitment misrepresents some of the central distinctive features of the domain; religious truth and reality are seen as requiring a much more subtle and nuanced elucidation, and so forth. (1995b, 304)

These and other remarks in the landmark 1995 essay 'Wittgenstein, Education and Religion' – such as the provocative commentary on the 'limits to questioning' in the educational recognition of religious living and religious witness in schools – undeniably echo some of the restlessness of the postliberal theological currents of the time (in which Wittgenstein's thought was also prominent). But this is surely only a postliberalism lite, remaining fiercely loyal to the core principles of liberal educational aspiration whilst insisting eloquently that these principles are reinforced by a more inclusive definition of their meaning and a more receptive attitude towards the spectrum of human experience with which they must deal if their fundamental vision of the flourishing person in the flourishing *polis* is to be realized.

McLaughlin's key texts, then, positioned at what might seem to be the *boundaries* of liberal education, nonetheless draw their critical strength from principles sitting right at the heart of liberal education as McLaughlin had absorbed these from Peters (1966), Hirst (1972) and Dearden (1972). In response to the rise of what they considered to be an often substanceless progressivism of 1960s 'child-centredness', 'play' and 'creativity', Peters, Hirst and Deardon endeavoured to reassert the centrality of core liberal educational ideals such as the priority of educational content over style and medium; the rigorous formation of the mind through learning in 'worthwhile pursuits'; and the classical initiation of the individual into traditions of knowledge, understanding and truth as these were vouchsafed in, for example, the thought of Arnold, Newman and Oakeshott. The cultivation of that other signature virtue of liberal ethics – rational autonomy – they also prized highly, but only as part of moral and educational economy in which the development of the individual person evolved incrementally through the application of determinedly non-individualistic means. Indeed, the Hirst–Peters–Deardon suspicion of fashionable 1960s classroom dogmas was in essence a serious misgiving that the rational-autonomy strain in liberal theory was eclipsing through the elevation of these preferred methods of the day the altogether deeper and broader heritage of liberal humanist education as this had been protected for generations. It seems clear from the longer perspective on the subsequent British educational experience in particular that the 1960s and 1970s political investment in progressivism as part of a supposed emancipation from the educational failures of the past undoubtedly fortified immeasurably the rational-autonomy strain, according it at important junctures an almost totalizing grip on the meaning and the goals of liberal education. Hence McLaughlin's essays on the encounter of religion and education referenced above may now seem to anticipate some of the preoccupations of postliberalism mainly because of the trajectory assumed by liberal education in the period since they were written rather than because of any direct prescience on their author's part.

Nevertheless, a further strain of thought can now be perceived emerging from the 1990s nexus in which McLaughlin's thinking on these matters matured and where changes in theological thinking and shifts in educational theory briefly converged. Post-liberal theology has in many respects faded from academic and ecclesial attention, but its educational legacy remains powerfully present in the fierce debates around religion and liberal democracy occasioned by the surge of religious atavism reverberating across the world on the cusp of the millennium. The accompanying argument of influential philosophers and teachers such as Phillip Wexler that we have crossed a 'post-secular' boundary in understanding the forces at work in the globalized era – with dramatic implications for the politics of recognition and the way we deal with the question of 'postliberal' or 'illiberal' belief in our schools and universities – has also been of critical importance to education's reanimated dialogue with the experience of faith (Hotam and Wexler 2014).

Testing liberal education

Lest with even a philosopher of Terry McLaughlin's magnanimity and range, we consider the postliberal to be a remote or esoteric set of preoccupations, it is worth noting briefly two significant works that emerged at more or less the same time as McLaughlin's important essays and which also sought to probe the limits of liberal education in a rapidly changing culture. I take them in reverse chronology only because of the uses to which I will put them and the recursive and cross-over nature of the contributions they made at key milestones in the evolution of several distinct but related expressions of 'postliberal' sentiment.

The important *Festschrift* of 1993 for Paul Hirst, edited by Robin Barrow and Patricia White, *Beyond Liberal Education*, paid unstinting tribute to Hirst while recognizing that a singular achievement of his work was to raise questions of meaning and value in education that might be answered differently from the perspective of an altered society or the resources of philosophical and intellectual traditions (such as Platonism) that Hirst had consistently eschewed (Barrow and White 1993). Several of the essays in the collection skillfully draw out themes in Hirst's writings that require reconsideration (vocationalism for example) by the light of shifting economic and cultural realities. Others point respectfully to omissions in the priorities that he identified or in the sometimes limited range of examples of practice and application that he supplied on which the philosophy of education could deliberate to the point of consensual judgement.

Cooper amplifies in the collection some of the wider 'postliberal' anxieties of the day, and since, by returning in his own influential essay to the question of truth and by querying Hirst's investment in what Cooper labels (borrowing language from Dewey and Dummett) 'warranted assertability' (1993, 34). It is important to emphasize that Cooper's is not a fundamental rejection of Hirst's account of truth and its relationship to what human beings can reliably know, but simply an attempt to understand it and a recognition that Hirst's commitment to a 'public agreement' model of liberal education 'no longer backed', as Hirst famously stated, 'by metaphysical realism', may run the risk, despite its many merits, of depriving liberal education of other potential sources of secular transcendent meaning – handicapping the pursuit of goals dear to certain schools of philosophical training, for example, such as unconditional service or selfless fulfillment in the loving contemplation of an absolute reality.

Martin's essay in *Beyond Liberal Education* is in key respects a more direct dissent from the Hirstian construction of the curriculum and in many ways a foreshadowing of the much more agitated critical theory and poststructuralist critique of liberal education with which I associate the second strand of the postliberal experience, and to which I shall return below (1993, 107–129). While welcoming Hirst's attention to the need for the curriculum to explain itself in terms of an underlying rationale and a coherence with the forms of knowledge, Martin absorbs what were by 1993 very powerful impulses in the surrounding climate of critical theory and English Studies, energetically challenging the alleged ethnocentrism, antifeminism and seamless universalism of the Humanities and of the larger Enlightenment agenda of which they were the supposedly unimpeachable educational channels. Martin's attack on what she sees in the essay as the doomed attempt in schools and universities to preserve a 'white man's culture' from the polyvocal witness of the colonially excluded, the sexually abjected and the politically and economically oppressed is configured as a serious reproach to Hirst's supposedly 'settled' view of the curriculum and even to the discursive construction of the skewed 'Western' epistemologies underpinning it. It is worth observing in passing that Hirst may be something of a straw man in this argument and his account of the curriculum unduly flattened by a reading that excludes, for example, its signature scepticism towards the dominant styles of curricular integration favoured by postwar governments and its openness to practical reform as human knowledge advances. But Martin's is a strategic interpretation, striving to illuminate zones of human experience seemingly untouched by the liberal understanding of legitimated knowledge. In the 'beyond' of liberal education, she discerns a crowd of witnesses, a kind of wretched of the earth, whose testimony and passions are definitively excluded from the conversation of mankind but who – ominously – will not put up with this for very much longer.

One of the most ambitious and compelling attempts to draw out from the shifting and evolving patterns of the 1980s postmodern humanities to which Martin was also indebted a quite new but nonetheless sympathetic programme for the refurbishment of liberal education came in 1987 from the renowned American philosopher of education C.A. ('Chet') Bowers, in his controversial but highly distinguished work, *Elements of a Post-Liberal Theory of Education* (1987). Influenced by the readings of Foucault and Derrida that were by then strongly associated with the Yale School of Paul De Man and Harold Bloom – and reverberating with increasing volatility throughout the study of the humanities in the USA and Europe – Bowers mounted a concerted re-reading of some of the canonical philosophers, psychologists and champions of the Liberal Educational tradition as he surveyed it: B.F. Skinner, Carl Rogers, Paulo Freire and, above all, John Dewey himself. At the same time, Bowers was also highly sensitized to what he took to be (misleadingly perhaps) the 'Conservative' tradition in English-speaking educational thought, most obviously represented by Oakeshott, but also present in the Transcendentalists, and drew this body of literature into his overall examination of the strengths and limitations of the liberal theory of education as it responded to the social, economic and cultural pressures of the late modern world.

The key insight that Bowers brings to his close reading of Dewey, Freire, Rogers, and Skinner is that whatever their very substantial differences, they share a common worldview the roots of which lie in the Enlightenment and the Enlightenment's hopes for the emancipatory potential of popular education. Each figure is committed, he argues, to the power of critical reflection, to the sovereignty of the individual and to education as a path to individual freedom and collective social progress. What the four systematically neglect, according to Bowers (though Dewey and Freire are much less culpable in this regard), is the extent to which humans are *embedded* in a material *mesh* of economic, social and biopolitical relations which conditions both their possibilities for individual autonomy and corporate solidarity *and* the inescapable limitations placed upon both. In keeping with the Foucauldian 'unmasking' of the technologies of disciplinary regulation held to be discursively implicated in even the most progressive forms of education, this embeddedness implies that only a decidedly limited spectrum of life can at any time become the object of deliberate reflection, appraisal and control at the levels prized by popular education. Liberal education in other words works, but only on a limited bandwidth of human experience, which it covertly modulates and confines in the interests of its own reproduction. In keeping with the organicism and intuitionism of Oakeshott, recognition of embeddedness also implies that the traditions into which human subjects are socialized are not simply the inert demands of the past, which impede progress and self-realization, but the indispensable materials with which we forge whatever limited individuality and self-fashioning we can provisionally attain.

Once again, it is at least arguable that Bowers' is a selective reading of his subjects, most especially Dewey, with whom he has the greatest sympathy. The Dewey of *Liberalism and Social Action* or of *Democracy and Education* seems just as sceptical of evangelical autonomy and self-sufficiency and just as sensitive to interdependence as Bowers. For Bowers, however, Dewey consistently fails to acknowledge the full pressures of history on the actions of learning and teaching and is insufficiently sensitized to what Bowers terms the 'tacit dimension' in the iterative processes of human knowledge production and judgement formation. Perhaps understandably, a key characteristic of Bowers' subsequent work in more recent decades has been the urge to elaborate a progressive theory of communitarian education commensurate with the threats to human survival posed by the mounting crises of environment and climate. These twin themes now of course loom large in much popular contemporary literature on 'postliberal' ethics, (in the work of Fritz Oehlschlaeger, for example), where versions of liberal education are held responsible for cultivating the habits of possessive individualism and complacent materialist acquisition that now menace the planet (Oehlschlaeger 2003).

I suggested at the opening of this essay that the boundaries between the strands or styles of postliberalism with which I am concerned are fuzzy and confusing, sometimes even to the point of contradiction. In the 1990s, at least three working versions of 'the postliberal' were visible in the discourses of philosophy and the social sciences, particularly as understood and used in the UK. From the perspective of a seemingly triumphant yet paradoxically 'post-ideological' New Right, which had reworked even the politics of its party-political opponents in its own image, the philosopher Gray declared in his *Post-Liberalism: Studies in Political Thought* (1993) that

> The position defended here is post-liberal in that it rejects the foundationalist claims of fundamentalist liberalism. That is to say that it denies that liberal regimes are uniquely legitimate for all human beings. Human beings have flourished in regimes that do not shelter a liberal civil society, and there are forms of human flourishing that are driven out in liberal regimes. Liberal orders have, then, no universal or apodictic authority, contrary to liberal political philosophy. (1993, 284)

For Gray, the residual value of liberalism inhered only interstitially in 'the practice of liberty, that is our historical inheritance' (1993, 284). As I have suggested, however, quite different styles of 'postliberal' thinking in the same era were fueled equally vociferously by a totally contrasting conviction present in important centres of scholarly opinion and humanities polemic and which maintained that the energies of critique had forever broken open the postwar liberal consensus in favour of an emancipatory vision far to the left of mainstream liberal theory. Through the concentrated practices of reading, hermeneutics and educational encounters more widely and deeply conceived, these forces were both exposing what they saw as the restrictions and hypocrisies of liberal education whilst reimagining radically new paradigms for learning and teaching. The essence of their analysis – which of course remains very strong in the academy to this day – was that the practices of liberal education, for all their many imperfections, had slowly incubated movements of thought and feeling of a radically adversarial and committed cast deeply sceptical of the hegemony of the Western liberal-democratic educational consensus and the ambivalent purposes it had historically served. These subversive and insurrectionist critical movements such as multiculturalism, postcolonialism, feminism, psychoanalysis, historicism, post-structuralism and deconstruction clearly exhibited an obvious genealogical origin in the older liberal arts and humanities (and they often dealt with the same primary textual material), but they were each unswervingly committed to disclosing and interrogating the suppressed tensions, contradictions and exclusions of their shared ancestry through a radical decentring of high culture and a rejection of academic authority in the name of subaltern groups, silenced voices and marginalized witnesses part and present (Gottfried 1999).

Beyond liberalism

Of course it is important to note that for prominent strands of this movement, the overthrow or wholesale reinvention of the humanities as then constituted was to be welcomed and furthered. This objective would be central to the stances taken up by certain important philosophers of education such as Peters (2011), Giroux (2014) and Chibber (2013). For many of them, this inevitable development was not at all to be construed as a nihilistic undertaking, because it sought not the destruction of liberal education *per se*, but rather its comprehensive reimagining through a democratically empowered agonistic pedagogy of political struggle and passionate cosmopolitan dialogue, extending cultural admission to previously erased or forgotten groups. From out of this process of liberation and disruption, argued Trifonas, would swing into view the open-ended horizon of the so-called New Humanities of liberal education – enriched and transformed by their encounter with revolutionary impulses that the 'older' humanities helped inadvertently to bring forth and foster (Peters and Trifonas 2005). For other thinkers of course, such as Barnett (2014) or Fuller (2014) (channelling the cyberfeminism of Donna Harraway), the very idea of liberal education and education in the 'humanities' was simply too bloodsoaked and too crippled by histories of injustice and connivance with imperial and orientalist oppression to survive in any recognizable form. Inspired by inflammatory readings of Nietzsche, Adorno and Foucault, this adversarial stance demanded the epistemological and ethical repudiation of the Western modern or liberal education model and its replacement by a renovated aesthetic and heuristic order, the precise lineaments of which our own current limitations inveterately prevent us yet from seeing – a posthuman version, perhaps, of a Derridean or Levinasian 'Education to come', forever testing the boundaries of liberal triumphalism (Rutten and Soetaert 2014).

If I am correct in my judgement that each version of postliberal education is imprinted by or contaminated with the versions that preceded or surround it, then I have complicated the task of assessing the nature of its current inflections, even if this is confined to mapping those movements active in the public and educational spaces that persist in calling themselves 'postliberal' on even a speculative or calculatingly tendentious basis. At the level of political philosophy, the intriguing synthesis to which Bowers aspired in his searching reading of some of the canonical narratives of liberal education is present in the cadences of David Chandler and Oliver Richmond's very recent 2014 synopsis:

> Postliberalism is driven by a subaltern and postcolonial thrust away from the dominance of the West, its political philosophy, and its ordering of rights and needs (Bhabha 1994). It represents a shift away from how the existing power and order were naturalised by a colonial liberalism, and presented as emancipatory (Locke 1689/1991; Mill 1869/2010), towards a new era in which a far broader range of agency is implicated in dealing with structures that both produce conflict and institutions that make peace.... For this reason, postliberalism is representative of forms of critical agency that draw on the local actors' subjective agencies.... Postliberalism redirects the social contract away from an elitist and managerial 'great arch' between elites and society (Corrigan and Sayer 1985, 2–3), to a flatter relationship within society between its different groups, formed less hierarchically and based upon its socio-historical continuities. (Chandler and Richmond 2014, 6)

Recapitulating Bowers, we see in this overview a genuine effort to describe in postliberalism itself an ethic that is continuous with the radical critique advanced by the poststructuralist turn in theory and philosophy, alongside an embrace of forms of decentred agency, localism, and 'socio-historical' and institutional continuity enshrined in, and protected by, much classical 'conservatism' of the Oakeshott or Scruton type. In the context of the post credit-crunch UK of today, governed by an edgy coalition of Conservatives and Liberal Democrats, mired in the austerity-driven tasks of shrinking dramatically the reach of the postwar welfare state, and trapped in a space of constitutional and economic self-doubt, British postliberalism is for some merely a consoling intellectual fantasy doing duty for the absence of authentic political vision. For others, it is a still more sinister camouflage for the massive responsibilization of an already beleaguered citizenry and the equally wholesale socialization of economic risk.

There remains, however, some sense that despite this confusion and understandable cynicism, faltering steps are being taken to interpret these developments and the choices they lay before us by the light of a repurposed political philosophy, influenced by Continental thinkers from Jean-Claude Michea, of *The Realm of Lesser Evil* (2009), to the revived civic republicanism of Philip Pettit's *Just Freedom: A Moral Compass for a Complex World* (2014) – and on even to the political ontology of the English theologian John Milbank in his *Beyond Secular Order: the Representation of Being and the Representation of the People* (2013). In terms of a viable political programme from which post-austerity *education* might draw some sustenance, analysis remains in my view almost 'pre-philosophical' in outlook, the preserve of think tanks, lobby groups and higher journalism, seeing in the making of educational policy a potential institutional arena for the development of a robust and thickly reasoned postliberal practice, but extremely wary of rationalizing this. Goodheart of the centre-progressive think tank Demos argues persuasively that

> Postliberalism is a child of the two liberalisms – the 1960s (social) and 1980s (economic) – that have, together, dominated politics for more than a generation. But it is a restless and critical child, and one that cuts across some of the old lines dividing left and right. It does not want to go back to corporatist economics nor to reverse the progress towards race and sex equality . . . . But post-liberalism does want to attend to the silences, overshoots and unintended consequences of economic and social liberalism . . . . It aspires to a more realistic account of the human condition than liberalism offers – based on the idea of formation through institutions and tradition, on freedom based on security and the nurturing of capabilities, on the common life and common purpose. Autonomy and choice are not rejected but are understood in the context of the frameworks and institutions within which we know people flourish such as loving families or workplaces where employees have voice and recognition. (2014, 12)

Now this kind of platform may offer much that is attractive and compelling to philosophers and practitioners of education, even if only as an invitation to reason about the legacy of liberal education and its reinvention for the contemporary age. Yet along with several of the leading lights of the postliberal networks in the UK, Goodheart is a strong advocate of the employment-based pathway into school teaching, *Teach First*, and a stern critic of what he calls the complacent progressivism of Education faculties and Education professors, who he sees permanently seeking alibis for educational failure, trapped in producer-capture dogma and ideologically fastened to principles and to discourse with which few serving teachers can identify. It seems quite clear that 'postliberal' public intellectuals such as Goodheart or Maurice Glasman or Philip Blond are not intuitively hostile to philosophy or theory, yet they have come to identify much that many philosophers of education cherish as, in their terms, a sterile and doctrinaire form of progressivism by which Liberal Education has been almost completely subsumed. In this analysis, Liberal Education has *become* progressivism, and an incomplete, attenuated species of progressivism at that, quite reluctant to acknowledge its own shortcomings and bigotedly prejudiced against all that invokes tradition or custom in educational practice and pedagogy.

Equally challengingly, but at a more popular and demotic level, social media networks and associations of teachers, lobbyists and journalist-commentators, sympathetic to the evolving aims of postliberalism, have also furthered this critique of classroom 'theory' and progressivism in the name of a networked professionalism no longer dependent on the stifling credentialism of the universities or the professional regulatory bodies. The teacher, blogger and tweeter Tom Bennett – himself a distinguished graduate in Philosophy from the University of Glasgow and the holder of a PGCE from Kings College – now leads a powerful online chorus questioning the alleged 'cargo-cult' irrelevancies of much educational research and calling with the science journalist Ben Goldacre for a new clean-slate spirit of properly scientific investigation into 'what works' in schools for the improvement of outcomes for learners. Bennett's following of more than 15,000 is now organized and sponsored as *ResearchED,* a conference of teachers and their allies dedicated to the promotion of evidence-based education and research (2014). A hard-working and talented classroom professional, Bennett, presents himself as a pyrrhonist champion of inclusion, opportunity and the success and happiness of young people – and there is no reason at all to doubt the integrity of that claim. His aspirations would be consonant with many of the core 'liberal' values highlighted throughout this essay. Yet somehow the 'postliberalism' he represents (and I admit Tom Bennett may be averse to the imposition by others of a label he has never publicly endorsed) is largely disconnected from the institutional practices of philosophy of education and the broader reaches of pedagogical and cultural theory in universities and educational institutes. This seems to be both unsettling and portentous, suggesting that if an authentically refashioned 'postliberal' account of education is indeed steadily emerging, philosophers of education must do more to understand and engage with it – drawing out, perhaps, our previous experiences of the diverse cultural and intellectual movements attracted to this banner. While appreciating keenly that nothing propinques like propinquity, I would earnestly venture to suggest that Conroy's model of liminal education from his 2004 book *Betwixt and Between* may furnish one viable mode of engagement called for here, where Liberal Education is altered and enriched beyond its own imaginings by the threshold encounter with that which it has 'othered', deliberately and inadvertently, in the preservation of its fissiparous identity (2004).

The popular English school teacher and gifted educational blogger, Michael Merrick, recently offered an alternative agenda for English educational policy reform to the so-called Blue Labour grouping within the UK Labour Party – the interest group founded in 2009 by Maurice Glasman with the objective of reintegrating a postliberal 'politics of reciprocity, mutuality and solidarity' into mainstream Labour policy-making and planning (Blue Labour 2014). In a speech to Blue Labour early in 2014, Merrick argued that it was time for the Labour Party to rethink its educational philosophy in three broad and previously untouchable areas talismanic for the Labour Movement: Vocational Education, Social Mobility and the organization and governance of schools. Merrick's short argument in all three areas, whether commanding ultimate agreement or dissent, was erudite, reasoned and critically informed:

Blue Labour can also recognise the vital role of schools in forming our young and instilling within them the virtues that we have decided ought to be cherished, even where they might be rejected by wider society – but we must not think that such a thing can be contracted out over and against the family and the communities that act as both creator and guarantor of these institutions.

And lastly, Blue Labour can reject this obsession with social mobility as the judge and jury of educational success and offer an account of flourishing set within rootedness and love, rather than atomised and essentially selfish conceptions of success. (2014)

If arguments such as these represent an intervention typical of the current and expanding expression of postliberal educational thought in one of the crucibles of liberal and progressive education, then the philosophy of education as a discipline of thought and conceptual clarification should cease seeing it as either a reactionary neo-traditionalist threat, or ignoring it as an external unlicensed irrelevance, and instead seek out opportunities to bring its potentially absorbing philosophical contribution to the table of debate.

Acknowledgements

I am grateful to Paul Standish and Hanan Alexander for helpful comments on the original INPE McLaughlin Lecture.

Disclosure statement

No potential conflict of interest was reported by the author.

References

Barnett, R. 2014. "The Very Idea of Academic Culture: What Academy? What Culture?" *Human Affairs* 24: 7–19.
Barrow, R., and P. White. 1993. *Beyond Liberal Education. Essays in honour of Paul H. Hirst*. London: Routledge.
Bauman, Z., and Leonidas Donskis. 2013. *Moral Blindness: The Loss of Sensitivity in Liquid Modernity*. Cambridge: Polity Press.
Bennett, T. 2014. "ResearchED." Accessed 24 November 2014. http://www.workingoutwhatworks.com/en-GB/About
Blue Labour. 2014. Accessed 24 November 2014. http://www.bluelabour.org/who-we-are/
Bowers, C. A. 1987. *Elements of a Post-Liberal Theory of Education*. New York: Teachers College Press.
Brown, W. 2010. *Walled States, Waning Sovereignty*. New York: Zone Books.
Cathey, R. A. 2009. *God in Postliberal Perspective: Between Realism and Non-realism*. Farnham: Ashgate.
Cavanaugh, W. T. 2002. *Theopolitical Imagination: Discovering the Liturgy as a Political Act in an Age of Global Consumerism*. London: T&T Clark.
Chandler, D., and O. Richmond. 2014. "Contesting Postliberalism: Governmentality or Emancipation?" *Journal of International Relations and Development* 2014: 1–24.
Chibber, V. 2013. *Postcolonial Theory and the Specter of Capital*. London: Verso.
Conroy, J. 2004. *Betwixt and Between: The Liminal Imagination, Education and Democracy*. New York: Peter Lang.
Cooper, D. 1993. "Truth and Liberal Education." In Barrow and White, (1993), 30–49.
Dearden, R. F. 1972. "Autonomy and Education." In *Education and the Development of Reason*, edited by R. Dearden, P. Hirst, and R. Peters, 58–75. London: Routledge & Kegan Paul.
DeHart, P. J. 2006. *The Trial of the Witnesses: The Rise and Decline of Postliberal Theology*. Oxford: Blackwell.

Dewey, J. 1973. *The Philosophy of John Dewey*, edited by J. J. McDermott. Chicago, IL: University of Chicago Press.
Fish, S. 1997. "Mission Impossible: Settling the Just Bounds between Church and State." *Columbia Law Review* 97 (8): 2255–2333.
Fuller, S. 2014. "The Higher Whitewash." *Philosophy of the Social Sciences* 44 (1): 86–101.
Gaus, G. F. 2003. *Contemporary Theories of Liberalism: Public Reason as a Post-Enlightenment Project*. London: Sage.
Giroux, H. 2014. "When Schools Become Dead Zones of the Imagination: A Critical Pedagogy Manifesto." *Policy Futures in Education* 12 (4): 491–499.
Goodheart, D. 2014. *A Postliberal Future?* London: Demos.
Gottfried, P. E. 1999. *After Liberalism: Mass Democracy in the Managerial State*. Princeton, NJ: Princeton University Press.
Gray, J. 1993. *Post-Liberalism: Studies in Political Thought*. London: Routledge.
Hauerwas, S. 1997. *Wilderness Wanderings: Probing Twentieth Century Theology and Philosophy*. Boulder, CO: Westview Press.
Hirst, P. H. 1972. "Liberal Education and the Nature of Knowledge." In R.F. Dearden et al., (1972), 391–414.
Hotam, Y., and P. Wexler. 2014. "Education in Post-Secular Society." *Critical Studies in Education* 55 (1): 1–7.
Martin, J. R. 1993. "Curriculum and the Mirror of Knowledge." In Barrow and White, (1993), 107–129.
McLaughlin, T. H. 1995a. "Liberalism, Education and the Common School." *Journal of Philosophy of Education* 29 (2): 239–255.
McLaughlin, T. H. 1995b. "Wittgenstein, Education and Religion." *Studies in Philosophy and Education* 14: 295–311.
Merrick, M. 2014. "Blue Labour and Education." Accessed 24 November 2014. http://michaeltmerrick.blogspot.co.uk
Michea, J.-C. 2009. *The Realm of Lesser Evil*. London: Polity Press.
Milbank, J. 2013. *Beyond Secular Order: the Representation of Being and the Representation of the People*. Oxford: Wiley Blackwell.
Noddings, N. 2013. *Education and Democracy in the 21st Century*. New York: Teachers College Press.
Oehlschlaeger, F. 2003. *Love and Good Reasons: Postliberal Approaches to Christian Ethics and Literature*. Durham, NC: Duke University Press.
Peters, M. 2011. *Neoliberalism and After? Education, Social Policy, and the Crisis of Western Capitalism*. New York: Peter Lang.
Peters, M., and P. Trifonas, eds. 2005. *Deconstructing Derrida: Tasks for the New Humanities*. Basingstoke: Palgrave.
Peters, R. S. 1966. *Ethics and Education*. London: Allen and Unwin.
Pettit, P. 2014. *Just Freedom: A Moral Compass for a Complex World*. London: Norton.
Reinhert, S. A. 2011. *Translating Empire: Emulation and the Origins of Political Economy*. Cambridge, MA: Harvard University Press.
Rutten, K., and R. Soetaert. 2014. "A Rhetoric of Turns: Signs and Symbols in Education." *Journal of Philosophy of Education* 48 (4): 604–620.

Transition to parenthood and intergenerational relationships: the ethical value of family memory

Monica Amadini

> Inside the family, all individuals define their identity in relation to previous generations (those calling them to life), the present ones (those they share their life with), and the future ones (to whom they give life). This intergenerational exchange plays important educational roles: it fosters a sense of belonging and identification, promotes dialogue, and guarantees the passing down of ethical orientations. In addition to feelings of security and reliance on others, family memory creates a matrix that gives people a placement in the world, a sort of existential code through which to be located in existence. Fostering the habit of memory-making becomes therefore a major educational imperative, which however is not without challenges. The present contribution will consider those phenomena which can give rise to a weakening of bonds between generations and a growing exclusion of the ethical value of family heritage. The educational perspective that will be drawn is that of building a sense of alliance between generations, without being locked only on those aspects of psychological functioning or emotional ones. In order to explore the role of family heritage across the whole of a family life cycle, the article focuses on the identity and relational dynamics that come into being during a crucial phase that repeats itself across generations, i.e. the transition to parenthood and thus the arrival of a new family member. The reflections developed around the symbolic value of this transition will draw on the results of a qualitative research, conducted in order to analyze the ethical heritage passing through the bond between generations and to understand how the enhancement of an intergenerational pact may restore the ethical depth of parenting.

Introduction

Personal identity develops through a process of construction of the self, which in turn crystallizes by means of a network of relations across past, present and future. In this perspective, memory plays a crucial role, as it not only serves a cumulative function but also guarantees continuity across past, present, and future experiences (Gusdorf 1951). The subject, 'who is,' finds confirmation of his/her existence in 'what s/he was': the past belongs to him/her and connotes him/her. Memory thus contributes to the integrity of the self. As Ricœur posits, memory expresses the self-consciousness of a subject who perceives him/herself as unchanged through time. The permanence of the self in the subject's identity rests on memory, which enables him/her to recognize the memories of the past as belonging to him/her, as the result of experiences and relationships that contributed to the making of his/her history (2000).

From an educational point of view, it is appropriate to defend and promote the value of the past–present nexus – intrinsic to everyone's self-making path – with a view to favoring the acknowledgment of one's belonging to a history (both individual and collective). The past has to be discovered as a living presence that inhabits and supports the present (Agostino 2004, 238). Thanks to memory, the individual perceives him/herself as 'identity' that does not vanish, because past events impress themselves upon our emotional mind, leaving traces behind that turn the past into present: 'it's a living, never extinct past' (Hessen 1958, 19).

The family is an ideal environment for such memory-oriented work, not only because it is a primary relational and formative space but also because it keeps together all generations not just through blood ties but above all through symbolic and affective legacies. Family, as a whole, is a special relational system that lives across time, enduring across generations. In this perspective, family lineage is a privileged arena where intergenerational relationships find their most authentic expression: it represents a unique opportunity for parents to pass on a heritage to their children, enabling them to grow a sense of belonging and at the same time to continue to build up their history (see Halbwachs [1994] and Coenen-Huther [1994]). Family memory creates a matrix that gives people a placement in the world, a sort of existential code through which to be located in existence. The transmission of family memory, in addition to feelings of security and reliance on others, contributes to pass on ethical orientations. Family memory is not simply about 'what has happened in the past'; it is a part of the way in which families recreate themselves as an ethical unit in the present.

The fabric of family lines offers a firm reference framework for an individual's sense of identity, ensuring duration to personal histories (Bergson 1969, 240–251). Family history can be transferred across generations: it represents a way to make sense of where one has come from, to the extent that it offers a relational context that welcomes new family members, placing them in a dynamic bundle of individuals and histories that support them, in a dialectical interplay of identification and differentiation. Fostering the habit of memory-making becomes therefore a major educational imperative, which however is not without challenges. In the present contribution, we consider those phenomena which can give rise to a weakening of bonds between generations and a growing exclusion of the ethical value of family heritage. The educational perspective that will be drawn is that of building a sense of alliance between generations, without being locked only on those aspects of psychological functioning or emotional ones (Waiton 2008). Family today is at the crossroads of challenges that go far beyond an effective emotional and social adaptation. Fathers and mothers are called to rediscover the sense of generativity also in its ethical feature. Alongside the psychological and emotional dimension, therefore, it is important to emphasize the relevance of family history and the centrality of ethical issues resulting from exchanges across generations. It is within this family history that take shape the commitments of loyalty that bind family members to each other, as well as an heritage settled in norms, values, models.

In order to explore the role of family heritage across the whole of a family life cycle, we can focus on the identity and relational dynamics that come into being during a crucial phase that repeats itself across generations, i.e. the transition to parenthood and thus the arrival of a new family member. The reflections that will be developed around the symbolic value of this transition will draw on the results of a qualitative research. I have conducted this research in order to analyze the ethical heritage passing through the bond across family generations and understand how the enhancement of an intergenerational pact may restore the ethical depth of parenting. Parents' testimonies will allow to understand the relevance of the opportunity to address existential transitions, recognizing ethical resources and values transmitted within the family system.

The family as relational context of memory transmission

Inside the family, all individuals define their identity in relation to previous generations (those calling them to life), the present generations (those they share their life with), and the future generations (to whom they give life). Intergenerational relationships are characterized by interdependency and can play important educational roles: foster a sense of belonging and identification, promote dialog and guarantee the passing down of family traditions. Each family has its own distinctive stories, that express not only the interlacement of lives but also an ethical setting (Suissa 2006). With the passing of generations, the past, present, and future dimensions are joined together through the sharing of what has been constructed (heritage) and the introduction of new horizons (a life project). In this perspective, the development of a family memory offers a unique opportunity to become aware of one's history, but also to understand the present and shape the future. Memory and ethical heritage are continually reshaped to make sense of the past from the perspective of the present: it is a living and mutable force in the present (Samuel and Thompson 1990). As MacIntyre aptly argues, the family is a 'narrative unit of life'. In it, every single member can find the meaning of his acts, decisions, and behaviors, as if it were a narrative plot that keeps together and explains the experiences of all characters, by means of a binding force made of ethics and sense of identity (2007, 190–209).

It would be mistaken, however, to think that memory transmission always takes place in a linear and explicit fashion. In fact, each subject's ethical orientations result from the – often implicit – interpretation of the values, attitudes, behaviors, and experiences cultivated within the family. They develop in ways that often elude conscious appraisal: to a certain extent, they could be defined in terms of latencies that rest on very deep emotional nuclei (Brezinka 2003).

Memory transmission in a family is imbued with experiences that are 'not thought', not elaborated, but that significantly influence the individuals' ethical reference points. The events making up a family history and their affective connotations represent not only an important emotional heritage, but also a moral heritage as, in a sense, they pass down a sort of theory of life, a body of principles that orient it. Thus the history of a family takes on the traits of a symbolic reference framework that, though implicit, is not to be assumed passively or a-critically, since the function of family memory is not to preserve but to re-interpret. To be sure, belonging to a family means hosting a past made of traditions, models, and ethical values. This past, however, needs to be processed actively, so that family traditions can become a resource for the present, and not a burden. The transmission of family memory is thus a life-giving process that also takes place through departures from the inherited models.

In sum, the commitment to building bridges across generations has to take into account the need for patterns of meaning capable of highlighting common threads across different ages and histories, despite the specificities of each interpreting approach. All this requires an ongoing hermeneutic process on the part of all those involved, i.e. those who pass the heritage down to the new generations, and those who receive it. In this way, the family becomes a space of intergenerational dialog, dense with affection and meaning, where the heritages are not simply received but rather responsibly assimilated.

Family transitions and new intergenerational dynamics

A thorough understanding of the forms that intergenerational relations take in contemporary families calls for an in-depth analysis of the new stresses and strains impacting on family bonds and their symbolic contours. A comprehensive review of family relations in contemporary society is beyond the scope of this work. For the sake of argument, however, it is important to briefly touch upon some trends that have been highlighted in recent studies. Particularly worth mentioning among these is the weakening of intergenerational relationships, that drives the privatization and individuation of parenting. This phenomenon is placed into a broader 'problematisation of relationships', 'that is arguably undermining the spontaneous and autonomous relationships between people – and especially between adults and children. This is a process that despite its intentions should be understood as a form of antisocialisation' (Waiton 2010, 38) (see also Beck and Beck-Gernsheim [2002] and Howard [2001]). In such condition, the generational context that once used to frame the arrival of a child appears to have lost its original supportive power, leaving new parents more isolated and alone in their parenting role, and producing a sort of parental determinism. As for example Lee argues, 'the presumption of generational responsibility that has historically underpinned childrearing becomes disorganized, with adults positioned as both the omnipotent protectors of children and the ultimate cause of all their problems' (2014, 20).

Furthermore, the growing tendency toward exclusive, excessively sentimental parent–child relations in the family threatens to obscure the fact that being part of a family is a multifaceted experience, where manifold relations interlace diachronically and synchronically. The diffusion of intensive parenting models, centered on highly symbiotic ties, connoted on the simple affective pole, threatens to lose sight of the symbolic value of this family transition. The event of birth cannot trigger fathers and mothers only on the level of psychological functioning, but should open the doors to the possibility of access to the ethical heritage of the lineages. In this perspective, it is unwise to reduce the parenting role to the exclusive bond between father/mother and child, with a disproportionate preoccupation with the emotional connectedness of parents and children. Family relations are best understood as extended bonds: they require interaction not only with our closest loved ones, who share our everyday life, but also with family members belonging to past generations (Bengtson 2001).

The parent–child relationship does not just happen in a dyadic manner and *hic et nunc*. It is, inherently, an intergenerational bond that broadens the relational horizons, even across time and generations (Ramaekers and Suissa 2012).[1] To be sure, this event marks a critical and totalizing moment for the couple. But, at the same time, it gets inscribed in a horizon of generativity that transcends single individuals, as it belongs to a wider narration. The gift of life takes form within a history: it is given to the new parents, who in turn received it from their own parents, who had it from their own parents in their turn, on and on backwards in time. This chain of life transmission, serves the key role of constructing meaning and a sense of identity, both for the individual and for the wider family (Bertaux and Thompson 2005). Transition to parenthood has deep existential meaning for the individual. At the same time, it restructures the process of affiliation. The new parents are thus confronted not only with implicit, yet powerful, processes of identification with their families of origin, but also with a family heritage that they have to make their own and renovate. In other words, mothers and fathers face the challenge of shaping a new 'us,' which features traits of continuity with, as well as differentiation from, the respective families.

Being able to gauge these complex identity issues related to parenthood and the multilayered processes of coming to terms with family legacies, acknowledging one's roots, and distancing from internalized models represents a fundamental pursuit of education research. All this necessitates occasions to investigate the changing kinship-based patterns of responsibilities, loyalties, and rewards.

Transition to parenthood and family heritage: research perspectives

Investigating the diversity of intergenerational relations within the family as well as the building of a sense of family across generations requires a situated approach. A particularly appropriate methodology to these ends is a narrative approach, which allows the researcher to work on stories and with histories. Researchers use family narratives in a range of different ways (Pratt and Fiese 2004); in this case I attempt to illustrate a particular approach, focused on educational and ethical value of family legacy. Narratives are central as a method for exploring the representation and transmission of family and personal values in childrearing.

It must be pointed out that preferring a method over another also involves precise epistemological choices. In our case, narration is understood as a heuristic as well as reflective tool that triggers two fundamental processes:

- bringing to surface the meanings of family history: family memory may transmit a life-giving heritage and establishing shared ethical values within the family. The retrospective comparison with events can create the conditions to gain deeper insights not only into the intense emotional strains that the generative experience put on new fathers and mothers but also into the ethical heritage that this implies.
- valuing relations: narratives highlight the importance of our relations with people and make us gratefully aware of the heritage passed down to us. Parental identity cannot be defined in isolation from family's roots and affiliation and this is particularly relevant today: as stated earlier, too many parents raise children in a context where solidarity between other adults and relatives is undermined (Bristow 2014).

For those who are preparing for parenthood, dealing with family past is never mere information retrieval but rather a process of evoking a tightly interwoven fabric of feelings, faces, and events, i.e. a real story. This story is often neglected and unsaid. Our hectic daily routines, our exclusive focus on the here and now due to increasingly pressing professional and personal responsibilities do not often allow us to open our minds to the past and to memory. Furthermore, the overemphasis on the process of promoting the physical, emotional, and intellectual development of children (in order to be a 'good parent') often takes away fathers and mothers from the possibility to accept that universe of values and meanings they come from (Lollis 2003). Reflective devices are thus essential to the surfacing of those nodes that connect past, present, and future, giving voice to a family history that spans across time, generation after generation. The sense of belonging and the acknowledgment of one's gifts and debt emerging from reflective practices provide the new parents with a sort of anchor. Retrospection and the discovery of one's roots build a sense of continuity that is not limited to a mere replication of lived scripts but becomes an ongoing, dynamic exploration (Neuberger 1995).

This calls for methodological tools that activate memories, in all their semantic complexity, and that investigate the structure of intergenerational relationships beyond a focus on emotional, psychological, and transactional aspects of childrearing. Thanks to a qualitative research work carried out in 2012, I have had the opportunity to explore the early phases of parenting, in particular how mothers and fathers initiate the process of building their own and familial identity, and deal with family legacies and heritages.[2]

In order to explore the ethical aspects of lineage, I particularly used symbolic and evocative tools.

These were:

- A family heritage diary, focused on the three main relational dimensions underpinning parenthood, i.e. couple relationship, parent–child relationship, intergenerational bonds. The narrative approach is central to diary writing, as it raises awareness of the deepest ethical meanings involved in the transition to parenthood (Knowles 1989). Complementary to narration is an ample resort to photographs as a springboard for recollection of events and emotions that can be processed reflectively, in order to bring to the surface symbols, values, and representations. Diaries are written not only during parenting courses but also at home, to allow parents to carve some time out of their daily schedules and reflect on their history.
- A family tree, to raise a sense of lineage through the graphic representation of generational lines (great grandparents, grandparents, uncles and aunts, children, grandchildren, etc.), where each subject takes a specific place within the relational system spanning over time. From a symbolic point of view, the family tree also highlights the relational pattern underpinning the family: every node of the tree connects in ascending, descending and transversal order with other nodes. Further, this pattern also favors a reflection on the quality and typology of intergenerational bonds, highlighting aspects of continuity and discontinuity, cohesion and departure. From the clinician and therapeutic point of view, the construction of family trees (the genograms) is important in order to catch the symptoms arising from family interactions (or interactions of the patient and family with the outside world). In my case, family tree represents an opportunity for parents to reflect on transmitted beliefs, norms, values, and the way in which they want to pass them to their children, in a generational work.

Apart from these tools, I made use of an effective search device, shaped in order to catch the transmission of ethical guidelines and practices within the family, developed by the French sociologist A. Muxel. Her notable studies on 'Mémoire familiale' allow us to understand the fact that the way of affiliating are never simple and cannot be contained within a single mode of belonging. Family memory is an ambivalent memory, made up of joys and grievances, because it returns, for better or worse, the original collective history to which we belong. For new parents, it can thus represent an identity-defining resource that sets their lives in relation to a wider family history, despite the inevitable specificity and uniqueness of the family that they have just generated. The empirical studies carried out by Muxel offer valuable insights into the kind of connection linking individuals to their family memory and into the different identity levels affected by intergenerational legacies. The work of memory, fighting in the interaction between subjectivity and intersubjectivity, affection and norms, continuity and rupture, performs three mainly functions: reviviscence, transmission, and reflection (2002, 39).

Reviviscence is the act of bringing past experiences and events to the surface with a focus on affection. In a way, it refers to the intimacy of memories. Recollection, in this case, occurs in a sort of atemporal dimension, what Proust refers to in terms of involuntary memory. It is an inner, intimate form of recollection that searches time for eternal moments and events. Forgetfulness plays a central protecting role in this process, as it erases old wounds that inhibit one's progression in life. *Transmission*, on the contrary, meets the individuals' need to (re)discover the genealogical bonds that join them to other family members. It leads to the revelation of a 'we' that delineates one's sense of belonging as well as one's identity. Here forgetfulness guarantees the process of differentiation, i.e. the negotiation and personalization of one's family values, which prevent transmission from being reduced to mere replication. Finally, the third dimension of family memory, i.e. *reflection*, is the most analytical and evaluative of the set. It involves analyzing one's family overall experience as a basis for one's projection into the future. Acknowledging one's family past becomes, in this case, an opportunity to step back, recapitulate, recognize one's family heritage and plan one's future. Forgetfulness here supports one's quest for a salutary distance and for truth.

Parenthood, memory need, reflection

The research I did on the ethical implications of family intergenerational relationships allowed to investigate the educational value of heritage transmission across generations and to raise further questions and research into the field of parenting. The research purpose, in fact, was to investigate in an integrated way the affective quality of exchanges among family members and the centrality of ethical aspects in the definition of family ties. From the perspective taken here, ethical qualities are, alongside the relational ones, the backbone of parent–child relationships. Therefore, it is important to investigate the symbolic matrix of family past. Although we did not aim to present in detail the results of the above-mentioned research project, a clear focus on some issues emerged from the content analysis of the autobiographical materials, which allowed to reflect on the ethical and symbolical qualities of family memory. The analysis of parents' diaries, for example, showed that the families of origin are constantly referred to, though often unconsciously, in the processing of one's ethical values. Though with a fresh and modernizing approach, the new parents acknowledge – through recollection – the existence of a family heritage made of rituals, rules, traditions, caretaking practices, and so on. Some scholars have termed this 'the tent of values,' a safe place where family members can share beliefs, split responsibilities, and feel a sense of ethical belonging (Jacobson, Berry, and Olson 1975).

Drawing on the threefold approach of Muxel (2002), we can get more specific categories in approaching the narrative material and appreciate the complexity of meanings that are generated when memories are passed down from generation to generation, as well as the processes that underpin the development of parental identity.

Reviviscence

The function of this form of memory is to make the past 'living.' Through the re-enactment of scenes, past and present meet each other. Rather than as a nostalgic process, parents experience the recollection of family memories as an opportunity to better understand their personal history, through the lenses of a past that lingers in the present.

Although this is not the only function of memory, it is important to take into account also the emotional value of family memories. The affective dimension of reviviscence emerges clearly in the parents' discourse, especially when particularly intimate family scenes are brought to the surface. After rebuilding his family tree, a father shared this thought aloud:

> When I was working on my family tree, some memorable moments spent with uncle G. came to mind. He was my dear uncle, who took me to work with him in summer. How can I ever forget the utter joy of waking up at six in the morning to go to the market to get his fruits and vegetables stall ready? For me, he has been a real life mentor, he taught me the beauty of the relationship with people.

Transmission

This kind of memory is oriented to strengthen the sense of belonging and the respect of a sort of intergenerational continuity, precisely at the level of norms and values. The parents' written and oral narratives showed a degree of intergenerational convergence that had never been perceived before, when distance and indifference seemed to prevail. In the transition to parenthood, fathers and mothers discover a hitherto implicit sense of loyalty to their family heritage, as expressed by a father in his diary: 'Now that I'm a father, I know I want to live important life moments as a unique opportunity to be a family, as it used to be for my own family.' This continuity is not a mere replication of the same patterns of behavior, but rather the acknowledgment of a distinctive family style, of a rich heritage made of relational styles, of a body of meaning-making rules. These rules do show a path to follow, yet they simultaneously prompt a process of personal reinterpretation, as shown in the following excerpt by a mother: 'I treasure all the values I've been taught but since my daughter was born, I've found my own ways to live by them.'

Reflection

As mentioned earlier, the making of a family heritage requires interpretative and creative skills. It cannot freeze the past, because traditions need to push the individual forward, toward the future. This heritage is not a passive internalization, but rather a free interpretation, of the values from the past, in keeping with the individual's tension toward the new. Each generation needs to belong and to be free, in a dynamic play between connection and autonomy (Inowlocki 2005, 152).[3] As observed by Arendt, all human beings starting their life journey bring with themselves novelty as long as they are allowed to introduce changes. In other words, though belonging to a family, everyone is committed to generate his own history, by virtue of his uniqueness (1968).

In the research presented here, this interpretative and creative process – absolutely vital to the expression of one's ontological uniqueness – appeared to be the most fragile aspect of memory making. In their reflections, parents seemed only slightly aware of the intrinsic dialectic nature of intergenerational contact. The inevitable uncertainty (and novelty) involved in the task of personalizing the heritage received from one's own family is not verbalized spontaneously. Yet, the originality of the individual cannot emerge without a process of distancing from one's identity models.

This weakness points to the need to support parents in the process of coming to terms with intergenerational differences and with the new dimension that accompanies every next generation. This may well involve helping parents break with their past. A narrative tool as those discussed here can serve this function, as it raises the subject's awareness of both continuity and discontinuity. The development of one's personal identity is favored by the acknowledgment of difference and novelty. Through the dialectic of identification and differentiation, in the form of Ricœur's *idem-ipse* (1990, 12–13), each generation builds its own profile within the lineage.

The heritage of the past is not compromised if an heir interprets it freely and in ways suitable to his/her own context. A mother in our study writes:

> My parents taught me absolutely core values: resistance to difficulties, work ethic, responsibility, and discernment. Today I think I've found my own way to live those values, in terms of perseverance and determination, honesty and justice, to which I've added my own sensitivity.

Far from being a mere body of undisputable ethical rules and values, one's family heritage has to be understood also as a difficult though fruitful mediation between family past and individual conscience. Only in this way can the past inherited through the family heritage be really tangible. It may be uncomfortable but it is close and vital. In such dynamic memory work, past and present values interact for a richer construction of reality. Traditions are not handed down unchanged: they are transmitted through a creative process combining both continuity and enrichment. Family traditions remain open to new proposals, to the addition of new interpretations which draw on and disclose the dynamics of memory.

Parents' memory as 'dialogue of memories'

The examination of one's own family history through the threefold approach of reviviscence, transmission, and reflection is something that fathers and mothers do individually, gaining greater awareness of intergenerational relations in their own family line. If we conceived of this recollection process as a solipsistic one, however, we would lose sight of the fact that the development of parental identity is not only an individual pursuit but rather a couple event.

In this light, it is essential to present this process as fundamentally a co-participation, in which each single parent critically explores his/her own family heritage against the backdrop of the one received by his/her partner. On a biographical and historical level, parenthood is a dialogue of differences that, rather than developing into an undifferentiated whole, generates a relation of different existential paths.

If on the one hand we have to acknowledge the original difference of the two members of the couple, on the other it is essential to emphasize the dynamic process of synthesis they are expected to initiate when they become an 'us.' Both jointly rewrite their history, mediating what they have received with their uniqueness, both singular and dual (Pourtois and Desmet 2000).

The content analysis of parents' diaries and audio transcriptions revealed a large variation in the patterns of synthesis between past histories and future expectations. Among these are situations of complex intergenerational dialog, considerable imbalance in the recollection processes in favor of one family of origin to the detriment of the other, scant distancing alongside excessive idealization, or cases of enthusiastic attachment to one's roots alongside disapproving attitudes and division. The reflective work carried out with parents, intended as co-participation, may offer an opportunity to openly and confidently share biographical differences. Although this focus on one's past experiences, families of origin, and reciprocal representations may generate initial anxiety, it can develop into a precious unifying tool that supports one's commitment to the pursuit of a shared project.

When parents embrace this dialogic approach, the contact between the respective family histories can foster reciprocal understanding and involvement in the transmission (and revision) of family legacies to the new generation, as shown here:

> My wife and I wish that our respective families would go on teaching us the importance of family unity and that our son A. would always feel like spending time in the family, as is still the case with us, to experience that sense of connection and respect that we believe is a fundamental value to pass down to the generations to come.

Conclusive remarks

The foregoing reflections revolve around the contention that the family constitutes a fundamental relational environment, fostering the transmission of legacies and the development of identities. Being part of a family history gives the individual a sense of connectedness as well as reference points that, although bound to be critically assessed and personalized, still offer precious guidelines. The family heritage is not just a set of influences, less or more broader, but also a symbolical place for the individual to find sense of the self and others, of the environment and the history. The web of intergenerational relations offers knowledge, practices, values, and world representations, which taken together form a unique cultural heritage for all family members. From generation to generation the family hands down to its members a particular way to stay in the world, through paradigms, myths, rituals, stories which convey enduring views and values. This ethical heritage may be passed down through the generations as a result of family interaction, in this case parent–child interaction.

The examples depicted in the article may provide a window into this important meaning-making process that extends beyond parent–child relationships to the wider family unit. By processing this heritage, new generations can discover a precious body of models, rules, and values to draw on, feeling that they do not have to start from scratch building their own. Excessive centering on the psychological and clinical aspects could not encourage the understanding of this overall phenomenon of transmission. The research has been an opportunity to catch the richness of family memory, which demonstrates how the ethical dimension of transmission is inextricably mixed with psychological and emotional aspects, but not reduced to them. From an educational and philosophical point of view, it is important to grasp the opportunities which this perspective opens.

Popular and expert literature around parenting produces a sort of 'scientisation,' that encourage an ideal parenting which is emotionally intensive, but lacking on the ethical aspects of raising children. This sort of 'intensive parenting' is accompanied by increasingly weak patterns of belonging and fragile intergenerational ties. Passing through time and retracing the chain of transmission of life, it is possible to arrive at a symbolic overcoming of the narrow confines in which parenthood is often enclosed. Becoming parents is an experience that goes beyond the single story of a father and a mother, because it is part of a richer family history: a story that allows to feel connected with different generations and to recognize the symbolic heritage that is handed down over time. In this way, the intergenerational dialogue may help children to understand themselves as part of a family unit that shares a way to understand life events, perspectives, ethical guidelines.

Furthermore, the experience of research conducted with parents has given rise to the need to recognize the uniqueness of their family history, but also the need to compare their stories with those of other parents. By pooling experiences and feelings, many parents have discovered the beauty of sharing stories and come out of isolation. A large number of families that I have met in the research suffer from the lack of an informal supporting network. In view of this lack, I believe that it is appropriate to conceive parents' support also through the proposal of opportunities to socialize, to talk with other parents, to share the legacy receipts, to compare family traditions: in this way it is possible to get out of a widespread privatization of family ties, through a sharing of family memories. The comparison with other stories can break free from excessive concentration on one's own family dynamics. This decentralization helps parents to overcome the excessive self-reference, which often prevents to activate authentic reflective processes. The hermeneutic work done on the family legacy, through the comparison with other eyes, can be enriched by new perspectives.

With reference to this subject of family inheritance, I would like to conclude with a reflection on the symbolic bond that connects inheritance with responsibilities, receiving with giving. When we aim to interrogate family history and get the bond which links generations, it is restrictive only analyzing the processes of reception, that is what we have received from our predecessors. In a pedagogical perspective, it is important to make people aware of the fact that family memory is not only a gift but also a commitment.

Furthermore, fostering a reflective approach to intergenerational legacies enables new parents to reappraise their family history in terms of Godbout's threefold gift system of *giving, receiving*, and *reciprocating* (1992). These three steps are central to a family memory as well, a memory saturated with gratitude, innovation, and responsibility. Intergenerational relationships may provide an enhanced self-concept, sense of belonging, feelings of worth; but they also require to deal with family heritage in a responsible manner, as postulated by Jonas in his 'responsibility principle' (1979). The new parents' commitment to preserve and renovate their family heritage implies a responsible approach to their roots, so that the legacies passed down by past generations are not confined to the sole affective dimension but assume the form of ethical responsibility. In this perspective, addressing one's past means both searching answers to present and taking on the symbolic responsibility to give voice to a history to which we are all deeply indebted.

In a broader sense, this responsibility may open new spaces of encounter between individual, family, and society (Lahlou 2002; De Gaulejac 1999). Certainly intergenerational exchange strengthens the construction of memberships, but also carries a wealth of representations and rules that could drive individuals (parents in particular) to leave the confines of the private, to cross the home. In this direction, family memory could be opened to the perspective of a 'public destiny' (Vatz Laaroussi 2007). This would allow to draw unusual trajectories with respect to the educational role of intergenerational dialogue and family heritages. The ethical force of family memories could connect the nodes that bind the individual to the collective history, creating bridges among people, stories, and generations: in view of mutual responsibility.

Disclosure statement

No potential conflict of interest was reported by the author.

Notes

1. See in particular 'The Languages of Psychology and the Science of Parenting,' pp. 1–34.
2. The research was conducted in January, February, and March 2012 in three different preschools located in Brescia (Northern Italy) and its hinterland. In each school, six sessions (about 2–3 h) were performed. The sample was made up of parents with children aged between 2 and 5 years. Specifically, 62 parents were involved: 40% fathers and 60% mothers. Fifty percent of the sample took part in the research individually, the remaining 50% of participants followed the path with his/her partner. The research fits into the genre of narrative inquiry (Clandinin and Connelly 2000; Bodgan and Biklen 2007, Denzin and Lincoln 2011). The data, being of a linguistic nature (oral or written narratives), were analyzed using content analysis. After extraction of the 'nuclei of meaning,' content analysis was performed with the software T-Lab. For a more detailed account of the research project, see Amadini (2013).
3. In this article, it is possible to see how the meaning of the past and of traditionality is redefined by mothers and daughters to accommodate changes.

References

Agostino. 2004. *Confessioni*. Brescia: La Scuola.
Amadini, M. 2013. "Il sostegno educativo alla genitorialità: dar forma alla promessa custodita nel generare." In *L'attesa. Un tempo per nascere genitori* [The Wait. A Time to Born as Parents], edited by L. Cadei and D. Simeone, 135–144. Milano: Edizioni Unicopli.
Arendt, H. 1968. *Between Past and Future. Eight Exercises in Political Thought*. New York: Viking Press.
Beck, U., and E. Beck-Gernsheim. 2002. *Individualisation*. London: Sage.
Bengtson, V. L. 2001. "Beyond the Nuclear Family: The Increasing Importance of Multigenerational Bonds." *Journal of Marriage and the Family* 63: 1–16.
Bergson, H. 1969. *L'évolution crèatrice* [Creative Evolution]. Paris: PUF.
Bertaux, D., and P. Thompson. 2005. *Between Generations. Family Models, Myths and Memories*. New Brunswick: Transaction Publishers.
Bogdan, R., and S. K. Biklen. 2007. *Qualitative Research for Education. An Introduction to Theories and Methods*. New York: Pearson Education.
Brezinka, W. 2003. *Erziehung und Pädagogik im Kulturwandel* [Education and Pedagogy in Times of Cultural Change]. München: Ernst Reinhardt Verlag.
Bristow, J. 2014. "Who Cares for Children? The Problem of Intergenerational Contact." In *Parenting Culture Studies*, edited by E. Lee, J. Bristow, C. Faircloth, and J. Macvarish, 102–128. London: Palgrave Macmillan.
Clandinin, D. J., and F. M. Connelly. 2000. *Narrative Inquiry*. San Francisco, CA: Jossey-Bass.
Coenen-Huther, J. 1994. *La mémoire familiale* [Family Memory]. Paris: L'Harmattan.

De Gaulejac, V. 1999. *L'Histoire en héritage, roman familial at trajectoire sociale* [History in Heritage, Family Romance and Social Trajectory]. Paris: Desclée de Brouwer.

Denzin, N. K., and Y. S. Lincoln, eds. 2011. *Handbook of Qualitative Research*. Thousand Oaks, CA: Sage.

Godbout, J. T. 1992. *L'esprit du don* [The Spirit of Gift]. Paris: Editions La Découverte.

Gusdorf, G. 1951. *Mémoire et personne* [Memory and Person]. Paris: PUF.

Halbwachs, M. 1994. *Les cadres sociaux de la mémoire* [The Social Frameworks of Memory]. Paris: Albin Michel.

Hessen, S. 1958. *Fondamenti filosofici della pedagogia* [Philosophical Foundations of Education]. Roma: Armando.

Howard, P. 2001. *The Collapse of the Common Good*. New York: Ballantine.

Inowlocki, L. 2005. "Grandmothers, Mothers and Daughters." In *Between Generations. Family Models, Myths and Memories*, edited by D. Bertaux and P. Thompson, 139–153. New Brunswick: Transaction Publishers.

Jacobson, R. B., K. J. Berry, and D. H. Olson. 1975. "An Empirical Test on Generation Gap: A Comparative Intrafamily Study." *Journal of Marriage and the Family* 37: 841–852.

Jonas, H. 1979. *Das Prinzip Verantwortung. Versuch einer Ethik für die techologische Zivilisatio* [The Imperative of Responsibility. In Search of an Ethics for the Technological Age]. Frankfurt: Suhrkamp.

Knowles, M. 1989. *The Making of an Adult Educator. An Autobiographical Journey*. San Francisco, CA: Jossey-Bass.

Lahlou, M., (sous la direction de). 2002. *Histoires familiales, Identité, Citoyenneté* [Family Histories, Identity, Citizenship]. Lyon: Éditions L'Interdisciplinaire.

Lee, E. 2014. "Introduction." In *Parenting Culture Studies*, edited by E. Lee, J. Bristow, C. Faircloth, and J. Macvarish, 1–22. London: Palgrave Macmillan.

Lollis, S. 2003. "Conceptualizing the Influence of the Past and the Future in Present Parent–Child Relationships." In *HandBook of Dynamics in Parent–Child Relations*, edited by L. Kuczynski, 67–88. Thousand Oaks, CA: Sage.

MacIntyre, A. 2007. *After Virtue*. 3rd revised ed. London: G. Duckworth.

Muxel, A. 2002. *Individu et mémoire familiale* [Individual and Family Memory]. Paris: Nathan.

Neuberger, R. 1995. *Le mythe familial* [The Family Myth]. Paris: ESF.

Pourtois, J-P., and H. Desmet. 2000. *Le parent éducateur* [Parents Educators]. Paris: PUF.

Pratt, M. W., and B. H. Fiese. 2004. *Family Stories and the Life Course Across Time and Generations*. Hillsdale, NJ: Lawrence Erlbaum Associates.

Ramaekers, S., and J. Suissa. 2012. *The Claims of Parenting. Reasons, Responsibility and Society*. Houten: Springer.

Ricœur, P. 1990. *Soi-même comme un autre* [Oneself as Another]. Paris: Seuil.

Ricœur, P. 2000. *La mémoire, l'histoire, l'oubli* [Memory, History, Forgetting]. Paris: Seuil.

Samuel, R., and P. Thompson, eds. 1990. *The Myths We Live By*. London: Routledge.

Suissa, J. 2006. "Untangling the Mother Knot: Some Thoughts on Parents, Children and Philosophers of Education." *Ethics and Education* 1: 65–77.

Vatz Laaroussi, M. 2007. "Les usages sociaux et politiques de la mémoire familiale: de la reparation de soi à la reparation des chaos de l'histoire [Social and Political Uses of Family Memory: From Repairing Himself to the Repair of the Chaos of History]." *Enfances, Familles, Générations* [Childhood, Families, Generations] 7: 112–126.

Waiton, S. 2008. *The Politics of Antisocial Behaviour: Amoral Panics*. London: Routledge.

Waiton, S. 2010. "The Antisocialisation of Children and Young People: Undermining Professionals and Colonising Everyday Life." *Youth and Policy* 105: 37–49.

Exhausting the fatigue university: in search of a biopolitics of research

Florelle D'Hoest and Tyson E. Lewis

> Today it would seem that being fatigued is a fairly common physical and psychological effect of educational systems based on an increasing demand for high-yield performance quotas. In higher education, 'publish or perish' is a kind of imperative to perform, perform better, and perform optimally leading to an overall economy of fatigue. In this paper we provide a critical theory of what we are calling the 'fatigue university.' While highlighting the negative costs of fatigue, we also provide a philosophical distinction between tiredness and exhaustion that disrupts the biopolitics of fatigue from the inside. To do so, we turn to Gilles Deleuze and Giorgio Agamben whose writings on exhaustion point to its educational importance. Indeed, it is through the very 'illnesses' of exhaustion that the biopolitics of research can be problematized and opened up for new configurations.

Introduction

In a famous passage in Carroll's *Through the Looking Glass*, Alice and the Red Queen 'somehow or other, [...] began to run' (1872, 39). The little girl 'was getting so much out of breath [...] till suddenly, just as Alice was getting quite exhausted, they stopped, and she found herself sitting on the ground, breathless and giddy' (41). What surprises Alice is that, despite the race, she and the Red Queen are still at the same place. In our opinion, this scene could be a metaphor of our actual society, which is, in the words of the cultural theorist Han (2010), a fatigue society (*Müdigkeitsgesellshaft*). According to this German author, our society is not disciplinary anymore (Thou shalt not!) but based on achievement (Yes we can!). The subjects of this new society are constantly pushed to achieve goals and tasks, thus they are expected to be faster and more productive than ever before. The typical disease of this society of achievement is fatigue. Indeed, the fatigue society is so pervasive that even the last bastion of rest – sleep itself – is now under threat by the colonizing forces that emphasize productivity, efficiency, and constant self-monitoring (Crary 2013).

Alice and the Red Queen's race might also give a certain insight into research as it is experienced in what we would call the 'fatigue university.' Even more than knowledge, cleverness, or curiosity, a strong physical and psychological condition has become essential to survive research: we have to run, and keep running, in order to bear the current pace of publications, research project applications, etc. The old adage 'publish or perish' is an injunction to maximize one's utility to a knowledge economy through research, or else one will lose opportunities for grants, research positions, or tenure. Or, even worse, researchers are caught in the trap of publish *and* perish. It is not enough to merely publish but one must also publish in the highest ranked journals and the most competitive venues. If one submits to such an injunction, then researchers are more than ever exposed to the risks of escalating fatigue. All the while, this frenetic pace does not necessarily improve research; on the contrary, it often seems to lead us nowhere (D'Hoest and Bárcena 2011).

In this sense, fatigue would seem to be a kind of social and educational sickness brought about by the very real working conditions of a biopolitical knowledge economy – an economy that concerns the investment in and management of life itself (Foucault 1990; Hardt and Negri 2001). Indeed, it is only within a biopolitical framework emphasizing health, optimization, and achievement that fatigue would even register as a political, economic, and educational issue. Importantly, fatigue is not merely a regrettable result of the achievement paradigm but rather is its central product, for it is through fatigue that ever increasingly refined and sophisticated tools and strategies of self-improvement can be designed and implemented. And if such fatigue cannot be surmounted, then the individual will be abandoned by the system as a form of 'collateral damage.' In this sense, fatigue is *internal to* and *constitutive of* biopolitical logistics.

While critics are quick to point to fatigue as a symptom of larger forms of biopolitical control, is it not possible that tiredness and exhaustion, which are both expressions of fatigue, also have redemptive possibility overlooked by these very same critics? This is the clue given by two philosophers, Giorgio Agamben and Gilles Deleuze, whom we will explore in this essay. In dialog with Agamben and Deleuze, we analyze the conceptual space opened up by tiredness and exhaustion in relation to education, particularly with reference to the student–professor relationship within a university research framework. Our contention is that, nowadays, tiredness and exhaustion are necessarily at the heart of the research experience. In the following, we will study tiredness and exhaustion (1) in their common, philosophical, and educational meanings, (2) as concepts indicated (more than elaborated) by Agamben and Deleuze and, finally, (3) how these concepts relate to each other in a concrete educational situation that includes academic advising and research. Making a critical distinction between being tired and being exhausted will enable us to argue that only by thinking through the problem of fatigue can educational research become otherwise than a mere symptom of a fatigue society bent on producing quantifiable achievements in the name of optimal performance quotas. Indeed, it is through the very 'illnesses' of exhaustion in particular that the biopolitics of research can be problematized and opened up for new configurations.

A brief review of tiredness and exhaustion

What does research have to do with tiredness and exhaustion? Such an inquiry into the nature of being tired and/or being exhausted is of personal interest to both of us. We are researchers in the field of philosophy of education. One of us is a teacher at the university, and part of his job is to advise students on their dissertations; the other one is a Ph.D. student, who is writing a dissertation under the supervision of an academic advisor.

As such, we encounter valences of tiredness and exhaustion all the time in our professional lives, both in terms of our own work and in the work of other students/researchers. And yet, due to the emphasis on achievement that we encounter daily in terms of professional goals, standards, and expectations, speaking (let alone writing) about the topic of fatigue is accompanied by a certain taboo. For faculty, to admit fatigue is to admit to a 'lack of willpower' or to a 'lack of productivity' or to a 'lack of passion' or even worse, such admissions demonstrate a certain 'ungratefulness' for one's professional life. For students this means that they are labeled 'unreliable' or 'lacking promise' and thus are cut from large research projects, conference panels, and so on. In academic advising, fatigue is all-to-easily dismissed as a psychological problem that can be dealt with by seeing a psychiatrist or through medicalization. In all cases, it is something that is discussed in secrete, in whispers in hallways, or behind closed doors. The following is an attempt to break through this taboo on discussing fatigue in order to understand how society at large and philosophy in particular have constructed the complex concepts of tiredness and exhaustion. Our goal is to lay some groundwork for a much more in-depth analysis of the same concepts found in Agamben and Deleuze.

According to the Oxford Dictionary, 'tired' means 'in need of sleep of rest.' After the race, the Red Queen tells Alice: 'You may rest a little now.' Indeed, Alice may rest a little because the race has tired her. At this point, Carroll uses the word 'exhausted' ('just as Alice was getting quite exhausted...'). The same dictionary registers two meanings of 'exhausted': (1) 'drained of one's physical or mental resources; very tired' and (2) 'completely used up.' In the common, everyday uses of the terms, tiredness and exhaustion are thus clearly related: there seems to be a difference of degree between 'tired' and 'exhausted.' 'Exhausted' is *more than* 'tired' (a comparative), to the extent that it can mean *the extreme form* of 'tiredness' (its superlative). In the description of Alice after the race, the use of 'exhausted' instead of 'tired' indicates that Alice could not have run much more or faster than she did, since she was actually reaching her limits.

For the French historian of philosophy Jean-Louis Chrétien, fatigue is an essential phenomenon of existence, and, as such, it has always been a philosophical theme. In his book *De la Fatigue* (1996), the author surveys the history of philosophy and points to some interesting elaborations of fatigue by Aristotle, Sartre, Lévinas, and others. As Chrétien is right to point out, nobody gave more importance to 'tiredness' (*Müdigkeit*) and 'exhaustion' (*Ermüdung*)[2] in philosophy than Nietzsche; indeed the author dedicates a whole chapter to Nietzsche and the 'great fatigue.' Throughout his work, Nietzsche seems to refer to tiredness and exhaustion indifferently, and the various ways he describes the two are never fixed, yet he does suggest that there are different sorts of tiredness. When Nietzsche refers to tiredness, he usually points out a symptom we have to fight, for it is a sign of Christian decadence. Roughly speaking, tiredness deserves, in Nietzsche's thought, the same treatment as disease:

> Christianity was from the beginning, essentially and fundamentally, life's nausea and disgust with life.... Hatred of 'the world,' condemnations of the passions, fear of beauty and sensuality... – all this struck me, no less than the unconditional will of Christianity to recognize only moral values, as the most dangerous and uncanny form of all possible forms of a 'will to decline' – at the very least a sign of abysmal sickness, weariness, discouragement, exhaustion, and the impoverishment of life. (1967, 23)

Christian values provoke weariness, that is, make us weaker, and it is against these values that we have to struggle in order to recover our authentic forces from the grip of this 'will to decline.' Chrétien concludes: 'Fatigue becomes the more including, the more general denomination of everything we should say no to' (our translation 1996, 138). But sometimes Nietzsche refers to an original 'tiredness,' which is the reverse of the 'fatigue' we have just depicted: what Chrétien calls the 'fatigue of the fatigue.' In this sense, to be tired is to be tired of tiredness, of Christian values, and this is indeed a good sign. Nietzsche experienced original tiredness himself: there is a kind of tiredness that is a force, and not a weakness. It is to be tired of the tiring: to be tired of 'the good' (and not to be tired of the suffering).

Thus, according to Nietzsche, tiredness always carries a value, and it is usually negative, for it weakens us, making us decadent. The only case in which tiredness is positively considered by Nietzsche is when tiredness is a good sign: it is good to be tired when tiredness is a force that reacts against tiredness.

As we discussed previously, the current educational dogma emphasizes becoming an active worker, citizen, student who realizes his or her full potentiality in the name of economic efficiency and productivity (Lewis 2013); but, obviously, the more active you are, the more tired you become. Therefore, we can expect *more* tiredness from the current educational system: students, but also professors, are expected to be more tired than ever (given that, for example, there are more tests to pass, more student work to be graded, more papers to write, more grants to apply for, more conferences to attend, and so on). Thus, if activity is an educational goal, tiredness should be a healthy symptom, a sign that we are being truly active. And indeed, symptoms such as testing fatigue testify to the constitutive role of being tired under high-stakes testing. Interestingly, psychological research shows that this fatigue does not necessarily impair test-taking outcomes, and in this sense cannot be offered as evidence against high stakes testing (Ackerman 2009). Tiredness is not an obstacle to taking the test and maximizing outputs but is part and parcel of a fatigue society, becoming an opportunity for the student to continue to devise motivational strategies and skill sets in order to achieve optimal outcomes.

However, this natural tiredness which is internal to high-stakes testing and its fatigue cannot be drawn out to the point of becoming tired with being tired: activity has to remain permanent, the machine has to keep running, no matter which degree of tiredness affects us. We cannot avoid tiredness, but, as far as possible, we are expected to avoid its limit: exhaustion. We are educated to avoid exhaustion: we are educated in how to guard some reserve of our energy despite 'getting so much out of breath.'

This brief review thus leaves us with several remaining questions. First, is there a real difference between tiredness and exhaustion, and, if so, is it one of degree instead of kind? It would seem that common, everyday usage of the terms in the English language would suggest the former rather than the latter. Yet, being tired of being tired (as Nietzsche writes) could indicate a qualitative (rather than merely quantitative) transformation from tiredness to exhaustion. A second question then follows: Is there any space for rethinking being exhausted in the space of research? If exhaustion is the real taboo here (not simply tiredness), does this not indicate that there might be something fundamentally *disruptive* to the biopolitics of the knowledge economy about exhaustion? To further develop these lines of inquiry, we now turn to a careful reading of the themes in Agamben and Deleuze. What will emerge is a rethinking of the biopolitics of exhaustion as a kind of redemption of the tiredness of being tired.

Agamben on study, potentiality, and exhaustion

In this section, we would like to turn more explicitly to education and its particular relationship to fatigue. To do so, we will begin with an overview of Agamben's reflections on studying and their connection to exhaustion. In particular, his gesture toward Bartleby the Scrivener as the exhausted figure of study will lead us to Deleuze and a more in-depth discussion of the potentially positive powers of exhaustion. In short, we will use Bartleby as a hinge or fold between Agamben, Deleuze, and the concepts of education and fatigue. The result will be a new appreciation of exhaustion that is directly relevant to the question of research in the 'fatigue university.'

Before turning to Bartleby directly, it is important to understand the relationship between potentiality and education in Agamben's work. For Agamben, study is the quintessential educational experience of potentiality as such, freed from any ends or measurable actualizations (Lewis 2013). This is important because in the fatigue society, potentiality is usually only thought in relation to some actualization (which can be measured and thus improved upon). Indeed, for Agamben, the principle injunction of the fatigue society (as well as the fatigue university) might very well be 'Be all that you can be!' In this formulation, we must push ourselves to 'realize our full potentiality' without remainder. Potentiality must be put to work in order for the individual to be competitive in a fast-paced world of do or die, publish or perish. Yet what is missed here is any experience of our potentiality as such, or potentiality as a pure means rather than a mere means to another end. When we think of potentiality in and for itself, we realize that potentiality is not simply a capacity to do something but also and equally a capacity not to do something. To think potentiality is to think impotentiality. When thought on its own terms, potentiality, according to Agamben, has a particular tautological structure that holds within itself mutually exclusive opposites in a single formula. Speaking of potentiality, Agamben writes, 'the tautology "it-will-occur-or-it-will-not-occur" is necessarily true as a whole, beyond the taking place of either of the two possibilities' (1999, 266). In such a tautology, each alternative is returned back to a purely contingent state. Stated differently, in the tautology an event occurs *and* does not occur simultaneously. To be in potential, an occurrence cannot foreclose upon its contingency to not happen. Thus, potentiality is a suspension of distinctions such as occurrence and non-occurrence, being and not being, in order to keep open a perpetual field of contingent possibilities. The field of contingent possibilities is the precise location of human freedom as the opposite of necessity (something must occur or not occur) and impossibility (something that occurs cannot occur). As Agamben writes, '... the root of freedom is to be found in the abyss of potentiality.... To be free is, in the sense we have seen, *to be capable of one's own impotentiality* ...' (183).

What makes us human is the capability to *not* be: the impotential of our potentiality. This description is important for educators because, as Agamben argues (1995), study is an educational experience of potentiality: it is a time and space of rhythmic turning from undertaking to undergoing, stupidity to lucidity without necessary end. Held in this perpetual sway, when asked what one is studying, it is essential to answer with an indeterminate formula: 'I would prefer not to say.' In this formula, the studier remains indistinct, yet free in this indistinction. Freedom here is both positive and negative. The studier is free from the compulsions of an educational system obsessed with assessment of outcomes and measurement of potentialities, but also free to be continually *otherwise than* assessments and evaluations predict or society demands. Given that the fatigue university concerns itself with developing skills and capabilities for the purposes of actualizing these skills and capabilities in educationally and socially measurable forms, study seems to be nothing more than an obstruction or annoying rest stop on the way toward full optimization and thus economic utility. Indeed, the studier would most likely be labeled as suffering from depression – which is said to be a sort of fatigue,[3] and thus crossed off as a mere degenerate excess of the knowledge economy.

Interestingly, for Agamben, Bartleby the Scrivener is the 'most exemplary embodiment of study in our culture' (1995, 65). Bartleby, as a studier, withdraws his capabilities to copy from actualizing their potentiality in the form of work and prefers not to write. At this precise moment, when Bartleby famously prefers not to copy yet remains in the legal office as an 'employee,' he embodies the tautology of potentiality: no longer a worker he is not yet something else either. Indeed, his impotent gesture opens up a space and time that suspends the daily functions of the office: the formula 'I would prefer not to' spreading exponentially to the point of driving his employer to the brink of madness. As a studier, Bartleby is interminably moved between two antithetical poles: 'the potential to be (or do) and the potential not to be (or do)' (1999, 255). To prefer not to opens and sustains an indistinction to be and not to be that defines the tricky terrain of study. Only in this suspension is Bartleby freed to study and to become a paradigm of study. But to move in this space and time of study is to be exhausted by study. In a slightly different context Agamben again argues that the artist who puts down his/her pen and turns his or her back to Genius embodies 'exhausted and suspended time' (2007, 18) not unlike Bartleby who renounces the practice of his craft through the suspending function of his 'I prefer not to.' But what precisely is exhausting and exhausted about Bartleby? What distinguishes his exhaustion from the simple tiredness of his coworkers and employer, both of whom are frustrated by Bartleby's lack of willful intentionality?

For answers to these questions, we must now turn to Deleuze. But first, an important linguistic remark. 'Exhausted' is the word that has been used by the translators of Agamben's 'Bartleby, o della contingenza' and Deleuze's 'Bartleby ou la formule' and 'L'Épuisé.' The original words are 'épuisé' in French and 'stremata' in Italian; Agamben writes: 'Lo scriba che non scrive (di cui Bartleby è l'ultima, stremata figura)' (1993, 53). The adjective 'stremata' points at the extreme of the force, which has been reached, the limit of the energy that has been exceeded. We will see in the following that, whereas Agamben and Deleuze are not thinking through the same words, they are virtually drawing the same concept: 'stremata' and 'épuisé' point in the same direction. In this light, the clue given by the English language – the one word 'exhausted' – happens to be a good lead.

Deleuze: the positive power of exhaustion

'The Exhausted' was written by Deleuze three years before his death, as he was fatigued by a long standing lung disease (Cull 2011). Interestingly, the Spanish Dictionary *Maria Moliner* describes 'cansancio' ('tiredness') as provoked, sometimes, by a lack of breath; that happens to Alice, who, while 'getting quite exhausted,' ends up breathless. Besides, we often use this expression, 'breathless,' to indicate 'tiredness' or 'exhaustion': in French, 'breathless' can be translated by the expression 'être à bout de souffle' – like Godard's film – which literally means 'to the end of the breath.' Thus, Deleuze thinking concepts such as tiredness and exhaustion are no accident; rather, exhaustion and tiredness, that is, his permanent condition of breathlessness, have been the structural accident of Deleuze's life that have, like Nietzsche's various illnesses, pushed him to philosophize.

In 'M comme Maladie' ('M stands for Illness'), from *Gilles Deleuze from A to Z with Claire Parnet* (Boutang 2004), Deleuze expounds upon his fragile health condition. To him, illness ('maladie') is not something bad ('mal'), since illness serves the thought much better than a good health condition does. To think is to be attentive, to be listening to life, and illness sharpens life; in this sense, illness makes thinking easier. But Deleuze insists on the fact that tiredness and illness are not quite the same. Yet both concepts are existentially related: illness increases and brings tiredness forward. To be tired means: 'today, I have done what I could'; tiredness is the signal for the end of the day. In this interview, Deleuze never uses the word 'exhausted,' but it was recorded in 1988–1989, a few years before writing 'The exhausted.'

In this later text, which shows a shift in focus from the question of being tired to being exhausted, Deleuze provides a startling description which is worth citing in full:

> The possible is only realized in the derivative, through tiredness, whereas you are exhausted before birth, before self-realization or realizing anything whatsoever .... When you realize some of what is possible, it's in relation to certain goals, projects and preferences: I put on shoes to go out and slippers to stay in ... the realization of the possible always proceeds through exclusion, because it presupposes preferences and goals that vary, forever replacing predecessors. It is these variations, these substitutions, all these exclusive disjunctions (daytime/night-time, going out/staying in...) that are tiring in the end. (1995, 3)

In this passage, Deleuze begins by noting a difference between being tired and being exhausted. To be tired is to 'realize' some sort of potentiality in relation to certain goals, a possibility. Thus when one takes a test in order to measure skill acquisition, one is legitimately tired for one has attempted to realize a possibility: 'today, I have done what I could.' While it is perfectly acceptable and legitimate to be tired, Deleuze notes that such realization 'always proceeds through exclusion.' Thus the goal of taking the test produces a certain exclusion: not winning or not passing. When one is tired, sets of 'exclusive disjunctions' are produced such as 'going out/staying in.' Deleuze continues:

> Exhaustion is altogether different: you combine the set of variables of a situation, provided you renounce all order of preference and all organization of a goal, all signification. It is no longer so as to go out or stay in, and you no longer make use of days and nights .... That does not mean that you fall into indifferentiation, or into the celebrated identified contraries, and you are not passive: you press on, but toward nothing. You were tired by something, but exhausted by nothing. (1995, 3–4)

One is exhausted not by realizing a set of defined goals but rather by renouncing all preferences, all goals, and all determinate outcomes. Like Bartleby, Beckett's Mr. Knott 'does not reserve any combination for a singular use that would exclude others – whose circumstances are yet to come' (Deleuze 1995, 4). Rather than particular uses determined by particular goals, the combination holds within itself all possibilities equally: 'The combinatorial is the art or science of exhausting the possible, through inclusive disjunctions.' The exhausted tallies combinations, permutations, enumerations, and infinite lists to the point where he or she 'replaces projects with tables and programs denuded of sense' (5). In this sense, for Deleuze and Agamben, Bartleby and other enigmatic figures of study are exhausted because they are in a state of perpetual potentiality (perpetual combinatorials). Whether Agamben's tautology or Deleuze's combinatorial, contingent possibilities remain open, and thus withdrawn from all measure of success or failure.

'The Exhausted' is originally a post-face to a French publication of *Quad and Other Television Plays*[4] by Beckett. According to Deleuze, what makes these plays interesting are Beckett's different ways of exhausting the possible: meaningful sentences are exhausted by words, which are exhausted by voices, which are exhausted by space, which is exhausted by the image (which is the final exhaustion of the possible). This is not about tiredness, but exhaustion: here, it is clear that Deleuze traces a difference of nature between both concepts. Exhausted is not a comparative or superlative of tiredness, but something different. The exhausted does not rest, because he/she cannot rest. And the reason of this restlessness is the structural lack of rest (reserve) of exhaustion.

Deleuze does not use the word 'exhausted', but 'épuisé', which comes from 'puits': a well; 'épuiser' literally means 'dry up.' In Spanish, 'exhausted' is 'agotado', which comes from 'gota' (drop): someone who is 'agotado' has no drop left, no water reserve. 'Exhausto' is a synonym of 'agotado': 'exhausto' and 'exhausted' are built with 'ex' and 'haurire,' which means 'collect, draw water (haurire) outside (ex).' As has been indicated before, 'stremata,' the adjective used by Agamben to describe the figure of Bartleby as the last scribe, points at a limit that has been pushed to the extreme, exceeded. These linguistic facts put us on the way to understanding the radical difference between tiredness and exhaustion: admittedly, both states tend toward inactivity. But, first, after tiredness comes always rest, and rest is possible only because there is already some rest: not everything has been buried in the activity, something remains, and this remainder is the starting point for a new activity. But the exhausted does not rest: indeed, the exhausted does not lie in a bed but sits, like Dürer's melancholic angel, like the studier, like Bartleby. Second, someone gets tired after having done *something*, whereas the exhausted is exhausted 'already before his birth' *of nothing*. Third, you get tired because of a choice; you get exhausted when you do not choose, when there is no preference (we could perhaps say that exhaustion is an existential skepticism that prefers to withhold judgment at the very threshold of such judgment).

In 'M comme Maladie,' again, there is an interesting development and celebration of old age. To be old is to *be*; *Being*, full stop. When you are young, you have to be(come) this or that, you are tied to projects. On the contrary, to be old is to be free of projects, careless about the actualization of possibilities. To be old is to be exhausted, someone 'who has no other need than to be without need.' Bartleby has no age either, but we have the feeling that he is old: not that he has become old, but that he is (already old, already exhausted). And yet, isn't education about building and following projects, be(com)ing this or that? Are we claiming, as with Bartleby, that students who are already old are already exhausted?

Bartleby has no reserve, and he produces nothing. He does not tire himself, he is exhausted. But Bartleby is not only a character who has been fictionalized by Melville: we *are* Bartleby when we study, when we do research. To research is to re-search, to search repeatedly, and to search and search and keep searching means to have nothing to report, no conclusions to offer up. As studiers we are confronted not with meaningless materials or with meaningful results but rather with the exhaustion of an unfulfilled *potentiality of meaning*. When studying, we hold the various combinatorials in our minds without firmly committing to any particular thesis or conclusion. This is not a state of indecision but rather a firm commitment to our potentiality as such – our potentiality to do-this-and-that or to say-this-and-that. But such a commitment is not merely intellectual, it is also embodied, and thus written on and through our postures and gestures. Indeed, to be exhausted is to be haunted by the combinatorials that we not only think but also live. Exhausted studiers do not simply lie down and go to sleep. Rather they are always sitting, hunched over, carrying stacks of books, rubbing their eyes from the endless strain of reading and re-reading. They are, like Deleuze, out of breath. They are somewhat absentminded, jotting down this or that set of notes, which inevitably pile up on desks and in small, secret stashes only to be forgotten or eclipsed by new combinatorials that reveal themselves. As such there is a phenomenology of exhaustion that is very different from mere tiredness where one lies down and 'sleeps it off' to emerge refreshed and ready to begin work again early the next morning. Unlike this renewal, the exhausted is always dragging along ... he/she is always somewhat inoperative. His or her life appears suspended in a state that is neither moving forward nor retreating, but a constant series of hesitations and detours. As such, the economy of tiredness and renewal that is essential to the overall fatigue society is deactivated by a much more radical state whereby the studier is so exhausted that he or she *cannot be tired.*

Bartleby *looks like* a tired person, but he is not: he is exhausted *by nothing*. His exhaustion as a 'preferring not to' opens up a radically different possibility, one that has profound implications for research. Of course, the irony of this move is not lost on us: the character who appears to do nothing, research nothing, and fade away into nihilism does not seem a very efficacious paradigm for research, especially now in the day and age of 'publish or perish.' Certainly, Bartleby perished, his rhythm of study slid into nihilism. As such, if he represents – as we argue, drawing on Agamben and Deleuze – a point of suspension where the logic of tiredness is interrupted precisely through the limit case of exhaustion, this point of suspension must be further examined. How can the exhausted neither perish nor become yet another functionary of the biopolitical knowledge economy?

Tiredness and exhaustion in a concrete educational situation: academic advising and research

The exhausted departs from nothing and *does/goes to* nothing; the researcher lets idle everything he/she has learned before in order to study; he/she loses definitive destinations and prefers not to choose anything beyond his/her own potentiality without sacrifice; he/she dwells endlessly in the tautology or combinatorial. The research is exhausted and the research exhausts him/her: beyond the possibilities of supporting this or that theory/conclusion lies a preference not to actualize potentiality in a quantifiable form. All that is left is the potentiality to be and not to be, to do and not to do held together in the combinatorial that haunts the researcher day and night, never allowing him or her to rest.

As a teacher, one of us has often seen the advent of exhaustion overcome students when they suddenly open their mouths as if to say something profound only to fall quickly back into silence, when they retreat into hours of prolonged reading, when they doodle endless outlines and permutations of possible relationships between concepts, and when they postpone deadlines in order to keep tinkering with an idea. They define themselves in terms of some 'fixed' problem (we need to raise test scores for instance) only to realize that the problem pulverizes itself into multiple problems, dispersing into a series of pathways that, in the end, lead away from one another toward new horizons and new combinatorials that are loosely held together by the tautological potentiality of the study itself. In all cases, the students, heads bent down, back's hunched over with bags full of books, are not lazy or tired but rather caught in the interminable rhythms of research, the trace of which is written on the body through various signs of exhaustion – sitting in the library late at night or before the computer screen, finding themselves restless at the very moment when they should be tired out and going to sleep.

As teachers and advisors to future researchers, we have a role to play in bearing the burdens of exhaustion. Exhaustion should not be brushed off as merely an unsavory and thankfully temporary phase that will be eventually overcome through the completion of specific projects. This attitude again views exhaustion as a kind of deficit, but teachers cannot afford to be like the employer in Bartleby's office who is impatient, frustrated, and constantly agitated by this strange, interminable figure who is not productive or responsive to either commands or care. Exhaustion cannot be easily instrumentalized or absorbed back into the biopolitical economy of publish or perish. Indeed, there is a strange freedom from ends that is its own pleasure. Just as Deleuze found illness to be the very source of thought, so too bearing the burden of exhaustion need not be reduced to a psychological blip on the research ladder to success. It can and should be experienced as a state of freedom from determinant outcomes.[5]

Yet, sooner or later, the exhaustion of research will be pushed to publish something. Studies have to turn into dissertations – otherwise the result is infinite delay in the aporetic space of study, if not nihilistic dissolve as witnessed in the case of Bartleby. These goals are tiring, so it seems that the exhaustion of research is forced to live with the tiring pace of the fatigue university, but how? Tiredness and exhaustion are mutually exclusive: tiredness comes after realizing a possibility, to exhaust possibilities is to prevent them from applying to actualization; tiredness comes after having done something, the exhausted is exhausted by nothing; tiredness is a consequence of choice, exhaustion is the state of choosing not to choose, a permanent existential standstill (a radical gesture of academic 'preferring not to').

Like Alice, we are tired of this tiring research race. With this in mind, we would like to share a few questions that seem relevant to the concrete educational situation of research, and which it would be useful to think through for academic advising. These questions will not resolve the issues outlined here, yet we hope that they will break the taboo of the fatigue university, and thus enable us to question how exhaustion and tiredness shape the biopolitics of research.

(1) For the teacher/advisor: How can you open up the space and time of study so that students experience exhaustion as not simply an unwelcomed contingency that needs to be overcome but also as freedom to be otherwise than? As teachers and advisors, it is crucial that you open up the difficult yet free space and time of study so that students can come to experience exhaustion as a pure means.

(2) Yet if the teacher/advisor's role is to open up the space and time of study, is it not also true that something must in the last instance be produced? Does not some materialization of the work need to be brought into the world? But if this is the case, then have we not merely instrumentalized exhaustion, turning it back into a *resource* to be appropriated by the fatigue university on its quest for escalating efficiency?

(3) But this question leads to another: Can we think of a way to help students actualize the *impotentiality* of their thinking? With this question we enter a threshold that moves us beyond the fatigue university. If exhaustion is indeed the qualitative leap

that comes from being tired of being tired, then perhaps we can define *inspiration* as the second qualitative leap that comes from being tired by exhaustion. Indeed, Agamben argues that when Bartleby puts down his pen and ceases to produce 'evidence' of his potentiality, he opens up a space for action beyond any recognizable action – a space of 'inspiration' (1995, 65) that is also a space of nothing. And it is here that exhaustion suddenly morphs into a kind of inspiration. Exhaustion can push us to say, to write certain things, but in which way?

(4) In conclusion: What does it mean to *write* inspiration or to write impotentiality? To do research is, of course, to end up saying *certain* things (instead of *other* things, at least not at the same time), but in order to end up saying *certain* things, we have to re-search, that is, to come back to the ambiguous, the inclusive disjunctions, combinatorials. This means *saying things about the potentiality for saying things – saying certain things about that which remains uncertain* (our impotentiality). Is this not precisely the experience we have of reading Agamben's work – texts that appear to de-create themselves in the very moment of their appearing as texts? A new kind of research is thus made possible here; one modeled less on quantifiable and measurable outcomes or standardized/ recognizable formats and more on the aporetic practices of Beckett's plays or the novels of Walser and Kafka or the aphorisms of Nietzsche or the emphasis on problems over solutions in Deleuze. As both teachers and students, we should look for alternative forms of writing that interrupt, suspend, and render inoperative the fundamental logic of the research article that has been fully co-opted by the biopolitical knowledge economy. Such forms are tiring and tiresome. In other words: could we not make the most of the 'publish or perish' period by using these spaces and times to *exhaust* them, thus writing articles *as not* articles (returning them to their impotentiality to be otherwise than what they have become)? Only then can we discover the inspiration of that which remains in the remnants of the 'article.' Then, as Deleuze and Parnet suggested (1987) and performed, our academic writing would become completely different: … or …, … and … and … and …, it could be … or/and …, the … - … - … - ….

Disclosure statement

No potential conflict of interest was reported by the authors.

Notes

2. The German language seems to confirm what has been supposed above: that exhaustion (*Ermüdung*) is a degree of tiredness (*Müdigkeit*).
3. Before depression was officially recognized as a mental illness, it was usual to consider it as a form of fatigue. Someone depressed was someone who was extremely tired. We still hold fatigue for the essential feature of a depressive mood.
4. *Quad* illustrates (and probably inspires) the difference which Deleuze traces between 'tiredness' and 'exhaustion.' The central point o*f the square is a point of exhaust*ion/the exhausted point:

> There's no doubt that the protagonists tire themselves out and will drag themselves more and more. But tiredness is a minor aspect of the enterprise […]. The protagonists tire according to the number or realisations. But the possible is accomplished independently of this number, by the exhausted protagonists who exhaust it. […].

The protagonists realize and tire at the four corners of the square, along the sides, and the diagonals. But they accomplish and exhaust at the center of the square, where the diagonals cross. [...]. The center is precisely that place where they might come together; and their meeting, their collision, is not an event among others, but the only possibility of event -the potentiality of the corresponding space. To exhaust space is to extenuate its potentiality through rendering any meeting impossible. (Deleuze, 1995, 13)

5. The German historian of art Aby Warburg was said to be what we call today 'bipolar,' but we may read differently his psychiatric episode. In his essay 'Aby Warburg and the Nameless Science', Agamben writes that Warburg was tired of the divisions within and between knowledge systems, and he wanted to embrace everything in a 'science without name.' 'Depression' as a medicalized psychological state misses precisely what was his genius: from exhaustion, he created the unfinished *Atlas Mnemosyne,* 'a figurative atlas,' 'gigantic condenser that gathered together all the energetic current that had animated and continued to animate Europe's memory' (Agamben, 1999, 95) – a true combinatorial, as Deleuze might argue.

References

Ackerman, Philip. 2009. "Longer High-Stakes Testing May Result in a Sense of Mental Fatigue, But Not In Lower Test Scores." *American Psychological Association.* http://www.apa.org/news/press/releases/2009/06/mental-fatigue.aspx

Agamben, Giorgio. 1993. "Bartleby o della contingenza [Bartleby or on Contingency]." In *Bartleby: la formula della creazione.* Macerata: Quodlibet.

Agamben, Giorgio. 1995. *Idea of Prose.* New York: SUNY Press.

Agamben, Giorgio. 1999. *Potentialities: Collected Essays in Philosophy.* Stanford, CA: Stanford University Press.

Agamben, Giorgio. 2007. *Profanations.* London: Zone Books.

Boutang, Pierre-André. 2004. *L'Abécédaire de Gilles Deleuze avec Claire Parnet* [Gilles Deleuze from A to Z with Claire Parnet]. [Motion picture]. France: Montparnasse.

Carroll, Lewis. 1872. *Through the Looking-Glass, and What Alice Found There.* London: Macmillan & Co. http://www.gasl.org/refbib/Carroll__Alice_1st.pdf

Chrétien, J. L. 1996. *De la fatigue* [On Fatigue]. Paris: Minuit.

Crary, Jonathan. 2013. *24/7: Late Capitalism and the Ends of Sleep.* London: Verso Press.

Cull, L. 2011. "Deleuze's Bodies, Philosophical Diseases and the Thought of Illness." Paper presented at Philosophy on Stage 3, Vienna, November 24–27.

Deleuze, Gilles. 1995. "The Exhausted." *SubStance* 24 (3): 28. http://www.jstor.org/stable/3685005

Deleuze, Gilles, and Claire Parnet. 1987. *Dialogues.* New York: Columbia Press University.

D'Hoest, Florelle, and Fernando Bárcena. 2011. "Las voces del acontecimiento. Un ensayo sobre el aprendizaje filosófico [The voices of event. An essay on philosophical learning]." *Educaçao em Revista* 12 (1): 9–24. http://www2.marilia.unesp.br/revistas/index.php/educacaoemrevista/article/viewFile/1549/1343

Foucault, Michel. 1990. *The History of Sexuality, Vol. 1: An Introduction.* New York: Vintage Books.

Han, Byung-Chul. 2010. *Müdigkeitsgesellschaft* [Society of Tiredness]. Berlin: Matthes & Seitz.

Hardt, Michael, and Antonio Negri. 2001. *Empire.* Cambridge, MA: Harvard University Press.

Lewis, Tyson. 2013. *On Study: Giorgio Agamben and Educational Potentiality.* New York: Routledge.

Nietzsche, Friedrich. 1967. *The Birth of Tragedy and The Case of Wagner.* New York: Vintage Books.

Epistemic empathy in childrearing and education

Kai Horsthemke

> The question, what is it like to be a child?, is one that most of us, in our capacity as parents and/or educators, have probably asked ourselves already at some point. Perhaps one might go further and suggest that it is a question we *ought* to ask (or have asked) ourselves, insofar as the attempt to provide a meaningful response has a significant bearing on childrearing and education. It is a question that presumably frames the processes of cognitive and moral education – i.e. showing respect for the child's point of view and inducting the child into respecting the points of view of others. After briefly discussing the idea of empathy and relating it to ideas such as sympathy or compassion, this paper focuses on *epistemic* empathy in particular. The relevant characteristics in this regard are knowledge of another's internal state, including her thoughts and feelings; understanding how another is thinking and feeling and imagining how one would think and feel in the other's place. Regarding childrearing and education, the two central questions that concern us here are: what is the role of epistemic empathy in our dealings with our children, learners and students and how can we ensure that they become empathic individuals themselves? In other words, (how) can empathy be taught and learned? After examining several recommendations regarding the nurturing and development of epistemic empathy (exemplification, modelling, acquisition of poetic and general aesthetic skills, and sensitivity, induction, imitation, etc.), I pay closer attention to the idea of *modelling* epistemic empathy. I conclude the paper with a few thoughts about limits to epistemic empathy.

What is it like to be a child?

What is it like to be a child? This is a question most of us, in our capacity as parents and/or educators, have probably asked ourselves already at some point. Perhaps one might go further and suggest that it is a question we *ought* to ask (or have asked) ourselves, insofar as the attempt to provide a meaningful response has a significant bearing on childrearing and education. As I will argue below, it is a question that presumably frames the processes of cognitive and moral education – i.e. showing respect for the child's point of view and inducting the child into respecting the points of view of others.

The point of Nagel's question, 'What is it like to be a bat?' (1979, 165–180), is to draw our attention to the fact of the existence of a particular subjective point of view which necessarily always remains beyond the scope of our inquiry, an inquiry which – being objective – cannot, necessarily, assimilate the subjective point of view. One might argue that we *can* know what it is 'like' for a bat to be hungry, thirsty, to be afraid, to be in pain, to experience sexual desire, etc. One might appeal to knowledge by analogy (likeness due to function) as well as to knowledge by homology (likeness due to kinship), given facts about our biological constitution and kinship with animals in general and mammals in particular, and how their needs, habits and motives interact holistically. This, however, will – clearly – not do. As Nagel contends, 'we cannot expect ever to accommodate in our language a detailed description of ... bat phenomenology' (1979, 170). The point is that, although we can know what it is like for a bat to be *afraid* (even though our fears might be modified by our possession of language), we cannot know what it is like for a *bat* to be afraid. We may be able to know what it is like to be Dracula the man but not what it is like to be Dracula the vampire bat. 'What is it like to be ...' necessarily implies that there is a particular (set of) factor(s) beyond the grasp of the one who asks this question. The essential aspect always remains beyond,[1] as it does when I ask: 'What is it like to be a woman?' or more specifically, 'What is it like to be pregnant/to suffer from pre-menstrual tension?' or when a Caucasian asks: 'What is it like to be black?' The difference is that whereas the latter kinds of questions could be answered by women and by blacks (although I doubt that their answers could *really* be understood by men and by whites), the question 'What is it like to be a bat?' could only be 'answered' by bats. It is not only a matter of linguistic competence, but also a matter of the capacity to detect the meaning and relevance of such questions.

Our attempt at an empathic understanding of children is crucially different from the attempts of humans to understand bats, of whites to understand blacks and of men to understand women. The difference is that we were all once children. This, of course, introduces the problem of memory, or at least of its reliability. Although it is an important source of justification and indeed knowledge, our memory notoriously misleads or deceives us. It also tends to be selective, depending on what we (do not) want to remember. There are additional considerations. Thus, while I can claim greater authority to speak of the subjective point of view of a child (because I was once a child) than to speak of the subjective point of view of a woman (because I was never a woman), the following questions necessarily arise: what kind of child? belonging to which demographic group? what about geographic, cultural context? etc. There are arguably important differences in response to the questions, 'What is it like to be my son?' and 'What is it like to be Mowgli?' (see MacLean 1977).

Is it perhaps a matter of empathy gaining a stronger foothold in the former than in the latter case? But what exactly *is* empathy, and how is it different from related ideas such as sympathy or compassion?

Empathy (*Einfühlung*) and sympathy (*Mitgefühl*)

The notion of empathy (from the Greek word *empatheia* – 'affection', 'passion'; also related to *pathos* – 'suffering') refers to the ability to recognize and understand the experiences, thoughts, emotions, intentions and personal characteristics of another being. The intellectual history of this idea is arguably best traced via nineteenth-century German philosopher/psychologist Lipps (1913), whose notions of *Einfühlung* and aesthetic sympathy were equally influenced by David Hume and the father–son team Friedrich

Theodor Vischer and Robert Vischer, and to the work of Scheler (1954): 'In [Scheler's] projective empathy, one imaginatively projects oneself into the situation of another and envisions what one's own reaction would be in the other's situation' (Bein 2013, 11). Lipps and Scheler established a circle of the 'Munich phenomenologists' shortly after the latter's arrival in Munich in 1906. Inspired by their work, Edward Titchener (1909) developed the notion of empathy as an English conceptual translation of *Einfühlung* ('feeling one's way into another', 'taking up another's perspective, feeling another's emotions, or feeling *into* another's emotion and perceptions'; see Oxley 2011, 4, 5). Back in Germany, too, Edith Stein (Stein 1917/1989; Matzker 1991) deepened the conception of *Einfühlung*, as involving objective listening, followed by a deeper subjective connection, a tuning-into or 'feeling-into' another's subjective experience, rendered possible by our shared humanity. Stein's conception clearly rules out empathizing with non-human animals, but does it also rule out *sympathy* across the species barrier? Is sympathy *possible* without empathy?

Although there is a significant etymological connection between empathy and sympathy (or compassion), 'feeling-in(to)' (*Einfühlung*) is conceptually distinct from 'feeling-with' or 'feeling-for' (*Mitgefühl*). According to Bein, 'Empathy [but not necessarily sympathy, or compassion] is something we want out of, say, our psychoanalysts' (2013, 1). Nonetheless,

> ... something like empathy is indeed required in order to have compassion. In order to be compassionate one must have some means of detecting the suffering and satisfaction of others. If empathy serves this role, then empathy – or something functionally similar to it – is a necessary part of the cultivation and expression of compassion. Whether it is part of compassion itself or a complementary trait will be left for now as an open question, but any account of compassion that seeks to make the experiences of suffering and satisfaction in others available to the one who feels compassion must have some feature that serves the function of empathy. (Bein 2013, 4)

It seems to me that, *contra* Stein and others, it is easier for me to empathize with (*and* care more deeply for) my dingo than Rosemary's baby, Fritz the cat than Josef Fritzl, an escaped budgerigar than an escaped burglar. Part of the reason for this is that empathy is often biased. 'People', after all, 'tend to empathize to a greater extent' not only 'with family members, members of their primary group, close friends, and people whose personal needs and concerns are similar to their own' (Oxley 2011, 3) but also with their companion animals (who may be said to belong to the 'primary group' or indeed 'close friends' referred to by Julinna Oxley). I believe nonetheless that empathy has a significant function in normative ethics – but, in terms of defining normative moral obligations and principles (even in care ethics), this is an *instrumental* rather than a *constitutive* role (see also Oxley 2011, 6, 12; Slote 2013, 59[2]). This instrumental role is explained chiefly by the consideration that, unlike sympathy, 'empathy's most important functions are epistemic' (Oxley 2011, 6[3]): 'empathy can be used to acquire justified beliefs about others' mental and emotional states' (12). It

> performs a number of *epistemic* functions that enable us to reflect on our beliefs about others in a new way. ... Empathy enables people to understand how others see the world, helps them to appreciate others' perspectives and connect with them emotionally, eliminates the perception of conflict between oneself and others, and makes possible the perception of similarity between oneself and others.
>
> Focusing on empathy's epistemic dimension is an approach that has the resources for explaining how empathy and empathic thinking are relevant to ethical reflection, deliberation, and justification. (Oxley 2011, 5–6)

Perhaps the case might be made that, with regard to empathy in particular, the cognitive and the affective, reason and emotion, are indivisible (see also Slote 2013, 50, 54, 90/91: fn. 7[4]). The relevant characteristics in this regard are knowledge of another's internal state, including her thoughts and feelings; understanding how another is thinking and feeling; and imagining how one would think and feel in the other's place (see Oxley 2011, 7, 8).

The idea of epistemic empathy – and related notions like mindfulness

The idea of epistemic empathy is a fairly recent addition to discourses within social, moral and virtue epistemology. It has been employed in a wide variety of discourses. Thus, from a feminist perspective, Tong (1997) explores empathy as an epistemic skill in professional health care provision and practice. Gair (2011) is concerned with the cognitive and experiential role empathy can play in social work contexts. She draws on Stein's work on 'deep listening' and establishes links with the concept and process of mindfulness[5]: 'deeper listening facilitated through mindfulness approaches, in a way that incorporated deep learning models, may prove successful in cultivating greater empathy' (2011, 338, 339). Meissner (2010) focuses on the epistemology of empathy in psychoanalytic research.[6] Keskinen (n.d.) argues from a Quinean perspective that the use and the ostensive learning of observation sentences depend on empathy, i.e. the ability to understand what another individual is perceiving. Clark (2010) and Perlstein (2013) discuss epistemic empathy (or rather the lack of it) with particular reference to American conservatives (Clark) or right-wingers (Perlstein).[7] Clark maintains:

> Empathy is a way of seeing, and therefore a way of knowing.[8] To avoid empathy is to limit one's own perspective to only one's own perspective – to choose not to see and therefore to choose not to know. Worse than that – it is to choose not to be *able* to know. (2010)

Clark identifies a trend that he calls 'epistemic closure' among American conservatives: 'To choose not to see what empathy shows us is to *choose* stupidity' (2010). Considerably less prepared to attribute their attitude to some kind of voluntarism, Perlstein argues that a 'genuine right-winger will be so lacking in intellectual imagination – in cognitive empathy – that imagining how anyone could sincerely reason differently from them is virtually impossible', and that this is something 'beyond his poor powers of epistemological empathy to comprehend' (Perlstein 2013).

From the perspective of philosophy of history, Stueber explores the epistemic contribution of empathy (or what he calls 'reenactive empathy'[9]) to the explanation of action, in terms of a general endeavour to understand historical events and processes (2008, 34). Oxley devotes a whole chapter in her book to the epistemic functions of empathy (2011, 35–58), namely gathering information about the other person (42–46), as well as understanding others (46–48). She analyses the psychological experience of empathy and shows that it makes unique epistemic contributions to our understanding of other people. Since empathy brings information to our attention in a personal way, it has the potential to enrich moral deliberation. Nevertheless, it is not intrinsically moral and does not always lead to moral action. Given its role in helping us understand others, empathy is relevant also to Kantian ethics and contractual ethics,[10] not just to ethical theories that emphasize care and altruism. Citing empirical evidence, Oxley shows that the cultivation of empathy must begin early in life in order for people to be inclined to feel empathy for others in a way that informs their moral decisions. Slote (2013, 52) is concerned with the role that epistemic empathy ('empathy with another person's state of belief or knowledge or their intellectual/ scientific/ cognitive "point of view"') can play in the reconciliation of moral caring with the admission or recognition that there is such a thing as greater or lesser creativity (or intelligence or talent). He also introduces 'the epistemological ideals and intellectual/epistemic virtues of open-mindedness and fair-mindedness' as '(desirable) forms of epistemic empathy and epistemic *respect*' (50, 51). In what follows, I will assume – without additional argument – that open-mindedness and fair-mindedness are part and parcel of 'mindfulness'.

This paper owes a substantial debt of inspiration to the various works cited above, but it seeks to explore a particular, novel territory. My particular focus will be on the role (and also the limitations) of epistemic empathy in childrearing and education (teaching as well as learning). If, in what follows, I fail to distinguish sufficiently between the roles of parents and educators, between parenting/child-rearing and teaching/education, this is not because I do not recognize the important differences, the important ways in which parenting is not like teaching. Clearly, as parents we have a more intimate relationship with our own children, whereas teachers have a professional relationship with most children (see Suissa 2012).

Epistemic empathy in childrearing and education

The two central questions that concern us here are: what is the role of epistemic empathy in our dealings with our children, learners and students, and how can we ensure that they become empathic individuals themselves? In other words, (how) can empathy be taught and learned? These questions, and the responses that might be given to them, are not unconnected. If the function of epistemic empathy is to gain some kind of insight into the beliefs, ideas, thoughts, views, desires, aspirations, ambitions and experiences of those in our charge, then demonstrating such empathy and mindfulness is often likely to have a generative impact on the recipients of, say, our open-minded and fair-minded engagement. In other words, the epistemic respect that children, learners and students have experienced or received will often be likely to make them relevantly respectful persons themselves.

I think I have said enough above to indicate what counts as epistemic empathy in childrearing and education. Perhaps it will be instructive to examine examples of *lack* of epistemic empathy. One such example is what has become known as the 'substitute success syndrome', where 'parents try to live through their children and to impose their own needs, desires, aspirations on their child (or children) without taking the child's point of view into account in any significant way' (Slote 2013, 61). Similarly, the tough parenting methods employed by 'Tiger Mother' Amy Chua seem to be characterized by a lack of epistemic empathy. These methods have included calling her daughter Sophia 'garbage' in order to motivate her,[11] rejecting a birthday card on the grounds that 'I deserve better than this', and turning her house into a 'war zone' in order to coerce Louisa into learning a difficult piano piece, despite protestations from her husband Jed that she was insulting her daughter by calling her 'lazy, cowardly, self-indulgent and pathetic' (see Chua 2011a, 2011b). Chua asserts that

> Western parents try to respect their children's individuality, encouraging them to pursue their true passions, supporting their choices, and providing positive reinforcement and a nurturing environment. By contrast, the Chinese believe that the best way to protect their children is by

preparing them for the future, letting them see what they are capable of, and arming them with skills, work habits and inner confidence that no one can ever take away. (2011a)

Chua is clearly concerned for the welfare of her daughters Louisa and Sophia, and sincere and articulate in her views. Yet, her maternal (matriarchal?) bluster, confidence and claims to superiority, all based on the questionable assumption that child achievement is all-important, invite the suspicion that she is concerned as much about her own status in light of her daughters' success or failure as with their health and happiness. While one may agree with certain aspects of her objection to recent, approval-obsessed 'Western' styles of childrearing and education (which have led many children to narcissism or self-destructive anxiety), it is difficult to perceive any empathy (moral or epistemic) in her style of parenting – which appears to be anything but respectful. 'Letting them see what they are capable of' may *appear* to involve epistemic empathy but in the present context it is much closer to coercive bullying.[12]

Before Dewey, says Slote, 'subject matter and various "values" were in most instances simply imposed on school children "for their own good", and the children had little say in what and how they learned' (2013, 61). Dewey was of the opinion that teachers ought not to 'impose educational subject matter on an essentially passive child, but were to take the child's interests and points of view deeply into account throughout the teaching process' (61). There have been a range of suggestions by theorists as to how empathy is or can be taught – some of which are more useful than others. Thus, Dewey believed that 'open-mindedness and fair-mindedness should be exemplified, taught, and/or encouraged in schools' (60). Taking his cue from Dewey's emphasis on the importance of children learning to think for themselves, Slote contends that

> [i]f teachers listen to children's voices, the children will learn to respect their own voices much more than if everything were imposed on them. But *at the same time* those children will also be learning a lesson in open-mindedness (or fair-mindedness). If teachers listen to and are willing to be influenced by what students think and want, then they themselves exemplify open-mindedness [...] If parents are concerned with others (and are normally loving toward their child), that attitude will tend to seep into their child. And something quite similar to the empathic osmosis of parental attitudes can occur when teachers show respect for the ideas, aspirations and attitudes of their students. (2013, 62)

Parents show respect for their children when they take their point of view into account, and this 'very attitude is likely (in part via empathic osmosis) to translate into the children's eventual ability, as adults, to think and decide for themselves' (Slote 2013, 63). Similarly, if teachers model respect for the opinions and thinking of students, and

> if we add epistemic versions of inductive discipline into the mix, we end up with a student who balances the capacity and disposition to think for him- or herself with a capacity and tendency to tolerate, respect, and be open-minded about what others think (Slote 2013, 64).

As I mentioned earlier, Oxley discusses

> the different kinds of empathy that can be taught, the methods of teaching empathy (rationally, through induction, through interaction with a baby), and the purposes for which empathy can be taught (for the purposes of generating care, for cultivating understanding and diversity, or for developing the skill of reading others' emotions). (2011, 13)

Since 'the moral context of empathy varies from one program to another, ... teachers of empathy, including parents, need awareness of what they are asking students to do when they "empathize" with others' (Oxley 2011, 13–14). Oxley concludes that 'the cultivation of empathy must begin early in life in order for people to be inclined to use empathy in making a moral decision' (14).

Having identified a dearth in the pertinent literature in this regard, Gair makes a few suggestions regarding the cultivation, teaching and learning of empathy. She considers 'empathy as a skill that can be taught alongside positive regard and a non-judgemental, [recipient]-centred approach' and 'poetry writing to cultivate ... students' empathy' (Gair 2011, 331), and endorses 'increased opportunities ... for ... students to explore empathy through narratives, shared personal stories, and vignettes', and provision of 'cognitive, experiential, and perspective-taking opportunities for students to explore how they might empathically, mindfully, and compassionately engage with diverse [recipient] groups in practice' (339).

Tong, too, considers the development of 'aesthetic skills – that is, ... capacities to see, hear, touch, smell, and taste' so that we can become fully attentive to others.

> By learning to focus on nuances of colour and sound; to describe their emotional responses to novels, paintings, and symphonies; to interpret what is going on in fictional characters minds and hearts; to write poetry, to keep a journal, to play a role in a play, to listen to an oral history, to sit through a Japanese tea ceremony – the possibilities are myriad – [parents and teachers] can develop precisely those skills they need to *attend* to their [children, learners and students] as individuals'. (Tong 1997, 161)

According to Tong,

> empathy is an epistemic skill, an aesthetic sensitivity that can be learned. Using teaching techniques similar to the ones used in art, literature, and music courses, teachers can teach [others] how to understand and interpret [children's, learners' and students'] values'. (1997, 162)

Tong later all but endorses a process of 'imitation' (of the behaviour of a caring person) as a way of learning to become caring – but it is doubtful whether this can be applied to (epistemic) empathy (165).

Of all the recommendations regarding the nurturing and development of epistemic empathy (exemplification, modelling, acquisition of poetic and general aesthetic skills and sensitivity, induction, imitation, etc.), I want to pay closer attention to the idea of modelling[13] epistemic empathy.

Epistemic empathy and modelling

Borrowing some ideas from Noddings on modelling and caring (1998, 46), one might say that while modelling is important in most processes of cognitive and moral education, it is vital with regard to empathy.[14] Here, we are not trying to teach children and students principles and ways of applying them to problems through chains of mathematical reasoning. Rather, we have to show how to empathize in our own relations with those we empathize with. So we do not tell our children and students to empathize; we show them how to empathize by creating empathic relations with them. Still following Noddings (while bearing in mind that she is speaking about 'practicing caring' rather than 'practicing empathy'), an essential component of education is practice:

> Attitudes and 'mentalities' are shaped, at least in part, by experience. Most of us speak regularly of a 'military mind', a 'police mentality', 'business thinking', and the like. Although some of this talk is a product of stereotyping, it seems clear that it also captures some truth about human behaviour. All disciplines and institutional organizations have training programs

designed not only to teach specific skills but also to 'shape minds', that is, to induce certain attitudes and ways of looking at the world. (1998, 47)

So, if we want people to approach life prepared to empathize, we need to provide opportunities for them to gain empathic skills and, more important, to develop characteristic attitudes. 'Some schools', writes Noddings, 'have instituted requirements for a form of community service' which she considers to be 'a move in the right direction' (1998, 48). Modelling empathy in education is not only a matter of modelling specific conduct or behaviour but also – to borrow from Noddings – of 'shaping minds' and 'mentalities', that is, of inducing certain dispositions and ways of looking at the world. If we want our students to approach life prepared to empathize, to be open-minded, fair-minded and respectful, we need to provide opportunities for them to gain relevant practical knowledge and, more important, to develop characteristic dispositions. The practice provided must be with agents who can demonstrate open-mindedness, fair-mindedness and respect.

Aloni, similarly, refers to the pedagogical significance of 'personal example and the inculcation of habit' (2002, 162):

> The pedagogical challenge is to find adequate and efficient ways to translate the philosophical and pedagogical insights into... pedagogical practices. ... [E]ducators would have to take the responsibility to *set a personal example in the art of living* as well as to create at their schools a pedagogical atmosphere of care, trust, support, dialogue, respect, fairness, tolerance, inquiry, freedom, commitment, responsibility and reciprocity. (218; emphasis added)

Both childrearing and education arguably require a 'fit' between disposition and conduct, at least as far as this is possible. Like parents, educators need to be aware of their potential impact on the behaviour of their students, in terms of what they themselves model or live-by-example, especially in the lower grades. On this note, teaching care, trust, support, dialogue, respect, fairness, tolerance, responsibility, etc. (see Aloni 2002, 218) are not so much a matter of practicing *what* one preaches, but of practicing *before* one preaches – if it is necessary to 'preach' at all. In relation to what Noddings says about modelling caring in the classroom, we do not *tell* our children and students to be empathic, respectful, open-minded, fair-minded, etc. We *show* them how to be so by creating empathic, trusting, supportive, dialogical, respectful, fair, tolerant and responsible relations with them.

Limits to epistemic empathy

If the preceding arguments and examples are compelling, then it may indeed turn out that epistemic empathy is a desirable disposition for us as parents and educators to have *vis-à-vis* our children, learners and students. Whether or not we also have practical and moral obligations (and, in the case of educators, professional obligations) in this regard is an issue I cannot go into in much detail here. It is at least *conceivable* that one can be a good teacher without being notably empathic. Yet, I would be considerably more hesitant to say the same about a (good) parent. While empathy does not constitute the whole of what makes someone a good person, it is nonetheless instrumental in defining and motivating normative principles and obligations. It is probably at its most generative if it is employed in conjunction with specific principles and directives.[15] This is where respect for rights arguably fulfils a crucial function. Empathy and respect for rights are not identical, but they may well be coextensive. Rights-based moral action and respectful concern without empathy depict an unlovely, normatively impoverished scenario. Similarly, empathy without emphasis on rights is conceivable, but equally incomplete. My considered intuition about an effective and compelling approach to moral and epistemic interaction[16] sees respect for rights as its backbone, and empathy as its heart.

A discussion of epistemic empathy would also be incomplete without consideration of possible limits. It appears that there is an indirect limit and also a more obviously direct set of limitations. The former consideration concerns the extent to which epistemic empathy and mindfulness will eventually entail consensus or agreement. Given that such empathy will embody a certain favourable attitude towards others' beliefs, thoughts and ideas, one might ask whether such a pro-attitude will eventually lead to agreement. I do not think that it will – or that it should, for that matter. As an empathic parent, I may not wish to impose my desires, needs and ambitions on my child, to force my child to endure the violin, ballet and other lessons that may lead to the kind of success that has always eluded me, i.e. without taking the child's point of view, ideas, desires and aspirations into account. But this point of view counts for considerably less when there are other parentalistic[17] matters at issue, like a visit to the dentist or doctor, extra math classes and the like. Relatedly, if someone's belief is mistaken, or someone's point of view involves false assumptions, dodgy justification, etc., then empathy would not lead to endorsement of such a belief or point of view – quite the opposite. My open-mindedness and fair-mindedness, for example, would not require me to adopt and/or endorse a view or train of thought that, for good reasons, I may disagree with.[18] In fact, my empathic attitude and 'objective listening' may lead me to recognize and understand the kinds of perceptual and conceptual errors that have been committed here – just like it may lead me to change my own mind or outlook. It may – but it need not: epistemic empathy is not sufficient for eventual consensus. Furthermore, just as empathy, in 'being instrumental to moral action, ... must be employed in tandem with specific moral principles and directives to generate a moral response' (Oxley 2011, 5), epistemic empathy is instrumental in the acquisition of knowledge and the recognition of truth – if used in tandem with specific epistemic principles and directives to generate an epistemic response.

The second set of limitations concerns empathy with those who are either unwilling or otherwise unprepared to be empathic, mindful, etc. towards the positions, beliefs, thoughts and experiences of others. 'There are limits to epistemic empathy', Slote notes,

> just as there are limits to the empathy an empathic person will feel concerning other people's welfare. If people betray you, your empathy for them will likely diminish to the vanishing point, in the wake of the anger you feel toward them, and, more generally, we will tend to have less empathy for those who are themselves lacking in empathic concern for others. In parallel fashion, one will be much less epistemically empathic and open-minded about the views of those who aren't epistemically empathic and open-minded towards one's own views or those of others, and such reactions of understandable epistemic intolerance and of what might therefore even be thought of as mild *epistemic anger* are as much a part of epistemic empathy and open-mindedness as reactions of anger and lesser empathic benevolence towards those who hurt us or others are built into empathic caring as a concept and phenomenon.... (2013, 91, fn. 10)

There is, however, clearly no precise method for determining when a person's empathy is no longer morally and epistemically appropriate. Some of us seem to have, especially with regard to those we love, sheer inexhaustible empathic resources. As a guide for teachers, albeit perhaps not for parents, one might argue that neither too little nor too much empathy is desirable.

Acknowledgements
I wish to thank Jim Conroy, Christine Doddington, Alison MacKenzie, Paul Smeyers, Andrew Stables, Judith Suissa, Barbara Thayer-Bacon and especially Stefan Ramaekers for their thought-provoking input on earlier versions of this article.

Disclosure statement
No potential conflict of interest was reported by the author.

Notes
1. On the difficulty, if not the impossibility, of knowing an other, and the dangers of imposing one's self on an other (especially with reference to Emmanuel Levinas), see Sharon Todd (2001). 'The Other, for Levinas', writes Todd,

    is a concrete manifestation of absolute difference. ... His Other is ... an unassimilable and unknowable alterity. (2001, 69)

    Instead of 'knowledge about the Other', it is 'the self's susceptibility ['openness' or 'exposure'] to the Other ... to which education must address itself if it is not to inflict violence' (Todd 2001, 68; see also 71, 73).

2. Slote states that 'empathy is necessary to the fulfilment of both intellectual and moral ideals or objectives' (2013, 59). It is clearly not *sufficient* for such fulfilment: empathy is not a substitute for but, rather, defines and motivates both in-depth scientific knowledge and normative moral principles and obligations.
3. See also Clark (2010): 'Empathy, at its most basic level, is epistemic'. An objection that might be raised at this point concerns the apparent redundancy of the term 'epistemic'. Or perhaps we might do away with 'epistemic empathy' altogether, in favour of an idea like 'recognition'. In what follows, I hope to persuade the sceptical reader that the notion of epistemic empathy fulfils a distinct and irreducible function in epistemological discourse, especially in education.
4. In Slote's view,

    there are no strictly intellectual opinions. All genuine opinions involve a relevantly favorable attitude, and perhaps this emotional aspect of the opinions facilitates the osmotic transmission of opinions (e.g., from parents to children) and makes it more plausible to accept the common-sense view that they can be transmitted or soaked up in this way. (2013, 91, fn. 7)

5. 'Mindfulness' has become a rather loaded notion in recent times, owing to contemporary psychologized versions of it that seem to reduce it to a 'technique' and use it in terms of something like a heightened awareness of how one is feeling at that very moment. (I owe this point to Stefan Ramaekers.) As will become obvious in what follows, I am not using the term in this way.
6. The less-than-startling presumption here is that empathic affective attunement is manifest between analyst and analysand. Owing to Sigmund Freud's admiration of Lipps, *Einfühlung* became a useful and indeed important tool in psychoanalysis and psychotherapy, developed further by Carl Rogers in the 1950s and 1960s (see Oxley 2011, 10; Gair 2011, 331) and Heinz Kohut in the 1960s and 1970s (Gair 2011, 329, 330).
7. Slote mentions, as examples, the lack of empathy and open-mindedness not only of the Spanish Inquisitors but also of many Muslims and Westerners towards one another (2013, 56).

8. The equation of 'seeing' and 'knowing' is one that is obviously difficult to defend. At best it holds in a purely phenomenological sense – i.e. in the sense that one cannot be mistaken about one's sensations. After all, this is what distinguishes (mere) sensation from observation. Observations, unlike sensations, can be attested to by a multitude of witnesses – and one can indeed be mistaken about what one observes.
9. According to Stueber, 'in order to be able to grasp agents' thoughts as reasons for their actions, we have to re-enact their thoughts, beliefs and desires in our own mind while being simultaneously appropriately sensitive to relevant differences between ourselves and the people whose actions we want to understand' (2008, 36). In order to achieve this, '[o]ur only option is to use our cognitive capacities and to put ourselves imaginatively in their shoes in order to grasp their thoughts as their reasons' (36).
10. Empathy is relevant to Kantian and contractarian ethics in terms of recognizing others as rational agents and as rational (constrained) maximizers of self-interest (for example, in 'prisoners'-dilemma-type of situations), respectively.
11. Chua writes:

> Chinese parents can get away with things that Western parents can't. Once when I was young - maybe more than once – when I was extremely disrespectful to my mother, my father angrily called me 'garbage' in our native Hokkien dialect. It worked really well. I felt terrible and deeply ashamed of what I had done. But it didn't damage my self-esteem or anything like that. I knew exactly how highly he thought of me. I didn't actually think I was worthless or feel like a piece of garbage. As an adult, I once did the same thing to Sophia, calling her garbage in English when she acted extremely disrespectfully toward me. (2011a)

12. Judith Suissa has observed that it

> may be that Chua herself, in her self-appointed role as Tiger Mother, has become incapable of simply living with her children. It is in this sense that, as Stefan Ramaekers and I discuss in our 2012 book, 'parenting' approaches can, by reducing parent-child interaction to questions of effectiveness, have the effect of blinding parents to their own experience of their children; blinding them, too, to the moral significance of endeavouring to live with children as part of what it means to live in a social world. (2012, 12: see also Ramaekers and Suissa 2012)

13. A preferable concept in this regard may be that of *vorleben*, for reasons elaborated elsewhere (see Horsthemke and Kissack 2008). In this paper, however, for the sake of conceptual simplicity, I follow what seems to be a fairly standard use of 'modelling'.
14. Noddings, it must be noted, considers empathy to be 'peculiarly rational, western and masculine' in its Western usage (2002, 13; see also 1984, 30). She takes issue with the Oxford University Dictionary's definition of empathy as the 'power of projecting one's personality into, and so fully understanding, the object of contemplation'. Instead, she prefers a 'feminine' view of empathy that 'does not involve projection but reception' (1984, 30). She considers this receptivity view of empathy as more nearly capturing 'the affective state of attention in caring' (2002, 14).
15. As Oxley notes,

> empathy alone is insufficient and undesirable as a sole moral criterion; empathy is a psychological experience, not a normative principle. Thus, it cannot serve as a criterion of morally good action. (2011, 6)

16. Like other ideas usually employed in normative discourses, the notion of rights has also acquired an epistemic significance. Having 'the right to be sure' has been used as synonymous with possession of adequate justification (see Scheffler 1965; Ayer 1956).
17. I prefer this gender-neutral term to 'paternalistic'.
18. In cases where one knows [or has good reason to suspect] that someone is defending a position that is absolutely beyond the pale of rational discussion, it seems ... that open-mindedness and fair-mindedness don't require one to (try to) see what s/he is saying in a favourable light. (Slote 2013, 91, fn. 10)

References

Aloni, Nimrod. 2002. *Enhancing Humanity: The Philosophical Foundations of Humanistic Education.* Dordrecht: Kluwer.
Ayer, Alfred J. 1956. *The Problem of Knowledge.* Harmondsworth/Middlesex, NJ: Pelican.
Bein, Steve. 2013. *Compassion and Moral Guidance.* Honolulu, HI: University of Hawai'i Press.
Chua, Amy. 2011a. "Why Chinese Mothers are Superior." *Wall Street Journal* 8 (January). Accessed 1 February 2014. http://online.wsj.com/news/articles/SB10001424052748704111504576059713528698754
Chua, Amy. 2011b. *Battle Hymn of the Tiger Mother.* New York: Penguin.
Clark, Fred. 2010. "Empathy and Epistemic Closure." Accessed 2 January 2014. http://www.patheos.com/blogs/slacktivist/2010/04/30/empathy-and-epistemic-closure/
Gair, Susan. 2011. "Exploring Empathy Embedded in Ethics Curricula: A Classroom Inquiry." *Advances in Social Work* 12 (2): 329–344.
Horsthemke, Kai, and Mike Kissack. 2008. "*Vorleben*: Educational Practice Beyond Prescription." *Journal of Curriculum Studies* 40 (3): 277–288.
Keskinen, Antti. n.d. "Epistemology and Empathy: A Quinean Perspective." Accessed 2 January 2014. http://www.academia.edu/1522967/Epistemology_and_Empathy_A_Quinean_Perspective
Lipps, Theodor. 1913. *Zur Einfühlung* [On Empathy]. Leipzig: W. Engelmann.
MacLean, Charles. 1977. *The Wolf Children.* Harmondsworth/Middlesex, NJ: Penguin.
Matzker, Reiner. 1991. *Einfühlung: Edith Stein und die Phänomenologie* [Empathy: Edith Stein and Phenomenology]. Frankfurt/Main: Peter Lang.
Meissner, W. W. 2010. "Some Notes on the Epistemology of Empathy." *Psychoanalytical Quarterly* 79 (2): 421–469.
Nagel, Thomas. 1979. *Mortal Questions.* Cambridge: Cambridge University Press.
Noddings, Nel. 1984. *Caring: A Feminine Approach to Ethics and Moral Education.* Berkeley: University of California Press.
Noddings, Nel. 1998. "Caring." In *Philosophy of Education*, edited by Paul Hirst and Patricia White, 40–50. London: Routledge.
Noddings, Nel. 2002. *Starting at Home: Caring and Social Policy.* Berkeley: University of California Press.
Oxley, Julinna C. 2011. *The Moral Dimensions of Empathy: Limits and Applications in Ethical Theory and Practice.* Basingstoke: Palgrave-Macmillan.
Perlstein, Rick. 2013. "Thinking Like a Conservative (Part Five): Epistemology and Empathy." Accessed 31 December 2013. http://www.thenation.com/blog/177025/thinking-conservative-part-five-epistemology-and-empathy#
Ramaekers, Stefan, and Judith Suissa. 2012. *The Claims of Parenting: Reasons, Responsibility and Society.* Dordrecht: Springer.
Scheffler, Israel. 1965. *Conditions of Knowledge: An Introduction to Epistemology and Education.* Chicago, IL: Scott, Foresman and Company.
Scheler, Max. 1954. *The Nature of Sympathy.* London: Routledge & Kegan Press.
Slote, Michael. 2013. *Education and Human Values: Reconciling Talent with an Ethics of Care.* New York: Routledge.
Stein, Edith. 1917 (1989 transl.). *On the Problem of Empathy.* Washington, DC: ICS.
Stueber, Karsten R. 2008. "Reasons, Generalizations, Empathy, and Narratives: The Epistemic Structure of Action Explanation." *History and Theory* 47: 31–43.
Suissa, Judith. 2012. "Tiger Mothers and Praise Junkies: Children, Praise and the Reactive Attitude." Accessed 31 August 2014. https://www.philosophy-of-education.org/uploads/papers2012/Suissa.pdf
Titchener, Edward B. 1909. *Lectures on the Experimental Psychology of the Thought-Processes.* New York: Macmillan.
Todd, Sharon. 2001. 67–74. Accessed 15 April 2014. http://ojs.ed.uiuc.edu/index.php/pes/article/view/1871/582 "On Not Knowing the Other, or Learning from Levinas." *Philosophy of Education Archive.*
Tong, R. 1997. "Feminist Perspectives on Empathy as an Epistemic Skill and Caring as a Moral Virtue." *Journal of Medical Humanities* 18 (3): 153–168.

For the sake of peace: maintaining the resonance of peace and education

Kanako Ide

> This article is an attempt to develop the idea of peace education for adults through the assumption that, compared to peace education for children, educational approaches for adults are as yet undeveloped. This article also assumes that the progress of educational approaches for adults is necessary to the further development of peace education for children, as well as to the expansion of the theory. In navigating the argument around issues of peace education for adults, the article uses the example of educational issues faced by Amerasians in Okinawa. The article argues that language education is a fundamental aspect of peace education for adults. It also demonstrates that the content of language education for adults is different from the content of language education for children. Furthermore, the article defends peace education for adults, through language education, as the very first step towards creating peaceful conditions for the education of Amerasians in Okinawa.

Introduction: Amerasians in Okinawa

This article demonstrates that the development of a theory of peace education for adults is the first step towards the practice of peace education for children. The article focuses in particular on the matter of the educational issues faced by Amerasians in Okinawa born to Japanese civilian mothers and American fathers who are either current or former US servicemen or civilian personnel in Okinawa Island in Japan. The article uses the phrase 'peace education' to denote a particular confluence in the thought of Maria Montessori, an Italian educational philosopher and pioneer of peace education study, as it appears in practice in the historical example of the Amerasian population in Okinawa. The phrase 'peace education' denotes making an educational contribution toward peace.

To realize peace, Montessori asserts, '[...] the world of adults must change' (Montessori 1972 [1949], 116). Montessori proposes that the importance of peace education is to recognize children as teachers of peace. She says, '[...] the child is our teacher. Adults must above all be educated to acknowledge this fact so that they may change their behavior toward the generations that come after them' (Montessori 1972 [1949], 47–48). Deliberating peace education for children is a way to change 'the world of adults.' However, the purpose of this article is not to urge a direct political campaign to influence immediate social change, but rather, after Montessori's model, to advocate a slower and more organic path of change, by way of the assumption that politics and education have different tasks to undertake in achieving the goal of peace. Peace education for adults requires an exploration of educational methods the reform 'the world of adults.' The case of Amerasians is a pertinent one in relation to this argument because (1) it demonstrates how the absence of peace education for adults results in a loss of peace education for children, and (2) it is a complex case which combines elements of both the educational and the political. The peace policy which led mothers and fathers of Amerasians to meet around US bases in Okinawa is supposed to realize peace on an international scale, but the policy does not seem to provide peace for Amerasian children. Why have Amerasians been disenfranchised?

In service of this argument, I begin by describing the political problems faced by Amerasians in Okinawa, and then critically examine the usage of the words 'peace', and 'education', and also their combined notion of 'peace education', to discuss Amerasian educational issues. I first demonstrate the necessity of peace education for adults by describing the details of Amerasians' struggles in Okinawa. I argue that, since the social situation in Okinawa is sustained and framed by the world of adults, it is necessary to consider some educational approaches for adults in order to create reform. I point out the ways in which the language pertaining to the situation of the political debate over US military bases in Okinawa is confused. Then, I explore language education as a means of achieving peace education for adults. For this part of the argument, I apply the theoretical secessionism between political and educational perspectives developed by Walter Feinberg and Minoru Murai. In order to convey the risks inherent in using vulnerable words such as education, peace, and the phrase 'peace education' itself, this article calls for the delicate treatment of these terms to ensure protection of their meaning, and to ensure that their vulnerability to distortion is not used to present political thoughts as educational thoughts. I offer this argument as a first step toward solving educational issues for Amerasians.

Absence of peace education for children

The Amerasian community spans various countries in Asia and the USA. Amerasians are those born after World War II in Asian countries such as Cambodia, Japan, Korea, Laos, the Philippines, Thailand, and Vietnam, where US military stationing has led to the existence of offspring of US military fathers and local Asian mothers.[1] This indicates that at root, Amerasians are byproducts of international peace policy – the long-term international peace diplomacy between the USA and Japan. The USA occupied Japan from 1945 until 1951, and the Okinawa islands until 1972. For 69 years, Okinawa has headquartered one of the largest US military stations in Asia. Because of that, unlike other children of mixed or international couples, the heritage of Amerasians is uniquely political and it is reasonable that their children's unique educational needs receive certain public consideration.

However, there are discrepancies between the international 'peace' policy and the lived experience of peace. Until now, there has not been a cooperative international educational policy for Amerasians between their mothers' and fathers' respective home countries. The educational policies for them are divided by national borders. Due to these borders, their mothers' home countries have varied policies toward Amerasians, whereas their fathers' home country (i.e. the USA) has a consistent policy on Amerasians. As part of Cold War policy, the Amerasian Act of 1982 and the Amerasian Home Coming Act of 1987 allow Amerasians in Asian countries to emigrate easily to the USA but with 'refugee' status. Thus, even though Amerasians in Okinawa have a legal right to dual citizenship (until age 22), their educational rights are limited. Amerasians have to 'choose' American or Japanese schools, and whether to become American or Japanese by school age, or at least during early school age.

Amerasians in Okinawa have a choice of four kinds of school in Japan. Besides private school, Amerasians in Okinawa can attend Japanese public schools, American public schools (called Department of Defense Dependents Schools, or DoDDS), or a non-profit school whose curricula is specialized for Amerasian attendance. Since tuition is required by all schools except Japanese public schools, the choice of school depends on the state of the father–child relationship or the economic strength of the mother's family (DoDDSs do not require tuition if pupils' fathers recognize them and are in service). In addition to the financial problem, the decision to attend public school (both Japanese and DoDDS) is difficult for Amerasians. Attending public school means not only having to choose either to live as an American by accepting American school curriculum or to live as a Japanese by accepting Japanese school curriculum, but also to face social discrimination arising from complex and multilayered colonial relationships, a byproduct of being caught in between two countries.

I now describe the social structure that maintains discrimination against Amerasians in Okinawa from the following perspectives: political dynamics, racism, and sexism.

Political dynamics

The political relationship between the USA and Japan has been a hierarchical one. As a result of the USA's defeat of Japan in World War II, the US military has been stationed at various locations throughout Japan, including the Okinawa islands. Even though the Japan–US Status of Forces Agreement and the Japan–US Security Treaty are celebrated as symbols of alliance, they frequently display an uneven balance of power.[2] For example, American soldiers are almost never charged with crimes in Okinawa under the US–Japan Status of Forces Agreement which grants leniency even to those who are guilty of committing crimes. In addition, there is the matter of the hierarchical relationship between Japan and Okinawa, which has been a colonial one since the Japanese government established the Okinawa prefecture in 1879.[3] According to Fujisawa (2005), colonial assimilation policies were justified because Okinawa needed 'modernization', and this discourse continues to be used.

In a sense, Okinawa has been doubly colonized. For example, even though anti-US-base movements have been continuous in Okinawa due to the perception that the US military disturbs the 'peace' of the local community, these Okinawans' protests have been disregarded by the Japanese government as well as the US government. Here is a recent example. In January 2014, the anti-US-base candidate won a mayoral election in the Okinawan city of Nago. Two days after the election, however, the Japanese government ignored the local decision and called for bids for landfilling contracts to build the new base in Nago. This not only demonstrates the hierarchical relationship between Okinawa and Japan, but also between Okinawa and the US, because the establishment of a US base in Nago was originally planned by the USA in 1966, when Okinawa was occupied by the

USA. Washington D.C. and Tokyo have the authority to decide Okinawa's fate and to neglect local opinion. And, for Okinawans, it was apparent that a locally made and democratic decision had been ignored at a higher level of power.

Racism and sexism

The colonialism faced by Amerasians is additionally complex due to elements of anti-Asian racism as well as sexism against women. Kazumi Uezato pointed out that in Japanese public schools, for mainstream Okinawans and Japanese, Amerasian children are often made the objects of a more general hatred against US forces in Okinawa, visible in the abusive language used against them such as 'Yankee Go Home' (Uezato 1998, 28) or 'dirty' (Uezato 1998, 28). 'Yankee Go Home' is a slur that seeks to deprive Amerasians of their Okinawan and Japanese heritage, and the abusive epithet 'dirty' is suggestive of the shameful stereotypes of the sex trade. At the same time, the society has been viewing those Japanese women who fraternized with American men as being somehow socially abnormal, engaging in activity that was not considered respectable.[4] Furthermore, DoDDSs are not places of acceptance for Amerasians either. The racism contains undercurrents of sexism. Within American society in Okinawa, hate speech against Amerasians takes the form of phrases such as 'Japanese Trash!' (Uezato 1998, 116), indicating that Americans in Okinawa know the social status of Amerasians in the Japanese community.

According to Uezato, a non-profit school for Amerasians in Okinawa was established by mothers and advocates in an effort to solve the risk of mistreatment in schools and the curriculum mismatch. The school has developed an alternative educational curriculum to achieve its ends, which it calls 'double education'. Double education proposes to '... develop students who can be effective citizens of both the US and Japan and attempts to enable students to value and become part of both cultures/countries' (Noiri and Janes 2008, 172). As discussed earlier, Amerasians have a legal right to dual citizenship until they become adults, but the current educational system and school curriculum, which are divided by national borders, do not address the right to hold dual citizenship. Rather, schooling limits Amerasians' right to dual citizenship. Thus, double education tries to provide a double US/Japanese curriculum to prepare for American as well as Japanese citizenship, but also promotes a suitable identity development for students as Amerasians in a stress-free school environment.

The idea of double education might be an epoch-making educational approach because it tries to ensure, at the very least, that Amerasians' educational needs are met. However, the social conditions that Amerasians have to deal with in Okinawa are far more complicated. The double education curriculum includes the teaching of both Japanese and American social systems, and offers bilingual teaching in certain subjects including mathematics. However, despite its good intentions, this double education in fact promotes the Amerasian identity crisis through its treatment of the peace policy between Japan and the USA. In Japanese public school curricula, it is considered to be a crucial part of peace education to discuss the existence of the US bases in Okinawa. Since this educational model interprets the US bases as a symbol of war and other social problems, especially those encountered in Japanese public schools in Okinawa, it covertly teaches negative images of Amerasians at the same time. On the contrary, in DoDDS curricula, Okinawa's US bases are taught as symbols of peace, virtue, and justice. Teaching the peace policy in this way does not meet Amerasians' needs either because it interprets Amerasians' struggle as trivial in comparison with the missions authorized by the peace policy. The point at issue here is that the educational discourse surrounding international 'peace' policy in both American and Japanese public school curricula contradicts each other. Both interpretations make Amerasians feel out of place in the classroom. However, double education does not solve the problem either, because it leaves no room for Amerasians to take both sides. Double education and peace education, therefore, are incompatible.

The absence of language education

Although the purpose of peace policy is supposed to realize peace on an international scale, it does not provide peace for these children. Thus, it is necessary to discern the obstacles which prevent the development of educational cooperation at the conceptual level. However, peace education for adults should not simply become a means of speaking up on behalf of the subaltern. Rather it should reflect the social assumptions hiding behind the attitude against the subaltern. Why have children of Amerasians been neglected in the context of peace education at school?

The omission of Amerasians' perspectives in peace education can be seen as an assumption that to engender a truly inclusive approach to the topic would be to start a debate about whether the existence of US forces in Okinawa is just or unjust. This assumption is visible in the different approaches taken by Japanese and American schools, and the politics influencing these approaches. For example, peace education in the DoDDS curriculum sees the stationing of US bases in Okinawa as just, likely because DoDDSs exist as an outcome of this stationing. In contrast, the approach to peace education within the curricula of Japanese public schools in Okinawa takes the opposite position, at least partly because it offers a way to protest the damage inflicted by US forces and suffered by the local community and environment. These contradictory educational approaches do not simply reproduce certain political positions; they also reveal 'peace' diplomacy as a central issue of conflict. In other words, Amerasians displace the justice issues from the political debate over the existence of US bases in Okinawa into the educational discussion about what peace education means for Amerasians. If the educational approach focuses only on the debate about existing conditions, it is at risk of not taking into account the Amerasian minority who are unlikely (for various reasons) to take either position in the debate. Thus, the way to explore some educational approaches that would go beyond the current debate is to examine the causes which sustain the current debate.

Gavan McCormack and Satoko Oka Norimatsu (2012, 2013) point out that one of the features of the debate over the existence of the US bases in Okinawa is the US and Japanese governments' extravagant use of pleasing sounds in the form of words and phrases such as peace, justice, humanitarian aid, appreciation, sincerity, wholeheartedly, promise, apology, reduction of the burden, elimination of the risk, and sympathy budget allocation.[5] McCormack and Norimatsu quote an Okinawan blogger (Miyagi 2010) as a symbol of the counter arguments, who revealed the underlying quality of those sweet sounds: 'No need to say thank you, but take your trotter off my foot.'[6]

Paul Standish makes an argument that vagueness in language use causes problems in educational discussion. Standish examines the specific term 'social justice'. 'Social justice,' he says, 'is a phrase that recurs with some force in contemporary political and academic discussion' (Standish 2012, 17), but the term 'does bear some critical examination' (Standish 2012, 17). Standish says that 'there is a continuing need to be sensitized to the rhetorical inflation of this and similar terms' (Standish 2012, 25). He says that, because of the rhetorical correctness of the sound of the term 'social justice', people have taken advantage of the term to justify their political positions within the context of educational policy. As a result, its theoretical background marks a distance from 'certain central aspects of education' (Standish 2012, 25).

This is also the case in the debate over the US bases in Okinawa. The sweet sounds have been taken advantage of in justifying certain political positions as well as neglecting other issues about the US bases such as Amerasians' educational needs. Standish's claims about the use of the term 'social justice' offer an important angle from which to examine issues of peace education for Amerasians. The term 'peace education' itself is also at risk of being used lightly and distorted, due to its inference of rhetorical correctness and innocence. As already described, the easeful use of the phrase 'peace' can be seen in the political debate. Here, skepticism should be applied. Are the words 'peace' or 'education' being used appropriately, if 'educational approaches for peace' involve the exclusion of certain demographics?

Standish claims that in order to understand the risks inherent in using such vulnerable words, it is necessary to pay some attention 'to the nature of the language itself' (Standish 2012, 19), and to 'experience a difference between semantic fields' (Standish 2012, 21). There will be a struggle to capture the meaning, but nevertheless, the seriousness of the language demands critical examination by those who use it. Thus, a language education for adults is especially important when the meaning of words such as education and peace are at stake. I want to emphasize here that language education does not refer to the understanding of grammar or syntax, or to the acquisition of new words or foreign languages. Rather, language education here means examining the quality, sense, and sound of words which people are already familiar with. This type of language education is not aimed at children who are in the process of acquiring language skills, but rather at adults. It is important to check the chaotic condition of the usage of these words. The purpose of this language analysis is to be a stepping-stone: to develop the discussion for Amerasians' educational needs. In a sense, language education for adults is recognized as an important component of peace education for adults.

I examine the resonance of the words 'peace' and 'education' from two different angles in the next section.

Tuning into peace and education

Walter Feinberg provides an idea regarding the impasse of peace education for adults by highlighting the importance of the theoretical distinction between educational thought and political thought. Feinberg says:

> [...] if it is argued that the state has the authority to require children to experience certain kinds of education on the grounds that this advances a legitimate state interest, this argument is a political one, and it may still be questioned on educational grounds. The distinction between education and politics is important to maintain, as is the distinction between what should be educationally allowable and what is educationally desirable. Without these distinctions it will be largely impossible to sort out the issues that confront us in terms of identity and cultural recognition. Of course, the distinctions are only markers. (Feinberg 1998, 29)

Feinberg discriminates between two different ways of discussing education. We might consider what is 'educationally allowable' as in fact a question about what is politically allowable, because it requires the consideration of educational issues from within social, economic, and cultural conditions. However, a discussion of what is 'educationally desirable' goes beyond actual social contexts and political dynamics. Feinberg claims that both discourses are important to develop because they have different roles in educational theory. Feinberg's position therefore is that educational discourse differs from political discourse at the theoretical level. This secessionism is supported by Montessori's argument on peace education. She says:

> Peace is a goal that can be attained only through common accord, and the means to achieve this unity for peace are twofold: first, an immediate effort to resolve conflicts without recourse to violence, to prevent war – and second, a long term effort to establish a lasting peace among men. Preventing conflicts is the work of politics; establishing peace is the work of education. (Montessori 1972 [1949], 30)

Montessori attempts to detach the work of politics from the work of education, seeing them as having different tasks to undertake in achieving the goal of peace. Feinberg, however, fractionalizes the educational approach to peace into educational and political aspects. Viewed through his theoretical framework, the two different educational approaches to the US bases in Okinawa which arise in American public schools and Japanese public schools are politically contrastive, but neither one is an 'educationally desirable' narrative.

Feinberg also points out how difficult it is to decouple educational issues from political debate, using the notion of democracy as an example. He says:

> I believe that there is an important distinction between political democracy and educational democracy that can help us to sort out different kinds of claims regarding the responsibility of schools in promoting certain identities. This distinction is frequently overlooked by educators who wish to use education to advance a certain form of enlightened, democratic understanding and who believe that one can determine the right thing to do politically on the basis of deciding what the right thing to do is educationally. It is also overlooked by political theorists who hold that the right thing to do educationally can be deduced by determining what the right thing to do is politically. (Feinberg 1998, 27)

According to Feinberg, the very existence of different ways of understanding the same issue tends to be easily dismissed or overlooked at the practical level as well as at the theoretical level, with the result that political discourse is confused with educational discourse.

Minoru Murai, a contemporary Japanese educational philosopher, critically examines the replacement of educational discussions with political debates from a different perspective (Murai 1996). Murai claims that many 'educational issues' have been distorted into political arguments because educational studies have been held to be parasitic upon other disciplines. As a result, the role of education is misidentified as being merely to fulfill economic and political needs. Thus, Murai proposes exploring an educational way of thinking as a way to promote the independence of educational theory. To address this, Murai (1994) proposes two things. First, that an educational way of thinking, which foregrounds education itself as an academic discipline, should be pursued. Second, that the status of this educational thinking should be respected. According to Murai, there are diverse ways of interpreting the same condition within various academic disciplines. For example, a criminal mind is treated differently by law and education.

Judges use the context of law to decide on the appropriate punishment, whereas educators seek the improvement of a criminal's life through edification. Each academic discipline has its own emphasis. However, for Murai, due to lack of a sense of the independence of educational theory as an academic discipline, many other disciplines and perspectives dictate what they want schools to do under the name of education, and schooling thus is always influenced by the political and social climate. In other words, Murai argues for a democracy of educational theory and other academic disciplines.

Again, for Murai, the foundational problem of education is that 'educational' questions should be answered by 'educationally desirable' enquiry such as discussing how the notion of peace resonates with Amerasians in Okinawa as members of the educational community. In the process, he says, the concepts of schooling and education should be corrected and the ideas of education and politics should be decoupled. Here, he argues that the primitivity of educational studies is a demerit to the development of the modern school system, especially in Japan. Murai claims that, in order to understand the weakness of educational discussion over political thought, it is important to rationally reflect upon the positive and negative effects of the development of the modern school system (Murai 2000), which recognizes that children have the right to receive basic education. The idea of basic education has been guaranteed by political institutions as compulsory school education. Here, he points out a confusion of the language[7]. Even though the idea of basic school education implies that it is the 'right' of students to receive basic education, political institutions express it as 'compulsory' school education, as if it is an 'obligation' (Murai 2013). The idea of 'obligation' in this context lies not with students, but with governments and parents. However, due to a contradiction in the language, the opportunity arises to organize the subjects in question as if political institutions have the 'right' to educate students at their schools, and as if children have an 'obligation' to be educated by them. As a result of the confusion of these subjectivities, the language of political ideology takes over the territory of education. This is how the structure of modern schools, according to Murai, ironically restricts the development of educational thought.

Murai (2013) also points out that the development of the modern school system led by modern states is creating confusion between the terms 'education' and 'schooling'. The term 'schooling' is originally a category of the term 'education'. However, the development of the school system created an illusion that the term 'schooling' is a synonym of 'education'. For Murai, if 'schooling' is misunderstood as having the same meaning as 'education' it violates educational studies, because the term 'schooling' is already controlled by the political institution. If 'educational' discussion implies only issues on 'schooling,' it limits the discussion to 'politically allowable' education. Moreover, because of the myriad potential language confusions, if the only kind of discussion that happens in schools is 'politically allowable', then it is a misidentification to refer to it as 'educational discussion.' The debate over the US bases in Okinawa is a reflection of this. It is a political matter, but it directly shows up in school curricula without discussion as to whether or not existing approaches to teach 'peace' policy are grounded in educationally desirable thinking. As a result, Amerasians have been disenfranchised in their school settings. In applying Murai's idea to the case of the Amerasians' educational issues, what resonates is the need to explore a peace education which is educationally desirable.

Murai proposes that the development of language education is a way of rectification. According to Murai (2013), the distinction between edification and education is one of the most delicate issues in educational studies as these words are two sides of the same coin. Similar arguments were developed by analytic philosophers in the 1970s. Ivan A. Snook, for example, tried to define education by contrasting it with indoctrination (Snook 1970). However, historical fact teaches that his attempt seems to have failed. Murai's theoretical framework helps to explain why. First, even though Snook applied the method of analytic philosophy as a way to define the terms of education and indoctrination by de-contextualizing them, his argument seems to have been contextualized and influenced by the political environments of the period, especially the Cold War. From a present-day viewpoint, his argument distinguishing indoctrination from education echoes the discrimination between schooling in communist countries and schooling in the Western bloc.[8] Thus, Snook's language analysis does not meet Murai's idea of language education because the purpose of the research (to define the term 'education' by way of defining the term 'indoctrination' in the period) was not to contribute to the development of an educationally desirable way of thinking, but rather to demonstrate the ways in which educational discussions are skillfully occupied by political discourses. Furthermore, Snook focuses on children and schooling in the analysis of indoctrination and education, whereas for Murai, it is really a question of confusing the meanings of schooling and education.

Conclusion

John Dewey says that '...the important thing is that thinking is the method of an educative experience' (Dewey 1916, 163). Applied to the Amerasian case, this approach reminds us that, even though it is difficult to include Amerasians' educational needs in a formal educational framework at the practical level, and to overcome the barriers of national frameworks, political tensions, and social discriminations, it is still important to practice analytical thinking as a way of overcoming. Educational practice (what Dewey called 'the production of good habits of thinking'[9]) should provide a sense of independence. But this does not mean that these approaches are isolated from political activity. Instead of encroaching upon the political sphere of influence in educational studies, it can be useful to examine political thought from educational perspectives. In other words, the Amerasians' case requires a consideration of whether it is suitable to refer to 'peace' policy as peace in an educational context. It is important to establish a discussion of what is an educationally desirable use of the term 'peace' because it is otherwise impossible to establish a recursive connection between educationally desirable peace and politically allowable peace. Having one's own voice is the way to contribute to reforming the social framework. It also promotes the creation of independent but recursive relationships between education and other disciplines.

It is correct that this habit of analytical thinking is necessary to learn from an early age, but it is also very important for adults who are familiar with this language. Peace education for adults teaches that language education is important, even as using language becomes more ordinary. Peace education for adults should be identified as a kind of daily maintenance, like washing bodies and brushing hair. This is because peace is maintained daily with the maintenance of the term. It is an educational activity to continuously reclaim the resonance of 'peace' and 'education.' It is also an educational activity to reexamine consistency in the meaning and usage of peace in context. These activities need to be constantly renewed. If we proclaim that the definition of peace has a fixed sense, we are at risk of losing the quality of peace. What we need for peace education for adults is to recover the subjectivity of both peace and education. Moreover, the term 'peace education' needs doubly delicate treatment to ensure protection of its meaning, and to ensure that its vulnerability to distortion is not used to present political thoughts as educational thoughts.

In conclusion, I return to Montessori's claim that children are the primary teachers of peace education for adults. She argued that children can teach peace to adults because they are peaceful and innocent. I agree with her idea but for different reasons, namely that children provoke adults to become more aware of what is an educational voice and what is a political voice, as the example of the Amerasian children demonstrates. The delicate case of the Amerasian children, and the political complexities it invokes, calls for adults to reform educational practice not within the current political framework, but beyond it.

Acknowledgements

The author thanks Dr. Walter Feinberg for his generous support and encouragement throughout the writing of this article.

Disclosure statement

No potential conflict of interest was reported by the author.

Funding

This work was supported by JSPS KAKENHI [grant number 23730770 and 26780456].

Notes

1. For more details see Murphy-Shigematsu (2002).
2. For more details see p. 193. In McCormack and Norimatsu (2013).
3. For more details see Fujisawa (2005).
4. For more details see p. 167. In Noiri and Janes (2008).
5. For more details see McCormack and Norimatsu (2013).
6. For more details see p. 170. In McCormack and Norimatsu (2013). Also, see http://miyagi.no-blog.jp/nago/2010/06/post_53a0.html
7. It is important to note that Murai wrote in Japanese, and thus the translation of this confusion into English does not translate perfectly across.
8. For more details see Snook (1972).
9. See p. 163. In Dewey (1916).

References

Dewey, J. 1916. *Democracy and Education: An Introduction to the Philosophy of Education*. New York: The Free Press.
Feinberg, W. 1998. *Common Schools/Uncommon Identities: National Unity and Cultural Difference*. New Haven: Yale University.
Fujisawa, K. 2005. *Okinawa/Kyouiku Kenryoku no Gendaishi* [Contemporary History of Authority in Okinawa and Education]. Tokyo: Shakai Hyoron Sha.
McCormack, G., and S. O. Norimatsu. 2012. "Resistant Islands: Okinawa Confronts Japan and the United States." In *Asia/Pacific?Perspectives*, edited by M. Selden. New York: Rowman and Littlefield.

McCormack, G., and S. O. Norimatsu. 2013. *Okinawa no Ikari: Nitibei heno Teiko* [Okinawa in Anger: Protesting against Japan and the United States]. Kyoto: Houritsubunka Sha.

Miyagi, Y. 2010. "yekaramono no kouta." In *Ten Thousand Light-Years from Home*.

Montessori, M. 1972 [1949]. *Education and Peace*. Translated by H.R. Lane. Thiruvanmiyur: Kalakshetra Press.

Murai, M. 1994. *Ningen to Kyouiku No Kongen Wo Tou* [Fundamantal Questions about Human and Education]. Tokyo: Shougakukan.

Murai, M. 1996. *Shintei Kyouiku Karano Minaoshi: Seiji, Keizai, Housei, Shinkaron* [Rethinking from Education: Politics, Economics, Law, and Evolutional Theory]. Tokyo: Toyokan Shuppan.

Murai, M. 2000. *Kindai Nihon No Kyouiku to Seiji* [Education and Politics in Modern Age Japan]. Tokyo: Toyokan Shuppan.

Murai, M. 2013. *Nihon Kyouiku no Konponteki Henkaku* [Fundamental Reform for Japanese Education]. Tokyo: Kawashima Shoten.

Murphy-Shigematsu, S. 2002. *Amerasian no Kodomotachi: Shirarezaru Minority Mondai* [Amerasian Children: Unknown Minority Issue]. Translated by J. Sakai. Tokyo: Shueishashinsho.

Noiri, N., and D. Janes. 2008. "Preparing for Double Citizenship: Educational Innovation at the AmerAsian School in Okinawa." The 10th Anniversary of the AmerAsian School in Okinawa, Okinawa.

Snook, I. 1970. "The Concept of Indoctrination." *Studies in Philosophy and Education* 7 (2): 65–108.

Snook, I., ed. 1972. *Concepts of Indoctrination: Philosophical Essays*. London: Routledge & K. Paul.

Standish, P. 2012. "Social Justice and the Occident." In *Proceedings of the 5th International Symposium between the Graduate School of Education*. Vol. 5, 17–27. Kyoto University and the Institute of Education, University of London.

Uezato, K. 1998. *AmerAsian: Mouhitotsu no Okinawa* [Amerasian: Another Okinawa]. Kyoto: Kamogawa Shuppan.

Education in times of fast learning: the future of the school

Jan Masschelein and Maarten Simons

>Against the background of the many attacks on the school as being outdated, alienating, ineffective and reproducing inequalities we offer a morphological understanding of the school as distinguished from functionalist understandings (sociological or economical perspectives in terms of functions and roles) and idealistic understandings (philosophical ones in terms of 'ideas of education'). Our educational morphology approaches the school as a particular scholastic 'form of gathering' i.e. a particular time–space–matter arrangement (including concrete architectures, technologies, practices and figures) that deals in a specific way with the new generation, allows for a particular relation to the world, and for a particular experience of potentiality and of commonality (of making things public). We elucidate how this form performs particular operations of suspension, profanation and formation of attention and how these operations imply a slowing down and an opening of future. Finally, we emphasise the potentially revolutionary character of the scholastic form and discuss contemporary attempts at taming or neutralising the school.

Introduction

The school's very existence has been called into question by radical deschoolers and unschoolers throughout the twentieth century. Schools, so they argue, rest on the false premise that we need them to learn, while we learn much better or faster outside school or outside the classroom (Illich 1970; Bentley 2000; Griffith 2010). Moreover, schools have been compared to prisons and camps (Gray 2013), they have been accused of being brutal colonisation machines. And all this seems to be based on sound observations and arguments. In today's era of lifelong learning and (digital) learning environments, perhaps one is allowing the school to die a quiet death. One anticipates now really the school's disappearance on the grounds of its redundancy as a painfully outdated institution. Indeed, besides the recurring charges and accusations levelled against the school (alienating and demotivating young people, corruption and abuse of its power, reproduction of inequality, lack of effectiveness and employability), we must take note of the recent development which states that the school, where learning is bound to time and space, is no longer needed in the digital era of online learning environments. A revolution fuelled mainly by new information and communication technologies makes it possible to focus learning squarely on the individual learner. In this new context, it is argued, the personalised learning process gains increased support through ongoing evaluation and monitoring, and learning itself becomes fun. Learning, it is stated, can take place anytime and anywhere. This means that the class as a communication technology is rendered obsolete. The school and classical education become redundant according to their critics: the entire concept of curriculum and classification based on age is a product of outdated ways of distributing knowledge and expertise. The school as a whole is determined by primitive technologies of the past. When listening to the critics of the school, it seems as if today learning becomes once again a 'natural' event, where the only thing that matters is the distinction between 'rich' and 'poor' or 'effective' and 'ineffective' learning environments.

Is all this indicating or announcing the end of the school? We hope not. In fact we want to offer some elements of a defence of the school, not in order to restore an old institution, but to develop a touchstone to reinvent the school. As part of this defence, we try to identify what makes a school a school and, in doing so, we also want to pinpoint why the school has value in and of itself and why it deserves to be preserved or, maybe better and more precise, deserves to be reinvented. We call this a morphological understanding of the school and we distinguish it from functionalist understandings (sociological or economic perspectives on the school in terms of functions, roles and societal needs) and idealistic understandings (philosophical ones in terms of ideas or meanings of education and schooling). Our educational morphology is, however, not a kind of elaborated theory, but more like a set of propositions or invitations to think about the school in a particular and perhaps more fruitful way in terms of 'forms of gathering and actions', rather than functions and institutions. Indeed, from a morphological perspective, the school is understood neither as an institution (obtaining legitimacy from a transcendent idea or ideal) nor as a (multifunctional) organisation (obtaining legitimacy from the performance of functions), but refers to a particular form of gathering. It is this 'scholastic form', what this form does (or creates) and the very concrete architecture, technologies, practices, figures, experiences and acts that constitute it, that we attempt to clarify, at least by pointing to some of its main features. It is important to be clear from the outset: we do not attempt to imagine an 'ideal school' or the school as 'idea', but to describe the school as a very concrete, material invention including a very particular form of (educational) gathering.

A particular invention

It may at first sound strange to inquire into the scholastic. Is it not obvious that the school is essentially a place of learning? Is it not self-evident that the school is about an *initiation* into knowledge, practices and skills, and about a *socialisation* of young people in the culture of a society? And is the school not simply the most economic, collective form to organise initiation and socialisation when society reaches a certain level of complexity? These are common perceptions of what the school is and does. In contrast to this view, it is very important to recall that the school is a specific (political and material) invention of the Greek *polis*, which implies that schools have not existed everywhere and always, and that schools might one day indeed also cease to exist (see also Stiegler 2006, 2008; Pena-Ruiz 2005). One could probably say that each society has its forms of learning and of dealing with knowledge and skills in relation to new generations, but the Greeks invented a very particular form (just as they invented the particular form to deal with our living together which is called democracy). In what follows, we make some further reference to Greek antiquity, but we do not intend to offer an historical account.

As part of our morphological account, we start from references to the Greeks in order to sketch some features of the school form.

In order to set the scene for our morphology, we want to start with four remarks. First, the school is not (just) about learning, and hence, we do not approach the school as one (formal) learning environment besides many other (informal) learning environments. Second, the school is not the economic solution for the impossibility of organising or financing individual teacher–pupil or master–apprentice relationships. Third remark: what we often call 'school' is in fact (fully or partially) a tamed, neutralised and hence de-schooled school. Thus, in this article we want to reserve the notion of the school for a concrete invention of a particular form of education. It is a form that throughout history was exposed to several attempts of taming and acts of neutralisation. Fourth, we hope the features of the school form that we elaborate here can function as a kind of touchstone in the true sense of the word; not as a kind of benchmark or set of principles to judge, assess or evaluate educational practices, but as a source of inspiration or point of reference in attempts to re-invent school practices. Let us now explore some of the features of the invention of the school. These could be approached as *materialised beliefs and decisions* or acts, written in practice and ethos (i.e. in a form), so to say.

Suspending the natural order

The Greek school emerged as an encroachment on the privilege of aristocratic elites in ancient Greece. Of course, from the very beginning there were operations to restore privileges, to safeguard hierarchies and classifications, but a major act that *makes school* is precisely the suspension of a so-called natural, unequal order. The school one could say is the materialisation of the belief that humans have no natural destination. It is the materialisation of the refusal of natural destiny and of the confirmation of *homo educabile*; since there is no (given) destiny, (wo)men can be educated. The school was doing this while providing *scholé* or *free time*, that is, non-productive time, to those who by their birth and their place in society (their 'position') had no rightful claim to it.[1] That is also the reason why Bernard Stiegler defines the school as 'otium/scholé for the people' (Stiegler 2006/2008, 150). School is literally a place of *scholé*, that is the spatialisation and materialisation of 'free time' and, thus, of the separation of two uses of time. What the school did was to establish a time and space that was in a sense detached and separated from the time and space of both society (*polis*) and the household (*oikos*). The invention of the school constituted an emancipatory rupture and provided the 'format' for time-made-free, that is, the particular composition of time, space and matter that makes up the scholastic. With the coming into existence of the school form, we actually see the democratisation of free time which at once is, as Rancière (1995, 55) argues, the 'site of the symbolic visibility of equality'. The school form should be regarded as the visible and material refusal of natural destiny. This also explains that the invention of the school form was at the same time the start of several attempts to tame or neutralise the school: time and again there have been attempts to reintroduce some kind of *natural* order (e.g. age, talent, capacity, natural development) and hence to claim a kind of natural destiny and to neutralise the free time. These are reactions to the fact that those who dwell within the school literally come to transcend the social (economic and political) order and its associated (unequal) positions. The scholastic format, as a consequence, suspended in various ways the urgency of the moment and enabled a particular dis-closure of the world.

Suspending the urgency of the moment: delay, suspension, profanation and attention

School is invented to develop faculties through study and exercise without the constraints of the moment. For that reason, school-children are not apprentices of a craftsman. School time is time of knowledge/matter for the sake of knowledge/matter (related to study), of capability for the sake of capability (connected to exercising) and of conversation/ argument for its own sake (which is at stake in thinking).[2] Time for study, exercise and thinking is time to bring oneself into (good) shape. In this sense, school time is freed from a defined end and therefore from the usual economy of time. It is 'un-destined' time where the act of appropriating or intending for a (immediate) purpose or end is delayed or suspended.[3] School time therefore is the time of delay and rest (of being inoperative or not taking the regular effect) but also the time which rests or remains when purpose or end is delayed. Study, exercise and thinking are thus, and importantly, practices which in themselves slow down and install a delay. Free time is separated from productive life, it is time where labour or work as economic or instrumental activities are put at a distance, and hence, study and exercise become possible.

A typical feature of this separateness, then, is suspension. Economic, social, cultural, religious or political appropriations are suspended, as are the forces of the past and the future and the tasks and roles connected to specific places in the social order. The school offers students for instance the opportunity to leave behind their past and family background, and indeed to become students like all the rest. Past and background, of course, do not disappear but when entering the school form they are suspended. And a similar suspension exists from the side of teachers (a profession that is not really a 'serious' profession), and from the side of subject matter (knowledge and other things that are not 'for real'). Clearly, suspension seems no longer to be part of education today; in contrast, there seems to be the opposite tendency, that is, to connect students to their past and family background, to transform teaching into a productive activity and to make subject matter directly useful. It is important to stress that to suspend means not to destroy or ignore, but to '*temporally* prevent from being in force or effect' (Oxford Dictionary). Education as a *form* of suspension is not destroying or denying anything, e.g. the past or the institutions, but is disorientating the institutions, interrupting the past. The necessities and obligations of professions, the imperatives of knowledge, the demands of society, the burden of the family, the projects for the future; everything is there or can be there but, as Barthes (1971) would say, in a condition of 'floating'.

Suspension could be regarded more generally as an event of de-privatisation; it sets something free. The term 'free', however, not only has the negative meaning of suspension (free from), but also a positive meaning, that is, free to. Drawing upon the terminology of Agamben, we use the term *profanation* to describe this kind of freedom. According to Agamben '[p]ure, profane, freed from sacred names is that thing that is being replaced in view of the common use by people' (Agamben 2005, 96). A condition of profane time is not a place of emptiness, therefore, but a condition in which things (practices and words) are disconnected from their regular use (in the family and in society) and hence it refers to a condition in which something of the world is open for common use (Agamben 2007). This is in line with Lewis (2013) who suggests to look at study as 'profanated learning'. Thus as part of practices of study, but also of exercise or thinking, things (practices, words, movements...) remain without defined end: means without an end (Agamben 1995; Simons and Masschelein 2009). It is in front of common things available as means that the young generation is offered the opportunity to experience itself as a new generation, i.e. the experience of (im)potentiality/beginning in front of something that is open for common use.

Things however are not only made profane but the school makes it possible for the new generation to become *attentive* to the world, to some-thing. Through the teacher, school discipline and architecture the school forms attention and makes attentive. According to Weil (1948) and to Stiegler (2010) this is even the most important issue when considering the essence of (school) education. The importance of attention can also be formulated differently: the school does not only make things known, but also exposes students to these things and gives them 'authority'. The school makes that the common things, or the world, can 'speak to them'. The magical event of the school – and hence, not the mechanical process of learning – invokes things to become 'alive', to come to speak, and hence, creates the possibility for students to become interested. The school does not just offer the opportunity to learn mathematics, but to become interested in mathematics. School than is also a space of *inter-esse* – understood as an in-between and a making of a relation (Stengers 2000, see also Sörensen 2009).

The form of *suspension, profanation* and *attention* is what makes school time a public time; it is a time where words are not part (no longer, not yet) of a shared language, where things are not (no longer, not yet) a property and to be used according to already familiar guidelines, where acts and movements are not (no longer, not yet) habits of a culture, where thinking is not (no longer, not yet) a system of thought. Things are 'put on the table', to use this wonderful image of Arendt (1968/1983), transforming them into common things, things that are at everyone's disposal for free use. What has been suspended is their economy, the reasons and objectives that define them during work or social, regular time. Things are thus disconnected from the established or sacred usages of the older generation in society but not yet appropriated by students or pupils as representatives of the new generation. In a way, school can be seen as the material, visible form of this 'not yet or 'gap'. It is in front of common things available as means that the young generation is offered the opportunity to experience itself as a *new* generation, i.e. the experience of (im)potentiality/beginning in front of something that is open for common use. The profane school or *scholé* functions as a kind of common place where nothing is shared but everything can be shared. In this view, schools are not public because of how they are financed, how they are regulated or by whom they are owned, but due to their form.

Opening a future

The school is the materialisation of the decision of a society to offer a time and space for study, exercise and thinking in order to give the young generation the opportunity to renew society. Therefore, the school form is also the way in which society puts itself at a distance of itself and brings itself into play as way to offer to itself and the new generation a future in the sense of the French 'avenir' (*à venir*), which is to come and radically unknown, i.e. not knowing what one does not know (Rheinberger 2007). To put it differently, school is the place where a world is dis-closed (its closure is removed) and where the belief that *'our children are not our children'* gets a concrete visible and material shape.[4] That our children are not our children, means that they are not to be reduced to members of a family or a community, state or society, and cannot be tamed by the destinies imposed on them.

To give a very simple example: the school is the place where the daughter or son of an engineer can become interested in arts or language. In a different register, Stéphane Moses (1992) argues, that school-time is 'a time of the possible' (23) or the materialisation of 'the time of the generations' (88).

As indicated before, school turns something of the world into 'school matter'. What is at stake is offering or presenting the world once more without trying to define how it should be continued or used, i.e. to offer it un-destined, without end, to set it free, so that students or pupils can begin anew *with* these things, *with* the world. For instance, at school it is not just about learning a language, but offering young people to possibility to become interested and hence to relate to it. These things can now get meaning again, or get a new meaning. That is also why Arendt writes:

> Our hope always hangs on the new which every generation brings; but precisely because we can base our hope only on this, we destroy everything if we so try to control the new that we, the old, can dictate how it will look. (Arendt 1968, 189)

Indeed, in all traditional and archaic societies knowledge and skill is protected and shielded and even kept secret. In contrast, knowledge and skill brought into the school becomes an affair of each and all and *in principle* does not presuppose any exceptional gift, particular talent, election or privilege. Of course, knowledge was, and still is, in fact not really equally available and public, and we are aware of the position of slaves and women in Greek society and several exclusions today. The point here is that in principle, that is, as part of the difficult act and belief of making and remaking school, it was, it is and hopefully it remains.

Again, to bring something (a text, for instance) into play and to set it free from regular usage is always risky. Without this risk, however, without offering the new generation time, space end material 'for play' – be it in study, playful conversation or exercise – there is no school. The school form discussed here clearly maintains something of a site of initiation: to conserve and pass on what the older generation knows about how to live together, about nature, and about the world. But the specificity, and the real 'school form' of this transmission or passing on, lies in what is transmitted being detached and released from any 'community' and 'position' (the older generation, the wise, the nation, etc.). This happens through a public time and place that brings knowledge (culture, habits, customs...) into play in a radical way. It is important to stress that these objects are not destroyed or radically criticised at school but they are turned into – drawing loosely on Latour (2005) – some-thing of concern, of common interest, and hence something to relate to. It is radical, and even possibly revolutionary, for at school everything can always potentially be put under discussion or be questioned. To put this in simple way, at school reasons can be asked for the most diverse phenomena: Why is the sun shining?, Where comes the rain from?, Why are there poor people?,...

Abandoning: an experience of 'being not unable'

Exercising and studying are forms of learning in which one does not know in advance what one can or will learn; it are open-ended events. Consequently, the experience of school is in the first place not an experience of 'having to', but of 'being able to', perhaps even the experience of pure ability (in relation to something) and, more specifically, of an ability that is searching for its orientation or destination. Conversely, this means that the school also implies a certain freedom that can be linked to 'abandon': the condition of having no fixed destination and therefore open to a new destination. Here, like elsewhere, we foremost point at the positive, educational understanding of 'being able to' and not, as Agamben (1997) elaborated, the negative condition of being banned in relation to sovereign power: *homo educabile* and not *homo sacer*.

That educational solitude, openness or indeterminacy is aptly expressed in the following excerpt from a novel by Duras (1990, 79–80) about a boy who does not want to go to school because there he learns what he does not know (which is of course the exact reverse of Meno's slave learning what he did know):

The mother: You notice how he is, schoolmaster?

The schoolmaster: I see.

The schoolmaster smiles.

The schoolmaster: So you refuse to learn, sir?

Ernesto looks long at the schoolmaster before he answers. He is so amiable.

Ernesto: No Sir, that is not the point. I refuse to attend school, sir.

The schoolmaster: Why?

Ernesto: Let us say that it makes no sense.

The schoolmaster: What has no sense?

Ernesto: To attend school (pause). It is useless (pause). Kids at schools are abandoned. The mother brings the kids to school so that they learn that they are abandoned. In this way she is released from them for the rest of her life. *Silence.*

The schoolmaster: You, Master Ernesto, didn't you need to go to school to learn?

Ernesto: Oh yes sir, I did. It is only there that I understood everything. At home I believed in the litanies of my idiot mother. It was only at school that I met the truth.

The schoolmaster: And that is . . . ?

Ernesto: That God does not exist.

Long and deep silence.

When Ernesto is confronted with the truth 'that God does not exist', we take that to mean that he has come to the realisation that there is no fixed (natural) destination or finality. But that does not mean that the school has no meaning. Quite to the contrary. What the school makes possible is 'formation' through encounters and opportunities to study and practice. In other words, the absence of any destiny does not make (school) education impossible or meaningless, instead it makes school meaningful: school is about the time and space offered to find a destiny.

Scholè, than, is not simply a time and space of passage (*from* past *to* future), project-time or initiation-time (*from* family *to* society). It is precisely an open event of 'preparation as such', that is, preparation without a pre-determined purpose other than to be prepared and 'in form/shape'. Being prepared must therefore be distinguished from being competent or being able to perform (well), and from the claims of employability that are associated with this goals. In this respect, it is not surprising that the most basic role of the school is to impart basic knowledge and basic skills. These are part of the exercises and study that prepare us and help us to 'come into shape'.

A form of gathering

We want to emphasise once more that the school is not an idea or ideal, but a form of gathering that is to be made. Education, or *pedagogy* if understood in its broadest sense, then could be regarded as being the art and technology to make school happen, that is, to spatialise and materialise free time. School pedagogy is about the tracing of spaces and the aesthetical arranging and dealing with matter that sets things free, makes students attentive, places them in the silence of the beginning and offers the experience of potentiality in front of something that is made public. School forms, then, are forms of suspension, profanation and attention, and pedagogy is the art and technology to give shape to these forms. It is beyond the scope of this article to discuss this in detail, but we want to stress here that a school pedagogy that aims at constituting the happening of 'free time' includes particular architectures and particular forms of discipline (intellectual and material technologies of mind and body, specific pedagogic gestures) and certain pedagogical Figures (persona characterised by a particular ethos, i.e. an attitude or stance such as embodied in the figure of the teacher) (Masschelein and Simons 2010; Simons and Masschelein 2011). Here, we just want to call out two often-neglected aspects of the school form.

First, as Stiegler (2006, 174–175) states, there is no school before and without writing and reading practices: these practices are not only about disciplining the body, but foremost about 'learning to sit still when listening attentively.' Without the school form, this particular kind of attention, and the related experience of being-able-to, would be impossible. In this context, it is interesting to remind that Isocrates, which is in fact for the school much more important than Socrates (e.g. being the inventor of particular school techniques such as the essay and the exam), emphasised the practice of writing as a way to install a delay and to suspend urgencies. More particularly, Isocrates is said to have offered 'the gift of time' to the art of rhetoric that by that time was enclosed in political and juridical practices:

> Away from the courtroom and outside the general assembly, rhetoric was no longer constrained by a sense of urgency and, in the absence of that constraint, did not have to sacrifice its artistic integrity to the contingent demands of a client's interests. (Poulakos 1997, 70).

The gift of time was related to the practice of writing that Isocrates favoured; writing being in itself a delay and being not only a way to make words readable and storable, but also a way to make 'things' audible, to liberate them from their muteness and to change objects into things that can concern us. Through and in writing, the world is materialised and is opened for study, that is, to reveal various, often unsuspected and uncontrollable, dimensions.

Second, and equally important, typical for the school form is that it involves more than one student. Of course, often we consider education in (large) groups to be a matter of efficiency, and hence, implicitly or explicitly a one to one relation between teacher and student is considered to be the most optimal learning context, but practically impossible or just considered to be inefficient. Individual education, or focusing exclusively on so-called individual learning pathways, is however not a form of school education. This is because it is only by addressing the group that the teacher is put in a vulnerable position and is *forced*, as it were, to speak to each one and to no one in particular and thus to everyone. In such a condition, a purely individual relationship is not possible, or is constantly interrupted, and the teacher is obliged to speak and act *publicly*. The scholastic discipline is imposed by the group on the teacher, and this discipline ensures that whatever she brings to the table becomes a common good. That also means that the typical scholastic experience on the part of students – the experience of 'being able to . . .' – is a shared experience from the outset. It is the experience of belonging to a new generation in relation to something – always for the students – from the old world (see also Arendt 1961). This something thus generates interest, calls for attention and attentiveness, and makes 'formation' possible. A community of students is a unique community; it is a community of people who have nothing (yet) in common, but by confronting what is brought to the table, its members can experience what it means to share something and activate their ability to renew the world. Of course there are differences between students, be it clothing, religion, gender or culture. But in the classroom, by concentrating on what is brought to the table, those differences are (temporarily) suspended or put between brackets – hence, not destroyed – and during that event a community is formed on the basis of joint involvement.

Taming or reinventing the school?

When considering the features of the school form, we can read the long history of the school as a history of continually renewed efforts to (intentionally or unintentionally) tame the school (and the teacher) and to rob the school of its scholastic, i.e. potentially innovative and even revolutionary character, that is, as attempts to de-school the school. Today, the school seems to be under attack more than ever before, because it concerns the very things that make a school to school. The attacks on the school today are lurking in the appealing calls to maximise learning gains and optimise well-being and pleasure in fast and personalised learning for each and all. Behind these calls lurks a strategy of neutralisation of the scholastic form, one that reduces the school to a service-providing institution for advancing learning, for satisfying individual learning needs and optimising individual learning outcomes. The focus on learning, which today seems so obvious to us, is actually implicated in the call to conceive of our individual and collective lives as an enterprise focused on the optimal and maximal satisfaction of needs (Simons and Masschelein 2008). In this context, learning appears as one of the most valuable forces of production, one that allows for the constant production of new competencies and operates as the engine for the accumulation human capital. Time as time to learn is equated here with *productive time*. Or more precisely, learning becomes a matter of constant calculation keeping one eye towards (future) income or return and the other eye focused on useful resources to produce learning outcomes. Learning becomes a personal business, a matter of productive and investment time, something that is open to endless acceleration.

Indeed, today as yesterday there are many strategies to tame the school.[5] However, today the most important one is to conceive of the school as a 'learning environment' helping students to produce essential 'learning outcomes'. The issue of offering good education now becomes the issue of the efficient and effective production of *employable outcomes* as being investments. It becomes unimportant where these outcomes are produced and therefore schools are challenged to prove their added value – just as teachers have to prove they are productive and become responsible in terms of outcomes, and as learners (learning coaches, etc.) have to manage their time investment in an efficient way. Therefore, the space of a learning environment seems to be the perfect mirror of our hyperactive, *accelerating* society, aiming at returns on investment in a way which is as effective and efficient as possible. The space of learning environments is no materialisation of free or public time, time of delay, but of time of investment and production. The school is no longer a place where society puts itself at a distance of itself. It becomes a (public) service delivered to individuals and to society, the community or the economy itself in order to reproduce itself, to strengthen, grow or expand.

Thinking the school space starting from outcomes actually prevents it from being a potentially revolutionary space, a space of renewal of society offering itself up in all its vulnerability. A society does not put itself on a distance of itself spontaneously, and certainly not at the moment that she is dominated, as Stiegler (2010) argues, by all kinds of (private) media powers that are used 'to form opinions' and 'capture attention'. Bachelard ([1934] 1967) once spoke about 'une société faite pour l'école' (that means a society that fits the school not a school that fits a society). He asked whether society is ready to recognise the school as such, as having its own public role and to provide it with means to work, a society which does not asks of the school what it cannot do but offers the means to be school: to provide 'free time' and transform knowledge and skills into 'common goods', and therefore has the *potential* to give everyone, regardless of background, natural talent or aptitude, the time and space to leave their known environment, rise above themselves and renew (and thus change in unpredictable ways) the world. The price such a society has to pay is to accept that it is *slowed down* (because there could be something more important), that it gives its future out of hands (and reconfirms that there is no destination, fundamentally accepting its finitude) and ready to trust people enough to free them of requirements of productivity in order to enable them to make school happen (and allow them to be teachers and students).

The assumption of our school morphology is simple in this regard: the school is a historical invention, and can therefore disappear. But this also means that the school can be reinvented (and re-decided), and that is precisely what we see as our challenge and as our responsibility today. Reinventing the school comes down to finding concrete ways in today's world to provide 'free time' and to gather young people around a common 'thing'. This reinvention could be guided by the touchstone we tried to sketch. But it definitely has to deal with an important challenge: the new information and communication technologies. ICT may have a unique potential to create attentiveness (indeed, the screen has the ability to attract our attention in an unprecedented way) and to present and unlock the world – at least when ICT is freed from the many attempts to privatise, regulate and market it. Many of these techniques are geared towards capturing attention and then redirecting it as quickly as possible towards productive purposes, that is, towards penetrating the personal world to meet predetermined targets (determined by the state or others), produce particular learning gains (as part of a learning capitalism) or to increase the size of the market (in advanced economies) (Stiegler 2010). In this case, we can speak of the capitalisation of attention, with the school being an accomplice in the effort to reduce the world to a set of resources. ICT certainly does make knowledge and skills freely available in an unprecedented way, but the challenge is whether and how it can truly bring something to life, generate interest, bring about the experience of sharing (gathering around a 'common good') and enable one to renew the world. In this sense, making information, knowledge and expertise available is not the same as making something public. Screens – just as a black board – might have a tremendous ability to attract attention, exact concentration and gather people around something, but the challenge is to explore how screens help to create a (common) presence and enable study and practice.

The challenge clearly does not only concern the reinvention of a school form, but also the decision regarding a (public) belief: a belief that there is no natural order of privileged owners, that we are equals, and that the world belongs to all and therefore to no one in particular. For us, the future of the school is a public issue, and our defence is meant to contribute to maintain it as a public issue.

Funding

This work was supported by the Research Council of the KU Leuven under Grant ZKC4752/OT/12/039/BOF. Title of the project: 'Under the spell of learning. The 'learning society' as a challenge for the public role of school, university and family education.'

Disclosure statement

No potential conflict of interest was reported by the authors.

Notes

1. The Greek word *scholè* means first of all free time, other related meanings are: delay, rest, study, school, and school building. Free time however is not so much relaxation time, but rather the time of play, study and exercise, the time separated from the time of production. *Scholé* as time to cultivate one self and others, to take care of the self, i.e. of one's relation to self, others and the world. See Masschelein and Simons (2010).
2. See also the remarks of Huizinga on some sentences from Aristotle (*Politeia* 1337 b 28) where he clarifies also that *scholè*/free time is opposed to labour-time and is the time in which we 'learn certain things – not, it be noted, for the sake of work but for their own sake' (Huizinga 1949, 161).
3. The *Oxford Dictionary of English* traces the original sense of 'destination' and 'to destine' back to the Latin destinare: 'the action of intending someone or something for a purpose or end'.
4. We give here a particular twist to the famous words of Kahlil Gibran's poem: 'your children are not your children' (Gibran n.d.).
5. For a detailed discussion of several taming strategies (such as politicisation, psychologisation, naturalisation, pedagogisation, flexibilisation and professionalisation), see: Masschelein and Simons (2013).

References

Agamben, G. 1995. *Moyens sans fins. Notes sur la politique* [Means Without End. Notes on Politics]. Paris: Payot et Rivages.
Agamben, G. 1997. *Homo Sacer. Le pouvoir souverain et la vie nue* [Homo Sacer. Sovereign Power and Bare Life]. Translated by M. Raiola. Paris: Seuil.
Agamben, G. 2007. *Profanations*. New York: Zone Books.
Arendt, H. 1961. "The Crisis in Education." In *Between Past and Future*, (1968/1983) 170–193. New York: Penguin.
Arendt, H. 1968 (1983). *Between Past and Future. Eight Exercises in Political Thought*. New York: Penguin.
Bachelard, G. 1934 (1967). *La formation de l'esprit scientifique. Contribution à une psychanalyse de la connaissance objective* [Formation of the Scientific Mind. Contribution to a Psychoanalysis of Objective Knowledge]. Paris: Vrin.
Barthes, R. 1971. "Au séminaire [To the Seminar]." In *Essais Critiques IV. Le Bruissement de la langue*, 369–379. Paris: Seuil.
Bentley, T. 2000. "Learning Beyond the Classroom." *Educational Management & Administration* 28 (3): 353–364.
Duras, M. 1990. *La pluie d'été* [Summer Rain]. Paris: P.O.L.
Gibran, K. n.d. "Children." http://allpoetry.com/Children-Chapter-IV

Gray, P. 2013. *Free to Learn: Why Unleashing the Instinct to Play Will Make Our Children Happier, More Self-Reliant, and Better Students for Life*. New York: Basic Books.
Griffith, M. 2010. *The Unschooling Handbook: How to Use the Whole World As Your Child's Classroom*. 2 ed. New York: Prima Publishing (Random House).
Huizinga, J. 1949. *Homo Ludens. A Study of the Play-Element in Culture*. Translated s.n. London: Routledge.
Illich, I. 1970. *Deschooling Society*. London: Marion Boyars.
Latour, B. 2005. "From Realpolitik to Dingpolitik or How to Make Things Public." In *Making Things Public. Atmospheres of Democracy*, edited by B. Latour and P. Wiebel, 14–41. Karlsruhe and Cambridge: ZKM & MIT Press.
Lewis, T. 2013. *On Study: Giorgio Agamben and Educational Potentiality*. Oxford: Taylor & Francis.
Masschelein, J., and M. Simons. 2010. "Schools as Architecture for Newcomers and Strangers: The Perfect School as Public School?" *Teachers College Record* 112 (2): 533–555.
Masschelein, J., and M. Simons. 2013. *In Defence of the School. A Public Issue*. Leuven: E-ducation, Culture & Society Publishers.
Moses, S. 1992. *L'ange de l'histoire. Rosenzweig, Benjamin, Scholem*. Paris: Seuil.
Pena-Ruiz, H. 2005. *Qu'est-ce que l'école*. Paris: Gallimard.
Poulakos, T. 1997. *Speaking for the Polis. Isocrates' Rhetorical Education*. South Carolina: University Press.
Ranciere, J. 1995. *On the Shores of Politics*. London: Verso.
Rheinberger, H. J. 2007. "Man weiss nicht genau, was man nicht weiss. Über die Kunst, das Unbekannte zu erforschen [One Does Not Know Exactly, What One Does Not Know. On the Art to Investigate the Unknown]." *Neue Zürcher Zeitung,* Mai 5.
Simons, M., and J. Masschelein. 2008. "The Governmentalization of Learning and the Assemblage of a Learning Apparatus." *Educational Theory* 58 (4): 391–415.
Simons, M., and J. Masschelein. 2009. "Towards the Idea of a World University." *Interchange* 40 (1): 1–23.
Simons, M., and J. Masschelein. 2011. "Un-Contemporary Mastery. The Ordinary Teacher as Philosopher." In *Lehr-Performances. Filmische Inszenierungen des Lehrens*, edited by M. Zahn and K. Pazzini, 17–35. Wiesbaden: VS Verlag für Sozialwissenschaften.
Sörensen, E. 2009. *The Materiality of Learning. Technology and Knowledge in Educational Practice*. Cambridge: Cambridge University Press.
Stengers, I. 2000. *The Invention of Modern Science*. Mineapolis: University of Minnesota Press.
Stiegler, B. 2006 (2008). *La télécratie contre la démocratie* [Telecracy against Democracy]. Paris: Flammarion.
Stiegler, B. 2010. *Taking Care of Youth and the Generations*. Stanford: Stanford University Press.
Weil, S. 1948. *La pesanteur et la grâce* [Gravity and Grace]. Paris: Plon.

Taking a chance: education for aesthetic judgment and the criticism of culture

Naoko Saito

This article explores the possibilities of the antifoundationalist thought of Cavell with a particular focus on his idea of *chance in aesthetic experience*, as a framework through which to destabilize the prevailing discourse of education centering on freedom and control. I try to present the idea of chance in a particular way, which does not identify it with chaos or limitlessness but takes it rather as a condition of meaning-making, and more generally of a perfecting of culture, of a conscientious sense of its further possibility and betterment. In Cavell's perfectionism, our aesthetic life models our political life, and such life requires our constant reengagement with our language. The cultural criticism this entails is to be understood not in merely negative terms but as itself a process of renewal. The interrelationship between the aesthetic, the political and language is at the heart of Cavellian education for self-knowledge, where this is understood as a matter of self-criticism. It connects, therefore, with Cavell's sustained commitment to challenging philosophy's self-knowledge. Along these lines, reference is made to John Cage's idea of chance in art. Cage is an American composer who was influenced by Thoreau and whose idea of chance has, perhaps because of this, some similarity to Cavell's. Discussing these antifoundationalist American writers, I argue that criticism of culture requires trust in one's taste, which is at the heart of aesthetic judgment. 'Taking a chance' is a mode of thinking and use of language that might replace a prevalent discourse of critical thinking in education and realize a possibility of liberal education beyond the dichotomy of freedom and control.

Beyond freedom and control

In *Experience and Education* (1938), John Dewey writes: 'the rise of what is called new education and progressive schools is of itself a product of discontent with traditional education' (18). In this more developed progressivism, Dewey came to express discontent with the misinterpretation of his idea of 'child-centered education'. Thus, in this book, he tries to restate what he means by progressive education: progressivism should not be interpreted simply as a shifting of focus from control to freedom and from an initiation into a culture to innovation. Whereas 'MANKIND likes to think in terms of extreme opposites', of '*Either-Ors*', Dewey affirms his own purpose of exploring 'intermediate possibilities' (17), in ways that speak beyond the dichotomy of freedom and control.

He raises the question: 'What does freedom mean and what are the conditions under which it is capable of realization?' (22). In giving the impression that he is merely shifting between freedom and control, however, Dewey shows us the philosophical and practical difficulty of living and thinking beyond '*Either-Ors*'. This still is a continuing challenge to education today. We live in an age when the neo-liberal discourse of the global market is encroaching upon the field of education and when it has become all the more difficult to trust one's own judgment. A simple dichotomization (and, hence, combination) of freedom and control cannot help us reorient our thinking about culture and its criticism. More than ever, we need the kind of education through which we can learn that criticism requires tradition, and that tradition awaits criticism, to renovate our culture from within.

In response to this continuing challenge, this article explores the possibilities of the antifoundationalist thought of Cavell with a particular focus on his idea of *chance in aesthetic experience*, as a framework through which to destabilize the prevailing discourse of education centering on freedom and control. I try to present the idea of chance in a particular way, which does not identify it with chaos or limitlessness but takes it rather as a condition of meaning-making, and more generally of a perfecting of culture, of a conscientious sense of its further possibility and betterment. In Cavell's perfectionism, our aesthetic life models our political life, and such life requires our constant reengagement with our language. The cultural criticism this entails is to be understood not in merely negative terms but as itself a process of renewal. The interrelationship between the aesthetic, the political and language is at the heart of Cavellian education for self-knowledge, where this is understood as a matter of self-criticism. It connects, therefore, with Cavell's sustained commitment to challenging philosophy's self-knowledge. Along these lines reference is made to John Cage's idea of chance in art. Cage is an American composer who was influenced by Thoreau and whose idea of chance has, perhaps because of this, some similarity to Cavell's. Discussing these antifoundationalist American writers, I argue that criticism of culture requires trust in one's taste, which is at the heart of aesthetic judgment. 'Taking a chance' is a mode of thinking and use of language that might replace a prevalent discourse of critical thinking in education and realize a possibility of liberal education beyond the dichotomy of freedom and control.

Cavell and the idea of chance in art

> Art is often praised because it brings men together. But it also separates them. (Cavell 1976, 193)

> The task of the modern artist, as of the modern man, is to find something he can be sincere and serious in; something he can mean. And he may not at all. (Cavell 1976, 212)

Unlike Dewey, Cavell does not discuss education directly. He does, however, make us see the implications of chance, beyond the dichotomy of freedom and control, for our rethinking in education. In an essay on radical experimentation in music and with a sharper focus on what is at stake, here and now, Cavell invites the reader to consider a dimension of aesthetic experience in which taking a chance is not simply a matter of adventuring into uncertainty. Through his antifoundationalist view on cultural reconstruction, Cavell points towards the role of aesthetic judgment in cultural criticism.

For Cavell, philosophy and art are inseparable from the human endeavor of creation. Like that of Dewey, his general position on art can be understood in terms of 'art as experience'. It is here that the idea of chance is crucial. In an early essay, 'Music Discomposed', he writes of 'composition, improvisation, and chance' (Cavell 1976, 193). Cavell's idea of chance is illustrated in his take on modernism in music, especially with reference to the radical innovations introduced by Arnold Schoenberg. This is brought into focus especially through an examination of Ernst Krenek's critical discussion of inspiration in Krenek's 1960 essay 'Extents and Limits of Serial Techniques'. As a 'faithful disciple of Schoenberg' and 'an important spokesman for total organization', in Cavell's words (195), Krenek tries to overcome the dichotomy of tradition, history, and copying, on the one hand, and inspiration, on the other hand. How to be released from the ghost of the past (which returns in the form of 'recollection, tradition, training, and experience') – how to overcome it has been the problem of modernism (ibid.). It is here that Krenek, following Schoenberg, makes a radical move with the introduction of the idea of total structure. In that total structure, Krenek claims, 'The unexpected happens by necessity. The surprise is built in' (Krenek quoted by Cavell 1976, 195).

In response to the new music, Cavell is suspicious both of responses that cling to traditional values and of unquestioning commitment to innovation, both of which become ideological, closing down the responsibility of critical judgment. He is critical of Krenek's distrust of inspiration and submission to the total organization of formal tonal structure and principle: 'In denying tradition, Krenek is a Romantic, but with no respect or hope for the individual's resources; and in the reliance on rules, he is a Classicist, but with no respect or hope for his culture's inventory of conventions' (Cavell 1976, 196). Here it should be noted that Cavell uses the term, 'resources', not 'sources'. A source might suggest a pure origin of inspiration, a well-spring, whereas *re*source, a reworking of source materials smacks of Heidegger's 'standing-reserve'. Yet for Cavell there are no firsts, no absolute beginnings: sources are rather constantly being renewed. Hence, continual exploration or unfolding is internal to music, and this is a pattern of inquiry within composition.

It is the idea of *chance* – or, to put it more precisely, the taking of chances (199) – that, Cavell thinks, plays a crucial role here. Chance is a part of the life we ordinarily live. Human life cannot be put totally planned. Contingency is the nature not only of art, but also of our thought in general. He writes:

> Within the world of art one makes one's own dangers, takes one's own chances. [...] And within this world one takes and exploits these chances, finding, through danger, an unsuspected security. [...] Within it, also, the means of achieving one's purposes cannot lie at hand, ready made. The means themselves are inevitably to be fashioned for *that* danger, and for *that* release. [...] The *way* one escapes or succeeds is, in art, as important as the success itself. (ibid.)

Pointing to a way beyond the dichotomy of absolute structure and pure chance, Cavell's idea of chance is close to Dewey's. Cavell, however, puts a sharper focus on the sense that it is 'you' who has a responsibility to take a chance: that 'the chances you take are your own', that '*every* risk must be shown worthwhile' and that you are marked by 'the fate of being accountable for every thing you do and are' (ibid.). Here is a poignant sense of *taking* a risk and of taking it up as one's own (202), and this requires 'exactitude' for it is by this and this alone that one meets the conditions of 'commitment and accountability' (200); call this the condition of being singularized. In Cavell's eye, Krenek seems still to be caught in polarization of mechanistic metaphysics, on the one hand, and chance as random, on the other. For Cavell, by contrast, individual inspiration and convention are thoroughly interwoven: inheritance and renewal are inseparable. Hence, composition always accompanies a new development. With his idea of chance in mind, 'convention' is said not to be a 'firm inheritance from the past' but a 'continuing improvisation in the face of problems we no longer understand' (201).

In the taking of a chance, or in taking a better chance, Cavell highlights the significant role of *taste* – taste in aesthetic judgment, on the part both of artists and their audience, in virtue of its 'partialness' (206). It is an illusion to assume that in aesthetic judgment we can close down the significance of taste. And again, for us to trust our taste and to express it involves a risk: that we stake ourselves in expression, stake ourselves in what we mean. 'The task of the modern artist, as of the modern man, is to find something he can be sincere and serious in: something he can mean. And he may not tell at all' (212). It is this sense of precariousness, of 'stand[ing] on tiptoe', as Thoreau says (Thoreau 1992, 71), that permeates Cavell's idea of taking a chance.

> I said: in art, the chances you take are your own. But of course you are inviting others to take them with you. And since they are, nevertheless, your own, and your invitation is based not on power or authority, but on attraction and promise, your invitation incurs the most exacting of obligations: that *every* risk must be shown worthwhile, and every infliction of tension lead to a resolution, and every demand on attention and passion be satisfied – that risks those who trust you can't have known they would take, will be found to yield value they can't have known existed. [...] In this way art plays with one of man's fates, the fate of being accountable for everything you do and are, intended or not. (Cavell 1976, 199)

Cavell's aesthetic theory is, indeed, inseparable from his ordinary language philosophy: contingency is there at the heart of meaning-making. As in the 'invocation of chance', even silence is conditioned by language, by the 'muse', as the articulation of the possibility of speaking for one another (202). Articulation of the relation to the muse is a condition of human being. Things are not raw data: sound is already interpreted. With reference to the idea of a repetition from within which the occasion of breaking out takes place, Cavell describes a conception of composition in which anything is altered by what happens next. This is what Cavell shows in his idea of the projective nature of words. There is no way to contain the concatenations and associations of meaning occasioned by words. This is illustrated in the learning of language by a child:

> Now take the day, some weeks later, when [the child] smiled at a fur piece, stroked it, and said 'kitty'. My first reaction was surprise, and I suppose, disappointment: she doesn't really know what 'kitty' means. But my second reaction was happier: she means by 'kitty' what I mean by 'fur'. [...] If she had never made such leaps she would never have walked into speech. Having made it, meadows of communication can grow for us. (Cavell 1979, 172)

Language learning involves such leaps in meaning-making. But the projective nature of language is not limited to children's language learning: it continues to be a task assigned to human beings life-long. This resounds with Thoreau's idea of speaking in 'extra-vagance': 'I desire to speak somewhere without bounds [...] In view of the future or possible, we should live quite laxly and undefined in front, our outlines dim and misty on that side' (Thoreau 1992, 216). To take up this responsibility is always to risk the rebuff, to risk being not understood, being rejected or dismissed. But to fail to do this is to deny the very possibility of oneself. With this projective nature of meaning-making, taking a risk, making a leap, cannot simply be a matter of making a random choice. Rather it is, against the background of linguistic and cultural practice, to speak in one's own voice. Without space for these new 'meadows of communication', there is no possibility of meaning-making, and hence no hope for education. In this sense, taking a chance constitutes the condition of cultural criticism. This is so because, as we have seen, language is inherently open to risks: the chains of association are never closed, and this is the very arena (these 'meadows of communication') for the exercise of the imagination. The aptness of words is continually put into question, and they are turned to new purposes. Thoreau explains that in order to build his hut, it was necessary first to borrow an axe; but he returned it sharper than when he borrowed it. The sharpening of words when we use them well constitutes a criticism that is internal to the renewal of which the culture necessarily stands in need. In the pages to follow, we see how the idea of criticism at work here becomes entwined with notions of attunement and of finding one's pitch. In the latter stages of the discussion, these are in turn shown to be anticipations of Emersonian moral perfectionism.

Cavell, Thoreau, and Cage: chance and freedom in music and meaning-making

Cavell's idea of chance in music theory and meaning-making is not simply a matter of a reaction to structure. In order to elucidate this point, it is helpful to examine its apparent contiguity with the views of John Cage. Cavell refers to Cage as follows:

> In the writing of John Cage, chance is explicitly meant to *replace* traditional notions of art and composition; the radical ceding of the composer's control of his material is seen to provide a profounder freedom and perception than mere art, for all its searches, had found. (Cavell 1976, 194)

It is difficult to judge only from this remark whether Cavell expresses some affinity with Cage or not, and perhaps it is not Cavell's intention to make his views explicit here. Still a brief, though indirect, exploration of the potential parallels in this respect may be a means of exposing further the radicalness of Cavell's idea of chance, and more generally the crucial role that it plays in antifoundationalist American philosophy.

Cage is known as the composer who introduced the idea of 'chance operations' into music. Under the influence of Thoreau, especially from the early 1970s (Nicholls 2002, 4), he introduced the noises and sounds of daily life into his music, explaining: 'In contrast to a structure based on the frequency aspect of sound, tonality, that is, this rhythmic structure was as hospitable to non-musical sounds, noises, as it was to those of the conventional scales and instruments' (Cage 1971, 19–20, quoted in Shultis 2002, 28). His famous piece, *4'33"* – which is 'about silence, about finding that silence is not silent, and about learning that the sounds in which we are immersed can be perceived as art' (Williams 2002, 232) – was completed in 1952 at Black Mountain College. The idea of chance operations is characterized by 'emptiness of purpose' (Cage 1971, 135, quoted in Patterson 2002, 89) and absence of goal (Cage [1976] 1982, 72). He takes the view that the complexity of our life is derived from chance, and hence that we need to give up the idea of dichotomous choice in our thinking (79). Like Cavell, Cage's introduction of chance into music does not mean the abandonment of structure as a whole. Rather he transcends the dichotomy of contingency and structure, and more broadly of the inheritance and renewal of traditions: his aesthetics is willing to 'place controlled systems and unpredictable processes side by side': for example, in his work, *Music of Changes*, there is an 'intersection of control and chance' (Williams 2002, 230, 231). Discussing the 'affinities between Cage and postmodernism', Williams locates Cage somewhere between 'modernist doctrine of structure' and 'postmoderninst notion of text as something built on contingence' (227, 231). He takes the view that some of Cage's music is 'so difficult that the violinist is forced to make decisions in order to render the music playable' (231). This is parallel to Cavell's idea of meaning-making in that Cage locates the authority of judgment somewhere between the score and the performer (and hence, a reader is freed from 'the person of the author' [Cavell 1984, 53]) – with the performer being asked to pay close attention to the score, and yet to exercise her own judgment. Similarly, the reader of Cavell's texts is forced to make difficult choices and to exercise judgment, in a way that is demonstrated in his rereading of Thoreau in his *The Senses of Walden* (1992). Furthermore, just like Dewey and Cavell, it could be said, Cage returns music to the everyday, experimenting with this in the experiment of *4'33"* (Williams 2002, 232–233). Noises are in the background of silence: in silence, we hear noise. Williams calls this Cage's attunement to the idea of 'art as experience' (234).

Indeed there are some striking commonalities between Cavell and Cage with regard to their ideas of chance. Gerald L. Bruns' article 'Poethics: John Cage and Stanley Cavell at the crossroads of ethical theory' (1994) is helpful in identifying some undeniable commonalities between the two, and hence in seeing the way that chance is a key to a dimension of thought that exceeds any simple dichotomy between freedom and control. Bruns introduces us to their common ground through Thoreau. In reference to Thoreau's senses of sound and silence, Bruns points out that for Cage 'the relationship between music and noise is no longer an aesthetic relation of harmony but (in Cavell's language) an ethical relation of acknowledgment – music letting sounds be themselves' (Bruns 1994, 214). Bruns also finds commonality between Cage, Cavell, and Heidegger in that they share the view that 'chance brings openness to mystery down to earth in the form of acceptance' (215). He quotes from Cage's statement that 'we are made perfect *by what happens to us rather than by what we do*' (Cage quoted by Bruns 1994, 215, my italics). For Cage, to succumb to chance is to accept disturbance and to allow 'chance to recompose the order and fixity', to release us from our mode of grasping and framing (Bruns 1994, 216). And yet, exposing ourselves to chance, for Cage, does not mean abrogating the sense of coherence: the music is – 'not chaotic, not incoherent or unintelligible, but anarchic and unassimilable' (217). Bruns finds in Cavell's ordinary language philosophy a parallel to this alternative route to coherence through chance in the view that 'imp-words' (as in '*impulse, impels, impatient, important, impertinent, impossible, imprisoned, impressive*') are resuscitated as 'necessary recurrences', as 'noises language makes on its way to being intelligible' (219–220). The peculiarly impish quality of these words is realized if one faces up to the fact that the connotations and associations project into new contexts and uses.[1] In a way this resonates with the idea of chance, the unexpected nature of imp-words is seen not only as a persistent, potential source of anxiety but also as a condition of human freedom. While the impish quality of words can surprise you, in music you lose yourself in repetition. From within repetition, something new and unanticipated emerges. Just as Cage pays attention to each sound in the noises he hears, Bruns points out, Cavell leads us via Thoreau (or is it that Thoreau comes to us via Cavell?) to a condition where we become 'attuned, open and responsive (responsible), to the sense we do make, taking responsibility for our words' (220) – where we can live through 'the accidents of ordinary life' (221).

Bruns' examination of the commonality between Cage and Cavell, with its reference to Thoreau, shows us how philosophy, aesthetics, and art join hands in the preconditions of meaning-making, which are inseparable from chance. In their different ways, Cage and Cavell confront the question of how it is possible to be engaged in the process of perfectionist mutual attunement without being constrained by fixed structures.

The beginnings of an answer to this question lie in taking a chance – taking a chance by loosening our grip. Cavell refers to Emerson's 'explicit reversal of Kant' in his picturing of 'the intellectual hemisphere of knowledge as passive or receptive and the intuitive or instinctive hemisphere as active or spontaneous' (Cavell 1992, 129); it is in this radical overturning of the active and the passive that Cavell and Cage find chance as a source of aesthetic creation.

In contrast with Cavell's emphasis on aesthetic taste, however, Cage claims that the continuity of music composition is 'free of individual taste and memory (psychology)' (Cage 1961, 72 quoted in Burns 1994, 215). In his reading of Thoreau, Cage seems to puts a stronger focus than Cavell on the forgetting of the ego:

> The fifth paragraph of *Walden* speaks against blind obedience to a blundering oracle. However, chance operations are not mysterious sources of 'the right answers.' They are a means of locating a single one among a multiplicity of answers, and at the same time, of freeing the ego from its taste and memory, its concern for profit and power, of silencing the ego so that the rest of the world has a chance to enter into the ego's own experience whether that be outside or inside. (Cage 1980, 5)

The idea of self-abandonment (Cavell 1992, 137) is also crucial to Cavell's replacement of the subject of philosophy and art. Cavell claims that for Emerson and Thoreau, in contrast, say, to Heidegger, 'the achievement of the human requires not inhabitation and settlement but abandonment, leaving' (138); and this leaving, the moment of taking a leap, requires, on Cavell's (Thoreau's) view, one's trust in taste. 'Unattachment' in *Walden*, Cavell emphasizes, is recorded as 'interestedness' (117). Without interest, you take a chance, and interest may be the motive for leaving. What matters to Cavell is how to relocate our interest in our own selves. By contrast, Cage says that his pedagogy includes the teaching of detachment, which he associates with nothingness in Zen (Cage [1976] 1982, 75–76). In view of Cage's later devotion to Asian aesthetics, it is not impossible to guess that here, at least, Cage and Cavell part company.

Taking a chance and finding perfect pitch

> Criticism stands, or could, or should stand, in an altered relation to the art it serves. (Cavell 1976, 207)

How can the antifoundationalist mode of thinking in American philosophy that runs through Dewey and Cavell (and Cage) be translated into education? How can we avoid that thinking in terms of freedom and control that was our starting-point? Cavell acknowledges chance in our reengagement with language and culture. This is not to abrogate rules, but to resuscitate the practice of rule-following, in a revision of the criteria for judgment. *A Pitch of Philosophy* (1994) presents the idea that finding one's voice is a matter of finding 'perfect pitch' (30, 48) – an attunement of my words with those of my culture, and this at each moment. But this is not to imply acquiescence in some kind of perfected state. It is rather, as Cavell puts this in a celebrated passage in *The Claim of Reason*:

> What I require is a convening of my culture's criteria, in order to confront them with my words and life as I pursue them and as I may imagine them; and at the same time to confront my words and life as I pursue them with the life my culture's words may imagine for me: to confront the culture with itself, along the lines in which it meets in me. (Cavell 1979, 125)

Thus I find myself singularized, testing and renewing the terms of the culture, and myself against them, in the very words I use.

To find the right tone, in the right moment, and through the right medium, is something in which one's aesthetic judgment is at stake. Again this requires 'exactitude'. Aesthetic judgment is the model for the wider role of judgment in our lives, including in our political lives: and hence its development is a task of education, education in the name of cultural criticism.

Cavell highlights the moment of departure, of taking a leap. His Emersonian 'onward thinking' (Cavell 1992, 135) puts a sharp focus on the critical moment of conversion, on the 'threshold' and the 'crossroads' (Cavell 1979, 19), moving 'from darkness to light' (102). This is different from a move 'from certainty to uncertainty' (ibid.). Perhaps more consciously than Cage, Cavell encourages us to release our power *from within*, in the process of finding our own voice, and this, though paradoxically, by disowning oneself, such that 'the inmost in due time becomes the outmost' (Emerson 2000, 132). Our own partiality, our own taste, never dissipates. Criticism of culture is to be conducted from within, and the test of its success cannot be known in advance.

> The issue is simply this: we know that criticism ought to come only after the fact of art, but we cannot insure that it will come only after the fact. What is to be hoped for is that criticism learn to criticize itself, as art does, distrusting its own success. (Cavell 1976, 209)

Only when one has been able to speak those words will one regain one's *desire* to express, an eternal resource of cultural criticism. As Cavell says, 'power seems to be the result of rising, not the cause' (Cavell 1992, 136).

This is Cavell's Emersonian perfectionism, goalless and echoing Emerson's idea of *finding as founding* (Cavell 1990, xxxiv). Emersonian perfectionism is 'a perspective from which it may be seen that with a small alteration of its structure, the world might be taken a small step – a half step – toward perfection' (Cavell 1994, 50). There is no absolute new beginning: we always begin anew, taking a chance. We need to learn to take risks in speaking, where risk implies not so much adventurous forward movement but rather a humble, receptivity in action, involving suffering and patience. It requires attention to 'a particular *sound*' (Cavell 1976, 200), with 'absolute attention to one's experience and absolute honesty in expressing it' (211). This will hopefully bring forth a transformation in the way we see the world, hear its sounds and words, in the everyday: to find the unfamiliar, the strange in the familiar, as Cage prompts in the experiment of $4'33''$. To take a chance in this sense is to destabilize the prevailing discourse of critical thinking, enhancing the possibility of a *liberal* education beyond the dichotomy of freedom and control: we must learn that we live a bipolar life of freedom and inheritance, that we must keep trusting and testing our aesthetic taste, that we must retrieve our desire to express and our capacity to speak, and that, by so doing, we can resuscitate and remember our *political* emotions – where "political" is understood in terms of democracy as a way of life (Dewey 1988). Aesthetic judgment models political judgment for the following reason: aesthetic judgment without authentic affective response is void – that is, it is hollow or a sham; and political judgment in the absence of appropriate political emotion is a prescription for a polity that is hollow and moribund. Both require the finding of one's voice, whose exercise will be a practice of criticism in which the possibility of renewal inheres. It is only through this that democracy can be the voice of the people – where individuals are prepared to stake their ways of life. Cavell's critique of a commitment to experimentation that becomes ideological, exemplified in the work of Krenek, helps to reveal the nature of aesthetic judgment and shows something of what an education in democracy must become.

Disclosure statement

No potential conflict of interest was reported by the author.

Note

1. See Cavell's discussion of Edgar Allen Poe's 'imp of the perverse' in his *In Quest of the Ordinary* (Cavell 1988, 122–128).

References

Bruns, Gerald L. 1994. "Poethics: John Cage and Stanley Cavell at the Crossroads of Ethical Theory." In *John Cage Composed in America*, edited by Marjorie Perloff and Charles Junkerman, 206–225. Chicago, IL: University of Chicago Press, 1994.
Cage, John. 1971. *John Cage*, edited by Richard Kostelanetz. London: Allen Lane.
Cage, John. 1961. *Silence*. Middletown, CT: Wesleyan University Press.
Cage, John. 1980. *Empty Words*. London: Marion Boyars.
Cage, John. [1976] 1982. *Kotoritachi no tameni (For Birds)*, trans. Mami Aoyama. Tokyo: Seido-sha.
Cavell, Stanley. 1976. *Must We Mean What We Say?: A Book of Essays*. Cambridge: Cambridge University Press.
Cavell, Stanley. 1979. *The Claim of Reason: Wittgenstein, Skepticism, Morality, and Tragedy*. Oxford: Oxford University Press.
Cavell, Stanley. 1984. *Themes Out of School: Effects and Causes*. Chicago, IL: University of Chicago Press.
Cavell, Stanley. 1988. *In Quest of the Ordinary: Lines of Skepticism and Romanticism*. Chicago, IL: University of Chicago Press.
Cavell, Stanley. 1990. *Conditions Handsome and Unhandsome: The Constitution of Emersonian Perfectionism*. Chicago, IL: University of Chicago Press.
Cavell, Stanley. 1992. *The Senses of Walden*. Chicago, IL: University of Chicago Press.
Cavell, Stanley. 1994. *A Pitch of Philosophy: Autobiographical Exercises*. Cambridge, MA: Harvard University Press.
Dewey, John. 1938. *Experience and Education*. New York: Macmillan Publishing Company.
Dewey, John. 1988. "Creative Democracy — The Task Before Us" (1939). In *The Later Works of John Dewey*, Vol. 14, edited by Jo Ann Boydston, 224–230. Carbondale: Southern Ill.
Emerson, Ralph Waldo. 2000. *The Essential Writings of Ralph Waldo Emerson*, edited by Brooks Atkinson. New York: Modern Library.
Nicholls, David. 2002. "Cage and America." In *The Cambridge Companion to John Cage*, edited by David Nicholls, 3–19. Cambridge: Cambridge University Press.
Patterson, David W. 2002. "Words and Writings." In *The Cambridge Companion to John Cage*, edited by David Nicholls, 85–99. Cambridge: Cambridge University Press.
Shultis, Christopher. 2002. "Cage and Europe." In *The Cambridge Companion to John Cage*, edited by David Nicholls, 20–40. Cambridge: Cambridge University Press.
Thoreau, Henry D. 1992. *Walden and Resistance to Civil Government*, edited by William Rossi, 1–307. New York: W.W. Norton & Company.
Williams, Alastair. 2002. "Cage and postmodernism." In *The Cambridge Companion to John Cage*, edited by David Nicholls, 227–241. Cambridge: Cambridge University Press.

Character education and the disappearance of the political

Judith Suissa

> In this article, I explore some contemporary versions of character education with specific reference to the extent to which they are viewed as constituting a form of citizenship education. I argue that such approaches often end up displacing the idea of political education and, through their language and stated aims, avoid any genuine engagement with the very concept of the political in all but its most superficial sense. In discussing some of the points raised by critics of character education, I defend the need for a more robust and radical conception of the political as a basis for a form of political education.

Introduction

Character education, for many years a deeply unfashionable idea due to its 'historical associations with various forms of religious and moral indoctrination of the young' (Grace 2003, x), is definitely back on the agenda in English education policy. There has, for some years, been policy interest in and support for a range of initiatives that promote a form of character education in schools.

Many such initiatives have been subject to criticisms from theorists and practitioners concerned with issues of social justice, who express worries about the political assumptions behind them, either in the sense that they are seen as inherently right-wing or conservative, or that they are, as part of the 'therapeutic turn', recasting social problems as individual problems.

While I have some sympathy for these criticisms, my focus in the following discussion is not on the alleged, explicit or assumed ideological assumptions behind current character education programmes, but on the way in which they displace the idea of political education and, through their language and approaches, avoid any genuine engagement with the very concept of the political in all but its most superficial sense. In exploring some of the points raised by critics of character education, I defend the need for a more robust and radical conception of the political as a basis for a form of political education.

Kathryn Ecclestone, one of the most prolific and rigorous critics of recent versions of character education, points out (Ecclestone 2012) that this new trend is broad enough to encompass theorists of different political persuasions. It can no longer simply be written off as a project of the conservative right or the religious lobby, and has attracted supporters from across the political spectrum, as reflected in the following statement from the think-tank Demos, whose influential Character Inquiry was published in June 2011:

> There is growing interest in the political and policy importance of a certain set of personal attributes – in particular emotional control, empathy, application to task, personal agency, an ability to defer gratification – that might be summarized as 'character'. [. . .] While the terminology differs – in different cases, terms such as emotional resilience, social and emotional skills, or life skills, might be used – the central, and perhaps growing, importance of character is being recognized across intellectual disciplines and across the political spectrum. (http://www.demos.co.uk/projects/the-character-inquiry)

Similarly, Learning for Life, an umbrella organization that coordinates the work of a number of bodies developing character education projects in the UK, in expressing a concern that too much emphasis in the education system has been placed on competitiveness and future employment prospects, states: 'A reinvigorated conscious focus upon character education in schools is a necessity, if a proper balance is to be restored to the educational process' (http://www.learningforlife.org.uk/about/frequently-asked-questions/).

Criticisms of character education

In spite of their allegedly broad appeal, many recent initiatives in the field of character education have been the target of rigorous criticisms from philosophers and others. I now turn to a discussion of some of these criticisms in order to address the important conceptual and political issues that they raise.

Boyd, writing in a North American context, has criticized an approach to character education that he claims 'has now achieved the status of a movement in the U.S.' (2011, 147), arguing that 'there is a highly conservative nature to almost all contemporary character education discourse' (ibid.). The programmes he has in mind, which draw on the work of Thomas Lickona, one of the most influential theorists in the field, are those that defend a list of 'essential virtues'. Boyd refers to the 'epistemological arrogance' (ibid., 150) typical of these programmes, which strive at consensus over items on such a list, thereby ruling out disagreement and, in doing so, promoting a kind of 'willful difference blindness' (ibid., 152) that ends up propping up the status quo. A central flaw in such approaches, Boyd argues, is their conceptual confusion between 'the good' and 'the right'. Boyd notes that 'it is the contrast between the work done by "the good" versus "the right" that is so critical to liberal political theory, particularly in its aim of addressing the inevitability of difference and conflict among citizens' (ibid.). In failing to acknowledge this distinction, and consequently blurring the distinction between the good person and the good citizen, such character education programmes end up being 'discursively productive of a very conservative political perspective that serves to protect the status quo of social relations [. . .], ignoring or hiding difference or conflict' (ibid., 162). Thus 'by ignoring these deeper, more insidious social conditions [of systematic oppression faced by women, members of the working class, or those in racialized and sexually marginalized groups] this movement becomes politically conservative by default, if not by design' (ibid., 148).

Boyd's solution is to offer a more 'left field' approach to character education which assumes the Rawlsian distinction between the right and the good and focuses on the central political virtue of justice, adding the important perspective offered by Iris Marion Young's work on the oppressive relations between relationally defined groups in order to articulate specific virtues required to address the oppression of racialized and other marginalized groups.

I find Boyd's analysis persuasive and am sympathetic to his argument that in a society such as the USA, where issues of oppression on the basis of class, race and gender are so deep-rooted and pervasive, educational interventions concerned with democratic citizenship need to have a far more rigorous and central concern with issues of justice, and a social ontology more akin to that of Young than to that of Rawls. Yet at the same time, I am concerned that the conceptual distinction between the right and the good that Boyd regards as so indispensable to a robust approach to character education, glosses over some of the political tensions within the liberal project itself.

Projects for character education in English schools, such as those developed and supported by the Jubilee Centre for Character and Values founded at the University of Birmingham in 2012, may seem on the face of it less politically worrying than the US programmes that Boyd discusses. While the Jubilee Centre website also makes prominent reference to the work of Thomas Lickona, many of the educational programmes developed and promoted by the Centre are explicitly concerned with the virtue of justice (see http://jubileecentre.ac.uk/userfiles/jubileecentre/pdf/other-centre-papers/Framework). However, statements such as the following, from the Centre's 'Framework for Character Education in Schools', 'Schools do and should aid students in knowing the good, loving the good and doing the good. Schools should enable students to become good persons and citizens, able to lead good lives, as well as "successful" persons,' suggest that there may be a similar conflation here to that which concerns Boyd, overlooking the central tenet of liberal theory that 'the "good citizen" is a distinct *role*, not to be confused with the more general one of "the good person"' (Boyd 2011, 154).

In fact, as I discuss later, the conceptual distinction that Boyd defends opens up more tensions and questions than it resolves. The way to address these tensions, however, is, I suggest, not by a theoretical debate conducted within the academic discourse of political philosophy, but by bringing them into the classroom. Without a more radical conception of just what 'the political' means, and without engaging children in debates about how political aims, ideas and values are intertwined with, yet importantly distinct from, moral values, there is no hope of engaging children in the pursuit of a more socially just and less oppressive society.

The problem identified by Boyd in his criticism of character education programmes is very different from that identified by critics such as Kathryn Ecclestone, who argues that 'discourses of well-being and character both recast virtues and moral values as psychological constructs that can be trained without requiring moral engagement' (Ecclestone 2012, 476). Yet both critics are concerned with the wider political issues behind problems that advocates of character education often claim to be addressing. As Ecclestone argues, contemporary initiatives in the field of character education are explicitly linked to the positive psychology movement and its focus on boosting and measuring subjective well-being. For example, the recent 'Positive Education Summit' held at Wellington College in 2013 and co-sponsored by the Jubilee Centre, was aimed at 'highlighting the benefits of placing character and wellbeing on the timetable'. Reflecting the general tenor of such projects, the statement issued by the organizers of the summit, who included Martin Seligman, the guru of positive psychology, and James O'Shaughnessy, a former adviser to David Cameron and one of the engineers of the UK government's recent 'happiness index', announced 'We are calling on all schools to embrace positive education and introduce explicit character education into the curriculum' (see http://lightsandcolors.com/pes/the-summit/).

Analysing this discourse, Ecclestone explains that 'emotional and psychological well-being' is an umbrella term that

> draws in an extensive set of 'constructs' seen as amenable to development. These include resilience, stoicism, an optimistic outlook, an ability to be in the moment (or 'in flow'), feelings of satisfaction, being supported, loved, respected, skills of emotional regulation, emotional literacy (or emotional intelligence) as well as empathy, equanimity, compassion, caring for others and not comparing yourself to others. (Ecclestone 2012, 464)

She argues that 'the revival of an old discourse of "character" incorporates concerns with morals and virtues within a psychological depiction that embraces all the constructs of well-being within a more inclusive set of "capabilities", and hopes to find ways to measure them.'

Ecclestone is careful to point out that 'Unlike earlier discourses of emotional and psychological well-being, the new discourse appears to encourage moral and political questions' (ibid., 270), and includes advocates with liberal-Left and communitarian sympathies. Nevertheless, the overwhelming therapeutic tenor of most educational interventions premised on such approaches inevitably, according to Ecclestone, 'psychologises moral dimensions to well-being and character in a social project that aims to engineer them through state-sponsored behaviour training' (ibid., 465), encouraging a diminished view of the subject positioned as in need of such interventions. Ecclestone argues, powerfully, that

> We need a political and educational challenge to a social project that hopes to engineer emotional and psychological well-being and character whilst avoiding civic engagement in the political questions this raises. The problem is that if the human targets of therapeutically informed behavioural interventions accept their underlying emotional determinism, they are in no fit state to engage in these questions. (ibid., 477)

My concern is that there is no clear conception, either within the theoretical literature or within current educational policy, of just what a 'political question' is, or what the very realm of 'the political' consists in and what it means to think about political questions and moral questions. My suggestion is that, as with the challenges raised by the conceptual distinction between 'the good' and 'the right', we try to bring such questions and challenges into the heart of educational practice. How can children be expected to play a part in political life if they do not understand what 'political' means, or what kinds of questions can be described as 'political'?

The political and the moral

Boyd, in defending a 'left field' approach to character education, cites the work of Ben Spieker and Jan Steutel, which draws on Joseph Raz's notion of the capacity for a sense of justice, in support of his argument that 'critical, reasonable engagement of difference and conflict' is an essential component of character education in a pluralistic liberal democracy. Spieker and Steutel argue that the virtue of justice, on the Rawlsian conception, is a distinctly political virtue and as such, 'although there may be overlap with the character traits of a moral person in general', they are different as they do not depend on any 'grounding in a particular comprehensive doctrine' (Boyd 2011, 157). Yet Boyd's discussion here glosses over the contested nature of these very distinctions, which have been the subject of a great deal of debate within political philosophy. Bernard Williams, for example (Williams 2008), has defended what he calls a 'realist' conception of political philosophy against the Rawlsian normative, 'moralist' conception, arguing that Rawls' conception of justice is itself moral. Similarly, Susan Mendus, discussing the related distinction between 'the right' and 'the good', points out that 'it seems optimistic to suppose, as Rawls must, that different conceptions of the good will not spill over into (or even arise from) different conceptions of the right' (Mendus 2006, 236). Disagreements in politics are, she says, 'not simply disagreements about the highest ideals but also about what justice consists in and requires' (ibid.).

This central debate in political philosophy is often framed as a conflict between two competing answers to the question 'What is political philosophy?', which are seen as reflecting two philosophical traditions, one of which considers political philosophy to be a special branch of the more general area of moral philosophy, while the other sees it as an autonomous discipline (see Larmore 2013). This conflict is echoed, yet not addressed, in a great deal of the character education literature, which either seems to assume one or other of the two opposing positions in the debate, or to simply elide the two.

Many proponents of contemporary character education initiatives in Britain draw explicit links with citizenship education, as in James Arthur's claim that 'character education can be understood to be a specific approach to moral or values education and is consistently linked to citizenship education' (Arthur 2005, 239), and such calls often invoke the notion of 'civic virtues'. Yet not all arguments for an education in civic virtues can be interpreted as belonging to a republican or Aristotelian tradition – the tradition most closely associated with the view that 'political philosophy must proceed within the framework of the larger enterprise of moral philosophy' (Larmore 2013, 9), nor do they necessarily accept the Aristotelian idea of the political life as the 'highest, most comprehensive form of human association since its principal aim is to promote the ultimate end of all our endeavours, the human good itself' (ibid., 8). In fact, as Eamonn Callan noted some time ago, 'An antipathy to talk of civic virtue runs deep in the liberal political tradition' (Callan 1998, 211). Liberal theorists, Callan explains, have often been suspicious of 'virtue-based politics' due to the worry that it will impose 'an illiberal character standardization on citizens' (ibid.), thus undermining 'the dissent and individuality that a free society will properly welcome' (ibid.). Yet Callan himself, along with several other theorists, has defended the idea that 'for people whose fundamental political orientation is democratic – including those who are quick to add that the only democracy worth having is liberal – a wholesale renunciation of civic virtue cannot possibly be appealing' (ibid.). Callan, along with other theorists such as White (see White 1996, 1983), has argued that civic virtues are necessary in a democracy, and has developed an account of liberalism as 'a politics of virtue' depending on the understanding that 'justice as reasonableness' is necessary for free and equal citizens (ibid.). Likewise, Kymlicka (2001, 294) claims that 'the health and stability of a modern democracy depends, not only on the justice of its "basic structure," but also on the qualities and attitudes of its citizens'.

One does not have to be a republican or a communitarian to accept, with White, (1980, 149) that 'democratic politics is a moral matter', and that it therefore makes little sense to have 'a privatized moral education, on the one hand, [...] and on the other a political education concerned only with a descriptive element of the society's political institutions' (ibid.). Yet to argue for a conceptual and practical connection between moral education and political education is not to endorse the kind of psychologically oriented forms of character education typical of recent initiatives that elide citizenship education and character education. Nor should the acknowledgement that moral and political philosophy both 'have to do with the principles by which we should live together in society' (Larmore 2013, 1), and that therefore, as White points out, moral considerations play a role in political argument, lead us to overlook the importance of the distinction between political questions and purely moral questions.

Yet what is remarkable in current calls for a form of character education seen as part and parcel of citizenship education is not just their confusion over these basic issues to do with how to conceptualize political theory, political education and their corresponding relationship to moral theory, but their complete expunging of the language of politics from their rhetoric. The notion of 'the political' has, it seems, been displaced by this emphasis on 'citizenship' and 'character'. The word 'political' rarely appears in the various statements and proposals issued by the Jubilee Centre, and when it is used in work by academics writing on citizenship and character education (see e.g. Arthur 2003; Arthur 2010; Althof and Berkowitz 2006), it is generally done so in the context of 'political participation', as if what is important is that children be prepared for participating in something already defined as the political system; not that they engage in meaningful thought and discussion about just what such a system is, what it should be, what participation in it consists in or why it may be valuable.

We need, I argue, to bring back a focus on the political, and an attempt to get children to see political thinking, argument and action as a particular form of human engagement concerned with particular kinds of questions. Larmore (2013, 4), attempting to move beyond the opposition between the so-called 'realist view' associated primarily with Bernard Williams and Raymond Geuss and the 'moralist view' associated primarily with G.A. Cohen, defends a view of political philosophy as concerned with 'the problem of how people like us are to live together'. What I want to suggest is that for educational interventions in this area to have any real political significance, what is important is not that proponents of various approaches to character education resolve their philosophical disagreements, get clear on the distinction between the good and the right, or identify themselves as Aristotelians or Liberals. What is essential is that *the political* – understood as that whole realm of human enquiry and experience that touches on the question of 'how people like us are to live together' – is brought back into the classroom as a live issue.[1]

For children in schools to develop any genuine understanding of the meaning of the political, they need to understand not only how moral questions can be conceptually distinguished from political questions, but how they interact. This may seem paradoxical, but Larmore explains the point well when he argues that 'the characteristic problems of political life include widespread disagreement about morality', and are as such a distinct realm from moral philosophy, 'yet it cannot determine how these problems are to be addressed except by reference to moral principles understood as having an antecedent validity' (Larmore 2013, 5).

I suggest, then, that children need to be given opportunities to think about what 'the political' means, and that in providing such opportunities, educators need to be prepared to embrace the complexity suggested by the above-mentioned discussion. Yet acknowledging this complexity and adopting a perspective like Larmore's is not sufficient for this task, for Larmore is afflicted with the 'state fixation' (Miltrany 1975, 98) typical of many liberal theorists, and thus his perspective is narrowly focused on the existing framework of liberal democracy. I explore this issue in detail later.

The absence of the political in character education

One way in which the political is written out of character education programmes is, as Ecclestone notes, in their failure to address the moral and political context of notions such as courage and resilience that are a central feature of many such programmes. To illustrate this point, I turn to an examination of the notion of resilience. As Ecclestone explains,

> Influenced strongly by positive psychology and cognitive behavioural therapy (CBT), resilience is one of several, inter-related constructs that comprise 'emotional well-being' [...] In interventions based on this understanding, resilience is a foundation for a broader set of desirable social and emotional competences. More recently, it has become a key construct in a politically endorsed revival of an old discourse around 'character building'. (Ecclestone and Lewis 2014, 196)

Yes while Ecclestone is keen to show how the notion of resilience in such interventions is premised on a narrow psychological-behaviourist approach, and to promote a more critical perspective, what I want to argue here is that the space in the curriculum allocated to such programmes of personal and citizenship education can perhaps offer opportunities for directly engaging in discussion of 'the political' as described earlier, and thus bringing back a more meaningful form of political education. One way into this, for example, is to ask students: Are there things we should not be resilient to?

The UK Resilience Programme, a version of the Penn Resiliency Program developed by Martin Seligman, was piloted in 22 schools in England in 2007 and has since been taken up by dozens of schools (see http://www.howtothrive.org/thrivingschools/penn-resilience-program). The Thinking Minds website, one of the key resources for the programme, states: 'Put simply, resiliency refers to the capacity of human beings to survive and thrive in the face of adversity.' While I share Ecclestone's worry about the way such ideas are framed as 'psychological constructs that can be trained without requiring moral engagement' (Ecclestone 2012, 476), my suggestion is that we take such 'moral engagement' into the school itself, and try to engage children in a real understanding of the political realm and political discussion as involving basic moral questions – questions, for example, about human needs and the social obligations related to these needs. As a way into this endeavour, the question 'Are there some things we shouldn't be resilient to?' has clear echoes of Martin Luther King's idea of 'creative maladjustment'. In his 1967 speech to the American Psychological Association, King said:

> There are certain technical words within every academic discipline that soon become stereotypes and cliches. Modern psychology has a word that is probably used more than any other word in modern psychology. It is the word 'maladjusted.' This word is the ringing cry to modern child psychology. Certainly, we all want to avoid the maladjusted life. In order to have real adjustment within our personalities, we all want the well-adjusted life in order to avoid neurosis, schizophrenic personalities. But I say to you, my friends, as I move to my conclusion, there are certain things in our nation and in the world which I am proud to be maladjusted and which I hope all men of good-will will be maladjusted until the good societies realize. I say very honestly that I never intend to become adjusted to segregation and discrimination. I never intend to become adjusted to religious bigotry. I never intend to adjust myself to economic conditions that will take necessities from the many to give luxuries to the few. I never intend to adjust myself to the madness of militarism, to self-defeating effects of physical violence.

As an aside, I think that the fact that Martin Seligman's Penn Resilience Training Program is now offering resilience training to soldiers in the US army at a cost of $125 million is enough to prompt the question whether there are some things we do not want people to be resilient to. My general point, though, is that asking children to reflect on this question seems like a good way to prompt them to engage in genuine political discussion, and to go on to think about what this question implies, both in relation to their own experience and in relation to wider normative moral questions about how society should be organized. However, this kind of questioning can only carry a powerful moral and political impetus if our political systems and institutions are from the outset conceived as essentially malleable.

Thus my call for the political to be brought back into moral and citizenship education is not a call to reintroduce the kind of 'political literacy' advocated by Bernard Crick, who argued, in his call for political education in schools, that

> a person who has a fair knowledge of what are the issues of contemporary politics, is equipped to be of some influence, whether in school, factory, voluntary body or party, and can understand and respect, while not sharing, the values of others, can reasonably be called 'politically literate'. (Crick and Porter 1978, 7)

There have in fact been some recent calls in the UK for a revival of this kind of political literacy. For example, in April 2011 *The Independent* reported that the President of the National Association of Schoolmasters had told their annual conference that 'Youngsters should receive compulsory lessons in political education before they leave school', as it would 'give them a grounding in democracy and encourage more to vote in later life', going on to claim that 'An impartial education in politics would increase participation in elections with electors voting armed with a knowledge and understanding of party politics rather than a reliance on spin and media prejudices' (*Independent*, April 23, 2011). Likewise, Harrison Jones (*The Independent*, March 15, 2013) complains:

> Why is it compulsory to learn about shape theorems, textiles and gymnastics, but not the political system under which we live? Secondary school pupils leave education without formal teaching in such basic things as how the British political system operates, an overview of mainstream ideologies – alongside their (apparently) corresponding UK parties, and the mechanics of different voting systems.

Such calls for political education in schools refer to voter apathy and low turn-out at elections. But what they have in common with contemporary character education programmes is that they see the political system as simply that – the system which we have. A similar perspective is implicit in the principles of effective citizenship education set out by the Advisory Group on Education for Citizenship and the Teaching of Democracy in Schools, namely that 'citizenship should develop social and moral responsibility, community involvement and political literacy' (Crick 1998).

Quotes such as the above-mentioned give the impression that the problem is children's lack of factual knowledge of central aspects of the existing political system. Yet this begs the question of whether children even know what 'political' means. My suggestion is that this is the more urgent educational task, and that if it is to be undertaken in a way which will encourage children to engage with political ideas, debates and processes, it must embrace both the idea of political questions as being basic normative questions about, as Larmore says, 'how to live together in society', and an understanding of political arrangements as essentially malleable. This requires far more than an idea of political literacy and a grasp of the institutions and mechanisms of democracy.

Patricia White, like some other earlier advocates of political education (see e.g. Wringe 1984), is careful to point out that educating children for the kind of democratic dispositions she defends does not imply being 'blindly committed to the arrangements of any particular democratic state' (White 1980, 149). Yet this view seems somewhat lacking from current character education programmes – perhaps unsurprisingly in a climate in which mainstream political debate is dominated by the discourse of no alternative.

Adopting a more robust conception of the political as a basis for political education requires that educators concerned with social justice be willing to entertain the idea that a reality characterized by radical problems of poverty, growing inequality and impending ecological disaster may require radical political solutions. Central to this approach is a view of our political structures as malleable and of politics as an ongoing process of engagement with moral questions, rooted in human experience, as to how to shape and organize society.

The absence of such a perspective from contemporary character education programmes is evident not just in the way in which citizenship is framed, as discussed earlier, but also in the way in which political issues are discussed within curricular resources on specific virtues. For example, the Jubilee Centre project, 'Knightly Virtues', which has been run in 65 primary schools across Britain, involving over 3250 students (see http://www.jubileecentre.ac.uk/417/projects/development-projects/knightly-virtues#sthash.EFOvivAe.dpuf), includes a supplementary pack on the story of Rosa Parks, designed 'to explore in greater depth the virtues of courage and justice'.[2]

The emphasis on the personal character of Rosa Parks in the presentation of and questions about her story suggests a view of the political as something out there and given, with the important questions being questions for the individual: 'What do you think were the different virtues displayed by Rosa Parks?' 'What do you think you might have done if you had been on the bus?' The image of Rosa Parks as an individual with particular character traits, acting on her own, is in fact reinforced by many standard narratives about her, which ignore the well-documented fact of her involvement with the influential Highlander Center, that provided education and leadership training for civil rights activists. As Morris (1984) comments, the educational activities that Rosa Parks participated in at the Highlander Center were part of a process that theorists of collective action and political movements define as 'cognitive liberation' (see McAdam 1999). Although Parks' involvement with the Centre and with the Association for the Advancement of Colored People is mentioned in the Jubilee Centre material, the focus on the question of her individual character, and the very framing of the question 'Can an individual change society?' shifts the emphasis away from these kinds of collective political movements and the hope and belief they embody that the political system can be radically changed.

This narrow view of the political in which it is implied that radical social change is less feasible than the cultivation of personal character strengths is supported in the work of academics involved in the Jubilee Centre, such as Kristján Kristjánsson, who has responded to the objection often raised that character and virtue education are individualistic notions. These criticisms, he argues, generally have as their target 'US-style character education of the 1990's and current positive psychological virtue theory' (Kristjánsson 2013, 279).

While acknowledging the primacy of 'inward gaze and personal achievement' in such programmes, their position, Kristjánsson argues, is that

> the question of individual versus societal reform is a chicken-and-egg one – we need to start somewhere and, for developmental and pragmatic reasons, it is more feasible to start with the individual child, student or classroom than the whole school system of society at large. (Ibid.)

This argument seems to me at best naive and at worst disingenuous. First, as even a cursory understanding of Marx's theses on Feurebach indicates, the 'pragmatic' solution proposed here by no means escapes the complex social and political questions raised by this issue. Crucially for educators, if one genuinely believes that radical social change is necessary to overcome urgent social problems of injustice, inequality and oppression, then surely an essential part of such an approach is convincing people that such change is both possible and necessary, and creating a climate of public political discourse where ideas about what and how to change, and why, are openly debated and argued for. An educational approach that puts all pedagogical emphasis on individuals and their character traits mitigates against this, both reflecting and reinforcing the dominant policy discourse that views the system as here to stay and individuals as to blame for social problems.

The political imagination

Taking the educational stance that 'the political' is a central and distinct form of human engagement, bound up with moral questions about how we are to live together, and that any political system is inherently malleable and subject to change through collective action, will perhaps do something to discourage the kind of apathy remarked on by commentators. The approach to political education that I am defending here requires a flexibility and openness on the part of educators, that acknowledges that the question of what form our society should take is not fully decided, that the kinds of crisis facing us today demand radical solutions, and that perhaps a way to encourage the articulation of and participation in such solutions is to foster imaginative political thinking about the kind of society we want.

In the context of calls for civic education, Dewey is often cited as a democratic thinker we need to heed more. John Covaleskie, for example, in calling for 'a deliberate and deliberative effort to foster the virtues of character and intellect that democracy requires of its citizens' (Covaleskie 2011, 168), argues that we need to take seriously the obligations implied in the idea of a public developed in Dewey's work. But what is often overlooked by such advocates of democratic civic virtues is that an important element of Deweyan Pragmatism is, as commentators like Paul Goodman and Richard Rorty have noted, its utopian aspect (see Rorty 1999). As Goodman remarks, 'in a climate where experts plan in terms of an unchangeable structure, a pragmatic expediency that still wants to take the social structure as plastic and changeable comes to be thought of as "utopian"' (Goodman 1952, 18–19).

At first glance, one of the 'Big Questions' posed on the Jubilee Centre's website: '
How does the power of good character transform and shape the future of society?' certainly suggests that proponents of this approach are hardly concerned with simply preserving the political status quo. Yet, as discussed earlier, the assumption here is that individuals can learn, through appropriate pedagogical interventions, something called

'good character', and that this in turn can lead to social improvement. What is lacking, I have argued, is an educational engagement in the moral and political questions about just what such improvement consists in, and a willingness to consider that asking such questions might lead us into political ideas that appear, in the sense described by Goodman, 'utopian'.[3] Developing the ability to imagine, discuss and defend – or object to – different political ideas demands that we encourage children to understand political questions as fundamental questions about how to live together in society, to see our current political structures as essentially malleable, and to engage with the intertwining of moral values and ideas about how to organize society. What this requires, I suggest, is a kind of 'politics of imagination' (Bottici and Challand 2012); an appreciation of the critical role of the imagination in political thought and action.

This conception of politics, which is prior to 'the bifurcation between the two classically opposed ways of understanding the task of philosophically reflecting on politics – namely the "normative" and the "realistic"' (Ferrara 2012, 40) has been articulated by Alessandro Ferrara, as follows:

> Only a human form of association to which unlimited resources were available and which could equally satisfy all the ends striven after by all of its members could dispense with politics. The important role of the imagination becomes manifest here: by enabling us to project an image of the world, the imagination allows us to perceive certain ends as deserving more or less priority over others. (Ibid., 40)

Ferrara insists that 'we should be wary of equating politics with the "institutional" and the *staatlich*', as many dictionary definitions of politics do. 'For politics is also the locus where new values and new needs are articulated. [...] Politics at its best is the articulation of reasons that move the imagination' (ibid., 42).

I have argued that, to respond to Ecclestone's plea for 'a political and educational challenge to a social project that hopes to engineer emotional and psychological well-being and character whilst avoiding civic engagement in the political questions this raises', we need to bring the political back into the classroom, and to do so in a way that offers real hope of radical social change. This involves, I suggest, engaging children in an imaginative, intellectually challenging encounter with political ideas, and helping them to understand the historical and social context of collective endeavours to translate these ideas into reality.

Disclosure statement
No potential conflict of interest was reported by the author.

Notes
1. In adopting this phrase of Larmore's, I do not want to imply (and neither, I believe, does Larmore himself) that there is an unproblematic sense in which 'people like us' can be used in a way that does not exclude others who are 'not like us'. Rather, I suggest that this idea can be used to open up discussion about what can be considered as basic human needs, which in turn should form the basis for any political system designed to ensure that these needs are met. I would like to thank Sharon Todd for alerting me to this point.
2. I leave aside the disturbing question of why 'The Knightly Virtues' are considered educationally and morally valuable or appropriate in twenty-first-century Britain, and why Rosa Parks' story is included as a supplement to the 'great stories of knights and heroes' that form the core of this educational programme.

3. Of course, one may disagree with the radical suggestions implied here, and may be of the view that the democratic, liberal state is the best and most defensible political system available, and that the primary educational task is to strengthen its institutions and values. This seems, indeed, to be the position behind many of the character education projects described here. Yet if it is, it needs to be explicitly articulated and defended. It is the absence of any such defence that reflects the 'state fixation' mentioned earlier. I would like to thank Hanan Alexander for drawing my attention to the importance of this point, the broader implications of which I cannot pursue in full here.

References

Althof, Wolfgang, and Marvin Berkowitz. 2006. "Moral Education and Character Education: Their Relationship and Roles in Citizenship Education." *Journal of Moal Education* 35 (4): 495–518.

Arthur, James. 2003. *Education with Character; The Moral Economy of Schooling*. London: Routledge.

Arthur, James. 2005. "The Re-emergence of Character Education in British Education Policy." *British Journal of Educational Studies* 53 (3): 239–254.

Arthur, James, ed. 2010. *Citizens of Character; New Directions in Character and Value*. Exeter: Imprint Academic.

Bottici, Chiara, and Benoit Challand. 2012. *The Politics of Imagination*. Abingdon: Birkbeck Law Press.

Boyd, Dwight. 2011. "Character Education From the Left Field." In *Character and Moral Education; A Reader*, edited by J. DeVitis and T. Yu, 147–164. New York: Peter Lang.

Callan, Eamonn. 1998. "Review of Patricia White, 'Civic Virtues and Public Schooling: Educating Citizens for a Democratic Society'." *Studies in Philosophy and Education* 17 (2–3): 211–215.

Covaleskie, John. F. 2011. "Morality, Virtue and the Democratic Life." In *Character and Moral Education; A Reader*, edited by J. DeVitis and T. Yu, 167–178. New York: Peter Lang.

Crick, Bernard. 1998. "Advisory Group on Education for Citizenship and the Teaching of Democracy in Schools Qualifications and Curriculum Authority (QCA)." Education for Citizenship and the Teaching of Democracy in Schools, Final Report, September 22.

Crick, Bernard, and Alex Porter, eds. 1978. *Political Education and Political Literacy*. London: Longman.

Ecclestone, Kathryn. 2012. "From Emotional and Psychological Well-Being to Character Education: Challenging Policy Discourses of Behavioural Science and 'Vulnerability'." *Research Papers in Education* 27 (4): 463–480.

Ecclestone, K., and L. Lewis. 2014. "Interventions for Resilience in Educational Settings: Challenging Policy Discourses of Risk and Vulnerability." *Journal of Education Policy* 29 (2): 195–216.

Ferrara, Alessandro. 2012. "Politics at Its Best; Reasons that Move the Imagination." In *The Politics of Imagination*, edited by C. Bottici and B. Challand, 38–54. Abingdon: Birkbeck Law Press.

Goodman, Paul. 1952. *Utopian Essays and Proposals*. New York: Random House.

Grace, Gerald. 2003. "Foreword." In *Education with Character; The Moral Economy of Schooling*, edited by J. Arthur. London: Routledge.

Kristjánsson, Kristján. 2013. "Ten Myths About Character, Virtue and Virtue Education – Plus Three Well-Founded Misgivings." *British Journal of Educational Studies* 61 (3): 269–287.

Kymlicka, Will. 2001. *Politics in the Vernacular: Nationalism, Multiculturalism, and Citizenship*. Oxford: Oxford University Press.

Larmore, Charles. 2013. "What Is Political Philosophy?" *Journal of Moral Philosophy* 10 (3): 276–306.

McAdam, Doug. 1999. *Political Process and the Development of the Black Insurgency, 1930–1970*. Chicago, IL: University of Chicago Press.

Mendus, Susan. 2006. "Saving One's Soul or Founding a State: Morality and Politics." *Philosophia* 34 (3): 233–241.

Miltrany, David. 1975. *The Functional Theory of Politics*. London: Martin Robertson.

Morris, Aldon. 1984. *The Origins of the Civil Rights Movement: Black Communities Organizing for Change*. New York: Free Press.

Rorty, Richard. 1999. *Philosophy and Social Hope*. London: Penguin.

White, Patricia. 1980. "Political Education and Moral Education or Bringing up Children to be Decent Members of Society." *Journal of Moral Education* 9 (3): 147–155.

White, Patricia. 1983. *Beyond Domination*. London: Routledge and Kegan Paul.

White, Patricia. 1996. *Civic Virtues and Public Schooling: Educating Citizens for a Democratic Society*. New York: Teachers College Press.

Williams, Bernard. 2008. *In the Beginning Was the Deed: Realism and Moralism in Political Argument*. Princeton, NJ: Princeton University Press.

Wringe, Colin. 1984. *Democracy, Schooling and Political Education*. Abingdon: Routledge.

Formal criteria for the concept of human flourishing: the first step in defending flourishing as an ideal aim of education

Lynne S. Wolbert, Doret J. de Ruyter and Anders Schinkel

> Human flourishing is the topic of an increasing number of books and articles in educational philosophy. Flourishing should be regarded as an ideal aim of education. If this is defended, the first step should be to elucidate what is meant by flourishing, and what exactly the concept entails. Listing formal criteria can facilitate reflection on the ideal of flourishing as an aim of education. We took Aristotelian *eudaimonia* as a prototype to construct two criteria for the concept of human flourishing: (1) human flourishing is regarded as intrinsically worthwhile and (2) flourishing means 'actualisation of human potential'. The second criterion has three sub-criteria: (2a) flourishing is about a whole life, (2b) it is a 'dynamic state' and (2c) flourishing presupposes there being objective goods.

Introduction

The concept of human flourishing has been gaining popularity in the field of philosophy of education for some time now. Children should be equipped, at home and in schools, to lead *flourishing* lives, instead of or in addition to merely living a *happy* life. De Ruyter (2004, 377) writes that flourishing is a 'common denominator' of what parents hope or wish for their children. Well-known proponents of making human flourishing an overarching aim of education are White (2011; Reiss and White 2013) and Brighouse (2006), amongst many others. Brighouse (2006) urges teachers, policymakers and parents to focus more on what is in the interest of children instead of for example politics or the economy. Both write that children should be broadly educated to be able to live flourishing lives, independent of their contribution to economy.

Virtually all academic writings on human flourishing refer to ancient Greek philosophy, especially to the work of Aristotle. In Aristotelian ethics, the highest good that everything aims at in life, if there is such a thing, is called *eudaimonia*. The concept of *eudaimonia* refers to a state that combines 'doing well, behaving well and faring well' (MacIntyre 1967, 59). *Eudaimonia* has been mostly translated as 'happiness' (according to MacIntyre [1967, 59] a 'bad, but inevitable' translation), but is in contemporary discussion often referred to as human flourishing.[1]

We think that if it is argued that human flourishing should be an ideal aim of education, the first step should be to clarify what we mean by 'human flourishing', and what exactly the concept entails. To gain the clarity we need, it is helpful to look into the roots of human flourishing and consider the relation between human flourishing and Aristotelian *eudaimonia*. Therefore, in what follows we take Aristotelian *eudaimonia* as an exemplar or prototype for the idea of human flourishing. From it we derive two formal criteria. We see that, although Aristotelian *eudaimonia* can be seen as the prototype or exemplar (see Gallie 1956) of human flourishing, and although virtually all conceptions of human flourishing hark back, in one way or another, to Aristotle, some conceptions of human flourishing have diverged so far from Aristotle's conception that they cannot be called eudemonistic or (neo-)Aristotelian. In other words, though formal criteria for the concept of human flourishing are best derived from Aristotle's work, Aristotelian *eudaimonia* itself is just one conception of human flourishing.

Readers should not expect a thorough Aristotelian exegesis. It has not been our main purpose to analyse Aristotle's ethics and argue what *we* think *he* wrote that is important for educational theory. We have looked into the roots of thinking about flourishing as a means to the goal of better understanding the concept of human flourishing, with which we hope to show that 'human flourishing' is not only a better translation of *eudaimonia*, but a substantive concept for which formal criteria can be listed that are independent of Aristotle's and (neo-)Aristotelian ethics.

We are convinced that it is of great importance to first set up a clear framework of the concept of human flourishing, by means of formal criteria, in order to contribute to the quality of substantive discussions about education for human flourishing, diverse as they are. Ideally, the presented framework will function as a tool for these discussions. It is not meant to force agreement on one strict idea of flourishing human beings; for that purpose one would need much more substantive criteria than the formal, open, criteria we present here. It does, however, aim to set limits to too loose a use of the concept of human flourishing. We want to emphasise in this article that the concept of flourishing is being used in various, but connected ways, and we make use both of the history and the current use of the concept to show this connectedness. However, those readers who expect a full elaboration on the importance of embedding the concept of human flourishing in the goals of education will be left unsatisfied. This article should be considered as a prelude to that kind of endeavour. In the last part of the article, we make a start by giving examples of what implications formal criteria for 'human flourishing' can have for educational theory, with which we hope to underline the relevance of our endeavour.

Flourishing in Aristotle's philosophy

In the Nicomachean Ethics, Aristotle aims to elucidate the highest good in human life, 'that at which all things aim'. It is not difficult to establish what that highest good is, since there is general agreement that all things aim at what he calls *eudaimonia*, which is a quite objective matter (Annas 1993, 41). *Eudaimonia* is the most final end, since it is always pursued for itself and never for the sake of something else (Aristotle 2009, 10, 1097b and see criterion 1). *Eudaimonia* has traditionally been translated as 'happiness', but is currently more often translated as 'human flourishing'. It is one thing to establish what the highest good in human life is, but another what eudaimonia consists in, or how one is supposed to live a life filled with it.

The first thing that becomes clear about *eudaimonia* is that it includes both ethics and subjective well-being (see also Perry 1986; MacIntyre 1967; Kristjansson 2007; Haybron 2008). A good life is according to Aristotle both a morally good life and an enjoyable life, a life in which things go well (MacIntyre 1967, 59; Kristjansson 2013, 29). Perhaps this is the reason that many prefer to translate *eudaimonia* as flourishing, instead of happiness, since the use of the word happiness seems to be restricted to subjective well-being in contemporary philosophy (and other disciplines).

In a sense, Aristotle makes an inventory of what men usually do in life to be able to answer what men best should do, in order for them to come in a state of *eudaimonia* (see criterion 2). 'Human good turns out to be activity of the soul exhibiting virtue, and if there are more than one virtue, in accordance with the best and most complete' (Aristotle 2009, 12, 1098a15–20). He adds immediately that this 'activity of the soul' needs to last 'a complete life', because acting virtuously for a moment will not get you a flourishing life; this activity will have to be maintained throughout an entire life (ibid Aristotle and see criterion 2a). Or as Kristjansson (2013, 29) summarises:

> According to Aristotle, by analysing empirically the proper "function" of human beings (just as we analyse the proper function of a good knife or a good field of wheat), we can ascertain that human flourishing consists of the realisation of virtues of thought and character and the fulfilment of other specifically human physical and mental potentialities over a whole course of life.

Virtues are stable 'characteristics of the soul', which show themselves in the action of choosing the right mean between two vices (excess and deficiency), which is always dependent on the situation and the involved person (see also Pakaluk 2006, 385). 'When our desire and our thinking co-operate in the best way, we have moral excellence or virtue' (Wivestad 2008, 314). For example 'courage' is a virtue, balancing between 'rashness' and 'cowardice'; what in some situation is courageous, could be judged rash and irresponsible in another (MacIntyre 1967, 66–67). Human beings need practical wisdom (*phronesis*) or the insights of a practically wise person (*phronimos*) in order to be able to act virtuously; to be able to differentiate rashness from real courage. *Phronesis* is considered an intellectual virtue, which 'binds all the virtues together' (Wivestad 2008, 314); it 'is not just one virtue among others but is rather a necessary ingredient in all the others' (Dunne 1999, 240).

Virtuous activity needs to be trained. Only by performing virtuous activity continually, by emulating how practically wise persons perform virtuous activity, a person can inculcate the habit and become a virtuous man (MacIntyre 1967, 64). Only by practise in finding a 'well-balanced co-operation' between what we desire and what we think we should do, we will incorporate the virtues (Wivestad 2008, 314). This notion of training is characteristic for Aristotle's theory. For Aristotelian *eudaimonia*, and for flourishing in general, a process of development is required (see criterion 2b).

However, virtuous activity is not all there is to it. It is possible, says Aristotle, to be a virtuous person without living a flourishing life, because people need external goods as well (Aristotle 2009, 14, 1099a30–1099b5). It is very difficult, he writes, to 'do noble acts' without the advantages of, for example, 'good birth', social relations, and beauty. People have to have a bit of luck as well in the course of their lives, it seems (see Nussbaum 1986; and see criterion 2c).

So, in order to life a flourishing life, a good life, an *optimal* life, which is a combination of 'faring well, behaving well, and doing well' (MacIntyre 1967, 59), human beings have to learn to become virtuous persons and have to be lucky to lead a prosperous life.

Eudaimonia is not 'a passive end state' (Kristjansson 2013), but an activity. It is what we shall be calling 'a dynamic state' (criterion 2b) later in this article. Perfect *eudaimonia* then is the state of a perfect fit between our desires and that what is the right thing to do in a given situation, or in other words; always desiring the right thing, without 'any counter motivation' being produced (Annas 1993).

The concept of human flourishing: two criteria

In most literature, human flourishing is perceived and put forward *as an ideal aim* of education (see for example Brighouse 2006; Reiss and White 2013; and Nussbaum 2010). We think it is important to pay attention to the ways in which an ideal can be understood, in order to make clearer how the proposed criteria should be understood. Ideally, a human being's life will develop in such a way – and education will contribute to this development – that all of her potential can be actualised, whilst creating a harmonious balance between her potentials and other goods she aims to realise and that she is happy with it too. This is 'picture perfect'; and it represents a conception of perfect flourishing, which is practically unrealisable. A more realistic 'picture' of a flourishing life takes into account that 'life will get in the way'. De Ruyter (2015, 89) writes that 'when one takes into account what people can achieve given their circumstances and abilities, one has a realistic conception of flourishing in mind'. The ideal of perfect flourishing is still being pursued, but one realises that we, human beings, cannot always create the best circumstances for us to flourish, nor are we able to fully optimise all of our abilities (see also Lawrence 1993). And above that, sometimes we just do not succeed in doing our best, or it is simply difficult to decide what the best thing to do would be (when values conflict for example). The ideal of flourishing functions as a regulative ideal to structure our development and give us (high) aims to strive at (see Emmet 1994). But we need not maintain that human beings do not flourish until their lives are perfect, nor that it is 'bad' to not have a perfect life; in fact, it is human. The formal criteria we propose reflect this high goal of perfect flourishing; but it is important to keep in mind that flourishing is a matter of degree, and that the criteria need not be applied so strictly as to demand perfection.

As said before, according to Aristotle we can only judge whether someone has had a flourishing life at the end of that life (Aristotle 2009, 12, 1098a17–19). One the one hand, it makes sense, in reference to the ideal, to attribute flourishing to an entire life. But on the other hand, that is not the only way in which the word flourishing is used in daily life. It is not awkward to speak of 'flourishing children' or to call someone a flourishing human being who is not dead yet (or on her deathbed). Therefore, we think that it is helpful to distinguish between 'a flourishing life' (being the ideal) and the verb 'to flourish' (representing an actual evaluation, e.g. De Ruyter 2007, 2015). A flourishing life refers to the (Aristotelian) ideal of flourishing throughout an entire lifetime while the verb 'to flourish' is used in situations where an evaluation is made about a certain time-slice in someone's life and in which less demanding standards are applied (see De Ruyter 2015, 89). That is why we, for example, can say that a child has a flourishing childhood. This gives her – no doubt – a large advantage for the rest of her life, but does not guarantee a flourishing life; we don't know yet if, and to what degree, this child will be able to fulfil the ideal of a flourishing life throughout the rest of her life. In the last part of this article, we further elaborate on the implications that the ideal of a flourishing life can have for education, but first we clarify the proposed criteria.

We propose two criteria, of which the second criterion has three sub-criteria. Every actual conception of flourishing should meet all five criteria. Other uses of the term (uses that do not meet these criteria) are possible, but fail to capture what is distinctive about flourishing as opposed to for instance happiness. The first criterion is the same as that which Aristotle starts his search with; establishing that man's final end is something that is always pursued for itself and never for the sake of something else (Aristotle 2009, 10, 1097b). Therefore, we propose that flourishing should be perceived as being intrinsically worthwhile. The second criterion is a broad definition of human flourishing; the idea of 'actualising your potential'. Criteria 2a, 2b and 2c are sub criteria, which give further content to this idea of 'actualising your potential'. These criteria have all been derived from Aristotelian *eudaimonia*. However, as has been said in the introduction, from comparing Aristotle with more recent conceptions of human flourishing, we conclude that the formal criteria are broader than the interpretation of and path to human flourishing that Aristotle had in mind, which shows that *eudaimonia* in itself is best considered a conception of human flourishing.

1. Flourishing is intrinsically worthwhile

Human flourishing is perceived as that-for-the-sake-of-which human conduct is done (Rasmussen 1999). It is, in Aristotle's terms, 'complete': while many activities or virtues can be pursued for themselves, we also choose them because we believe that we will be happy if we do so. Flourishing, however, is always chosen for itself and never for the sake of something else (Aristotle 2009, 10, 1097b). Thus, we do not strive to flourish in order to reach some other goal. It is the other way around.

We should add that there are also activities that contribute to a person's flourishing that are not necessarily done *in order* to flourish. For example, when a person prefers spending time and money on eating nice food, he might do that just to enjoy nice food. Or, think of someone who engages in a romantic relationship; she did not do that so she could lead a flourishing life, but because she fell in love. The enjoyment of good food or a loving relationship might be constitutive elements of flourishing, but they were not done *in order to* flourish. Sufficient for the purpose of our formal criteria is therefore to conclude that (a) flourishing is an intrinsic good, and that (b) flourishing is worth striving for, so that (c) flourishing should be perceived as intrinsically worthwhile.

2. The actualisation of the human potential

We state that the core of flourishing is that it focuses on a notion of optimising 'the human being qua human being'; the actualisation of human potential (for instance in Aristotle 2009; Kraut 1979; Rasmussen 1999; De Ruyter 2012; Huta 2013).

When we say someone is flourishing, we mean that someone is functioning at a top-level – an optimal level. This 'top' is agent-relative; how well someone's doing depends on her potential and the possibilities she gets in her life (see also Lawrence 1993), although a certain minimal threshold is defined objectively. If someone is not or barely capable of actualising any potential (because of, for example, congenital disabilities or severe trauma during life), we will not say that they are flourishing human beings. How well someone (who is above this minimal threshold) is doing in *developing towards* that optimal level can also be judged. People can, in that sense, be compared with each other on their level of flourishing, by comparing the progress they have made relative to their own optimum.

De Ruyter (2012, 28) uses the term 'optimiser' for someone who develops herself in an optimal way. Flourishing persons, in her words, are 'persons who have developed (and are still developing) their possibilities to the full' (27). Developing in an optimal way, and in that sense to the full, should not be mistaken for 'getting the most out of something (i.e. your life or a given situation)', a phrase that is popular in our current society. Children are sometimes encouraged to become the 'best', which can be very confusing if the difference between becoming 'the best version of yourself' and 'the best pupil in school' has not been made clear. The notion of 'actualising the human potential' shows that human flourishing is not the same as happiness (in a subjective sense). To feel happy, someone does not have to strive to actualise their potential. For example, the famous character Oblomov from the novel by Gontsjarow (1958) is quite happy living his life doing literally almost nothing, leaving a large part of his potential un-actualised. Unless it is argued that 'doing nothing' is what makes Oblomov the best version of himself he can be, we would not say that he has had a flourishing life.

2a. Life as a whole

To be able to say that someone is flourishing or has flourished, one has to look at her life as a whole (Aristotle 2009; Annas 1993; MacIntyre [1981] 2001). 'Life as a whole' can be interpreted in a temporal sense, as referring to life from birth until death, as we have already referred to previously when we made the distinction between 'a flourishing life' and the verb 'to flourish'.

However, there is still another way in which life as a whole can be interpreted, namely in a holistic sense, as referring to the whole of one's life spheres. This holistic interpretation is crucial for 'flourishing'. A judgement about whether someone is flourishing takes into account all life-spheres. In that sense it is about a whole life, rather than one or some of its parts. For example, when someone is a successful banker, has a booming career and makes a lot of money, but neglects his wife and three children, because he works for over 80 hours a week and is never home, we would presumably not consider him to flourish. We hesitate to attribute 'flourishing' to him, because he neglects a significant part of his life-spheres. He could be happy, though, in the subjective sense of feeling happy. Or, as for example MacIntyre (MacIntyre and Dunne 2002, 10) puts it:

> What is important is to recognise that each life is a single, if complex, narrative of a particular subject, someone whose life is a whole into which the different parts have to be integrated, so that the pursuit of the goods of home and family reinforces the pursuit of the goods of the workplace and vice versa, and so too with the other diverse goods of a particular life. To integrate them is a task, a task rarely, if ever, completed.

In the case of the successful banker there is not enough integration, no balance, because there is neglect; and his wife and children suffer from it.

2b. A dynamic state

Development is characteristic of human flourishing (for instance in Aristotle 2009; Lawrence 1993; Hurka 1999; Kraut 2007; Huta 2011; De Ruyter 2012). Development is necessary to actualise the human potential, because people cannot optimise themselves by pushing a button or drinking a magical potion. Nor can a person develop someone else's potential; it is a personal process (Annas 1993, 37, Haybron 2008, 157). In other words, one has to do something in order to become a flourishing human being. According to Kraut (2007, 140), there is a widely accepted framework for thinking about normal human development, which gives us 'platitudes' that help us determine what is good for us. There is no clear beginning or ending to the process of development. Only when a human being dies, development has ended for that particular human being (at least, for all we know).

We can characterise this process of lifelong development as a sort of 'dynamic state'. A 'state' because flourishing is an attainable state – but it is not a static condition, but characterised by ongoing development, effort to sustain it and striving to improve it. Thus, it is a dynamic state.

2c. Objective goods

It is characteristic of conceptions of human flourishing to acknowledge that there are things that are good for everybody. Some of these objectively good things are constitutive of a flourishing life, for example social relationships, other objective goods are good capacities, the development of which will contribute to the flourishing of human beings, for example *phronesis*, practical wisdom, which Aristotle deems necessary to exercise all other virtues. For our purpose (open, formal criteria), it suffices to say it is a common denominator in most literature on human flourishing that objectively good human capacities are being developed (see for example Hurka 1999; Kraut 2007; Huta 2011; De Ruyter 2012).

Happiness, however, does not need this kind of external judgement about whether something is good or not. Popular conceptions of happiness seem to centre on subjective feelings of well-being only. In conceptions of human flourishing, this is not the case (for example in Aristotle 2009; Anscombe 1958; Hurka 1999; Rasmussen 1999). We do not imply, however, that the concept excludes subjective assessments as part of human flourishing. Several authors argue that human beings do not flourish, unless they themselves know or feel that they do (De Ruyter 2007, 27; but also Aristotle 2009; Rasmussen 1999; De Ruyter 2004; White 2006; Haybron 2008; Griffin 1986). They make a plea for a 'mixed theory', a conception of human flourishing that acknowledges the importance of both objective and subjective goods.

Flourishing in Kant's philosophy

Five formal criteria for 'human flourishing' have been proposed for which Aristotle's *eudaimonia* functioned as a prototype. We have said in the introduction that although *eudaimonia* has been used as an exemplar, it is in itself a conception of human flourishing. In this section, we give an example of a conception of human flourishing that differs a great deal of Aristotle's, namely that of Immanuel Kant.

It has often been argued that Kant had limited or no room for a conception of human flourishing. For example, Hill (1999) writes that Kant's conception of happiness cannot be a conception of human flourishing, because happiness is not an important intrinsic goal of Kant's moral rules, which is a criterion (1) of flourishing. We argue that this explanation is based on the mistake of taking Kant's conception of happiness as a conception of flourishing. A conception of flourishing should not be sought in Kant's ideas on happiness, but in Kant's notion of the highest good, which is his 'final end' and an intrinsically worthwhile good (see criterion 1). For Kant, the highest good conceivable is a combination of moral perfection and (deserved) happiness (*Glückseligkeit*) (MacIntyre [1981] 2001, 85; Stange 1920, 98; Haybron 2008, 36; Denis 2008, 85). This optimal combination of striving for moral perfection and feeling happy, which we recognise in Aristotle, could very well be a conception of human flourishing. Kant has an ultimate goal of conduct in mind, which is some kind of optimal state of being.

Can we really say that this optimal state of being is flourishing, i.e. the actualisation of human potential? Denis (2008, 86) argues, following Engstrom (1996), that the similarities between Aristotelian *eudaimonia* and Kant's highest good suggest at least a 'rough' conception of human flourishing. The following discussion confirms this suggestion. We have already shown that criterion 1 has been fulfilled, since perceiving flourishing as intrinsically worthwhile has been our starting point.

Kant puts great emphasis on development in his description of the highest good 'of a possible world' (Denis 2008). He sees the full development of characteristic human capacities (see Kraut 2007, 140) as our 'destiny' and as necessary for realising a state of optimal being in the whole world (Denis 2008, 91). Kant sees some kind of threshold for human beings to reach in order to flourish, yet is at the same time convinced that human beings are always on their way towards that threshold, and that this dynamic is ongoing, from generation to generation (criterion 2b) (Kant 1996). He questions whether this optimal state of being can ever be reached. He devotes several comments to the practical possibility of the highest good, but he seems to conclude that it is rather impossible. It can only be found in 'endless progress' towards it (Kant 1996, 102).

The most comprehensive conception of flourishing in Kant's writings is informed by his account of duties to oneself (Denis 2008, 97). This is because many of our duties require us to do things in order to become the best version of ourselves we can be. 'We are to consider ourselves as moral beings who are human beings, with specifically human drives and capacities; to cultivate our innate capacities; and to bring our emotions into some measure of harmony with reason' (97). Denis shows that Kant had a view on development that focused on the human being qua human being, on actualising the human potential whilst fulfilling our duties (see criterion 2).

We have not yet discussed the remaining criteria of (2a) judging the flourishing life as a whole and (2c) the necessity of referring to objective goods. The criterion of objective goods is easily met. In the very first lines of the Critique of Practical Reason, Kant explains the difference between the maxims of someone's will, which are subjective, and the practical laws, which are their objective counterpart (Kant 1996, 17). Moral perfection, as part of Kant's conception of flourishing, presupposes obedience to these objective practical laws, which makes them a necessary part of his conception of flourishing as well.

It is difficult to explicitly clarify Kant's notion of 'life as a whole' on the basis of his writings. It is apparent from Kant's writings on morality that moral perfection should be sought after in all life-spheres. It is not good enough to just be morally good 'at home'. However, there is more to life than morality, as Kant too acknowledges. Whether or not one should flourish in the (non-moral) life 'as a whole', is not explicitly elucidated by him. We think that a holistic perspective in Kant's work is most clearly found in his thoughts on the full development of human capacities, assuming that full development means development in all life-spheres (Denis 2008, 91).

We conclude that Kant's notion of the highest good meets the five criteria and thus can be called a conception of human flourishing. There are similarities with Aristotelian *eudaimonia*, but there is also an important difference. Happiness remains conceptually distinct from virtue within the highest good (Denis 2008, 85). Kant thought they were 'extremely heterogeneous concepts' (Kant 1996, 93), whereas in *eudaimonia* they are intertwined. It is very important for Kant's moral theory that happiness is not part of moral goodness, because he claims that it should not be the ultimate goal of moral perfection. A person does not strive for moral perfection in order to become happy (99–100). Another difference noted by for instance Denis and Conly is that in Kant's ethics there is more attention for the differences in desires, temperaments and situations of different people, which leads to great differences in what their flourishing lives might look like (Denis 2008, 108). Although Aristotle also emphasises the individuality of flourishing, his view on 'the flourishing life' was more 'standardised' than Kant's (Denis 2008, 98; Conly 1988).

Implications for educational theory: conclusion

Two formal criteria of 'human flourishing' have been proposed: First, flourishing should be perceived as intrinsically worthwhile (1). Second, human flourishing means 'the actualisation of human potential' (2), which entails that to be able to say that someone flourishes, we argue that one has to look at her life as a whole in a holistic sense (2a); that in order to actualise human potential a continuous developmental process is required, which shows that flourishing is perceived as a 'dynamic state' (2b); and that there is a necessary reference to objective goods, in the sense that there are human capacities that are objectively good for a person as well as certain external goods people need in order to live well (2c). Aristotelian *eudaimonia* was used as an exemplar for these criteria, but it was also shown to be just one conception of human flourishing. Using Kant's work as an example, we have shown that the concept is wider, and allows for various conceptions.

Now, what does this mean for flourishing as an aim of education? It seems that 'human flourishing' as an overarching aim of education has been proposed out of discontent with the current school system (see Brighouse 2006; Reiss and White 2013). Philosophers of education have actually been asking themselves the same question as Aristotle did: what is *really important* in life? And if 'leading a flourishing life' is the answer, what then is *really important* to teach our children? Surely not (only) how to get a well-paying job and be 'profitable' to our society (Nussbaum 2010). We should equip our children so that they can contribute to society in a meaningful way and get the best chance of a leading a flourishing life.

We think that listing formal criteria for the concept of human flourishing can contribute to clarifying why *flourishing* is being defended as an ideal aim of education and not something else. We suspect that 'flourishing' is not an arbitrary word-choice, that philosophers of education have reasons to use it, and we believe it should not be chosen casually. We fear that without some limits (on a formal level) the concept of flourishing might devaluate until it is used indiscriminately. The reasons for using this particular concept would then evaporate, and flourishing would become 'just another' popular phrase to agitate against the current aims of education. Listing formal criteria, as we have attempted to do in this article, can facilitate reflection on conceptions of human flourishing, it might elucidate to which aspects conceptions are similar and where they differ, and third, as said, it can be a tool to discriminate between flourishing and related terms, such as (subjective) well-being and happiness.

For example; take criterion 1; 'flourishing is intrinsically worthwhile'. Sometimes well-being and flourishing are both used in the same context, suggesting that they can be used interchangeably (for example in White 2011; Keyes 2007; Fredrickson and Losada 2005; Seligman et al. 2009). White uses the word 'well-being' as the overarching aim of education in his 2011 book. He proposes that 'well-being' is an ideal aim that is intrinsically worthwhile, and although it is sometimes a bit confusing for the reader that besides 'well-being' White uses 'flourishing' and 'a flourishing life' as well, in principle 'well-being' and 'flourishing' can indeed be used interchangeably (assuming for now that the other criteria are also met). However, Seligman et al. (2009, 302) argue not only that well-being 'can and should be taught' in schools, but also that the well-being of children can enhance their school performances. In the description of criterion 1, we have written that flourishing is intrinsically worthwhile, and is not pursued in order to reach some other goal. Rather, it is typical of flourishing that it is the other way around. Therefore, it is likely that Seligman et al. mean 'subjective well-being' here (which might indeed contribute to better performances at school), and that in this case well-being and flourishing cannot be used interchangeably.

Due to the confines of this article, we are only able to hint in the direction of an answer to why *flourishing* is being defended as an aim of education, but one thing that we think has become clear is that striving for a flourishing life is a life long journey in which one keeps asking what might bring out the best of oneself. As we have written, flourishing is characterised by ongoing development, striving and effort to sustain it. We think that one of the reasons of using the concept of flourishing as an aim of education is the emphasis on development and the development of objectively good capacities. This appeals to a strong intuition of educators to want for children that 'they make something out of their life'. As said before, this distinguishes flourishing from currently popular conceptions of happiness that seem only to require that people 'feel good' about what they are doing, whatever it is that they are doing. Another, related, reason might be that 'flourishing' inevitably puts an ethical question in the centre of educational theory by asking what those 'good' capacities could be, and who can judge whether they are really 'good'.

But, is this not asking too much of children, risking to turn them into stressful, unhappy overachievers? Should we not just try to equip children to have a nice life, and focus on being satisfied with whatever it is that happens to them in life (be *happy* with it)? We don't think so. We believe it is worth defending flourishing as an aim of education, because we do think it important for both educators and children to have high aims, so that educators will strive to create the optimal conditions for children and for children to get the best chance to develop themselves towards the ideal of an optimal life. We side with Emmet (1994), where she argues that regulative ideals, impossible as they may seem or are to realise, give us direction in life (see for instance Emmet 1994; Frankfurt 1999; De Ruyter 2007, on the importance of ideals). However, we do understand that the open, formal criteria that we have proposed might invoke connotations of competitiveness or images of over-achieving, performance-oriented children (and educators). We can only stress once more that flourishing is a matter of degree, and that it is important to keep in mind the distinction between the ideal of flourishing and the expectations with regard to what human beings can realise – the criteria need not be applied so strictly to a 'real' life as to demand perfection. Moreover, flourishing is not about winning, or becoming better than the rest. Flourishing is about self-knowledge, making good choices and creating a balance in a 'whole' life.

Disclosure statement
No potential conflict of interest was reported by the authors.

Note
1. There is a lot of discussion about whether *eudaimonia* 'should' be translated as happiness or human flourishing. Annas (1993) and Kraut (1979), among others, translate eudaimonia as 'happiness'. We will not embark on this discussion here, since our interest is in the use of the concept of human flourishing. We think that it is important to bear in mind the strong subjective connotations happiness has in our current society, and recognise that our current ideas about happiness are miles away from Aristotle's (De Ruyter 2004; Haybron 2008). It is therefore at least 'practical' to investigate the concept of human flourishing instead of happiness, because flourishing has less strong associations in temporary debate.

References
Annas, J. 1993. *The Morality of Happiness*. New York: Oxford University Press.
Anscombe, G. E. M. 1958. "Modern Moral Philosophy." *Philosophy* 33 (124): 1–19.
Aristotle. 2009. *The Nicomachean Ethics*. Translated by David Ross and edited by Lesley Brown. Oxford: Oxford University Press.
Brighouse, H. 2006. *On Education*. London: Routledge.
Conly, S. 1988. "Flourishing and the Failure of the Ethics of Virtue." *Midwest Studies in Philosophy* XIII: 83–96.
De Ruyter, D. J. 2004. "Pottering the Garden? On Human Flourishing and Education." *British Journal of Educational Studies* 52 (4): 377–389.
De Ruyter, D. J. 2007. "Ideals, Education, and Happy Flourishing." *Educational Theory* 57 (1): 23–35.
De Ruyter, D. J. 2012. "On Optimal Development and Becoming an Optimiser." *Journal of Philosophy of Education* 46 (1): 25–41.
De Ruyter, D. J. 2015. "Well-Being and Education." In *Education, Philosophy and Well-Being. New Perspectives on the Work of John White*, edited by J. Suissa, C. Winstanly, and R. Marples, 84–98. Oxon: Routledge.
Denis, L. 2008. "Individual and Collective Flourishing in Kant's Philosophy." *Kantian Review* 13 (1): 82–115.
Dunne, J. 1999. "Virtue, *Phronesis*, and Learning." In *Virtue Ethics and Moral Education*, edited by D. Carr and J. Steutel, 49–63. London: Routledge.
Emmet, D. 1994. *The Role of the Unrealisable*. London: The Macmillan Press Ltd.
Engstrom, S. 1996. "Happiness and the Highest Good in Aristotle and Kant." In *Aristotle, Kant, and the Stoics. Rethinking Happiness and Duty*, edited by S. Engstrom and J. Whiting, 102–140. Cambridge: Cambridge University Press.
Frankfurt, H. G. 1999. *Neccesity, Volition and Love*. Cambridge: Cambridge University Press.
Fredrickson, B. L., and M. F. Losada. 2005. "Positive Affect and the Complex Dynamics of Human Flourishing." *American Psychologist* 60 (7): 678–686.
Gallie, W. B. 1956. "Essentially Contested Concepts." *Proceedings of the Aristotelian Society* 56: 167–198.
Gontsjarow, I. A. 1958. *Oblomov*. Translated by Wils Huisman. Amsterdam: G.A. van Oorschot.
Griffin, J. 1986. *Well-Being. Its Meaning, Measurement and Moral Importance*. Oxford: Clarendon Press.
Haybron, D. M. 2008. *The Pursuit of Unhappiness*. New York: Oxford University Press.
Hill, T. E. 1999. "Happiness and Human Flourishing in Kant's Ethics." In *Human Flourishing*, edited by E. Frankel Paul, F. D. Miller, and J. Paul, 143–175. Cambridge: Cambridge University Press.
Hurka, T. 1999. "The Three Faces of Flourishing." In *Human Flourishing*, edited by E. Frankel Paul, F. D. Miller, and J. Paul, 44–71. Cambridge: Cambridge University Press.

Huta, V. 2011. "Linking Peoples' Pursuit of Eudaimonia and Hedonia with Characteristics of Their Parents: Parenting Styles, Verbally Endorsed Values, and Role Modelling." *Journal of Happiness Studies* 2012 (13): 47–61.

Huta, V. 2013. "Eudaimonia." In *Oxford Handbook of Happiness*, edited by S. David, I. Boniwell, and A. C. Ayers, 201–213, chapter 15. Oxford: Oxford University Press.

Kant, I. 1996. *Critique of Practical Reason.* Translated and edited by Mary J. Gregor. Cambridge: Cambridge University Press.

Keyes, L. M. 2007. "Promoting and Protecting Mental Health as Flourishing. A Complementary Strategy for Improving National Mental Health." *American Psychologist* 62 (2): 95–108.

Kraut, R. 1979. "Two Conceptions of Happiness." *The Philosophical Review* 88 (2): 167–197.

Kraut, R. 2007. *What Is Good and Why?* Cambridge: Harvard University Press.

Kristjansson, K. 2007. *Aristotle, Emotions, and Education.* Aldershot: Ashgate Publishing Limited.

Kristjansson, K. 2013. *Virtues and Vices in Positive Psychology.* New York: Cambridge University Press.

Lawrence, G. 1993. "Aristotle and the Ideal Life." *The Philosophical Review* 102 (1): 1–34.

MacIntyre, A. 1967. *A Short History of Ethics.* London: Routledge & Kegan Paul plc.

MacIntyre, A. [1981] 2001. *After Virtue.* Notre Dame: University of Notre Dame Press.

MacIntyre, A., and J. Dunne. 2002. "Alaisdair MacIntyre on Education: In Dialogue with Joseph Dunne." *Journal of Philosophy of Education* 36 (1): 1–19.

Nussbaum, M. C. 1986. *The Fragility of Goodness: Luck and Ethics in Greek Tragedy and Philosophy.* Cambridge: Cambridge University press.

Nussbaum, M. C. 2010. *Not for Profit.* Princeton, NJ: Princeton University Press.

Pakaluk, M. 2006. "Aristotle's Ethics." In *A Companion to Ancient Philosophy*, edited by M. L. Gill and P. Pellegrin, 374–392. Oxford: Blackwell Publishing.

Perry, M. J. 1986. "Moral Knowledge, Moral Reasoning, Moral Relativism: A Naturalist Perspective." *Georgia Law Review* 20: 995–1075.

Rasmussen, D. B. 1999. "Human Flourishing and the Appeal to Human Nature." In *Human Flourishing*, edited by E. Frankel Paul, F. D. Miller, and J. Paul, 1–43. Cambridge: Cambridge University Press.

Reiss, M. J., and J. White. 2013. *An Aims-Based Curriculum. The Significance of Human Flourishing for Schools.* London: Institute of Education Press.

Seligman, M. E. P., R. M. Ernst, J. Gillham, K. Reivich, and M. Linkins. 2009. "Positive Education: Positive Psychology and Classroom Interventions." *Oxford Review of Education* 35 (3): 293–311.

Stange, C. 1920. *Die Ethik Kants. Zur Einführung in die Kritik der praktischen Vernunft* [Kantian ethics. An introduction to the Critique of Practical Reasoning]. Leipzig: Dieterich'sche Verlagsbuchhandlung.

White, J. 2006. "Autonomy, Human Flourishing and the Curriculum." *Journal of Philosophy of Education* 40 (3): 381–390.

White, J. 2011. *Exploring Well-Being in Schools: A Guide to Making Children's Lives More Fulfilling.* London: Routledge.

Wivestad, S. M. 2008. "The Educational Challenges of *Agape* and *Phronesis*." *Journal of Philosophy of Education* 42 (2): 307–324.

Index

Note: **Boldface** page numbers refers to figures and tables, n denotes endnotes

academic advising and research 57–9
'actualising your potential' 122
aesthetic judgment and cultural criticism: Cavell's idea of chance 97–100; finding perfect pitch 102–3; freedom and control 96–7; music theory and meaning-making 100–2
Agamben, Giorgio 53–4
Amerasians in Okinawa: language education, absence of 77–8; Montessori's model of peace education 73–4; political dynamics 75–6; racism and sexism 76; schooling and education 75
American Psychological Association 111
Aristotle's philosophy, human flourishing in 119–21
'art as experience' 97–8

basic school education 80
Bauman, Zygmunt 23
Bennett, Tom 33
Beyond Liberal Education 28
Bildung 7–10; alterity and withdrawal 11–13; notion of 4, 13; as regime of individualization 10–11
Bildungspläne 6
Blue Labour 33–4
Bowers, C.A. 29–31
Boyd, Dwight 106–9
British postliberalism 32
Bruns, Gerald L. 101
Bultmann, Rudolph 25
Butler, Judith 4, 5

Cage, John 97, 100–2
Callan, Eamonn 109
camera ethnography 20; material 6, 14n8; video-DVD 6–7

Cavell, Stanley 17, 20; idea of chance 97–100; music theory and meaning-making 100–2
CBT *see* cognitive behavioural therapy
Chandler, David 31
character education 105–6; criticism of 106–8; political absence in 111–14
Character Inquiry 106
childrearing and education, epistemic empathy in 61–70
children, loss of peace education 74–7
Chrétien, Jean-Louis 51–2
Chua, Amy 65–6
Claim of Reason, The (Cavell) 102
cognitive behavioural therapy (CBT) 111
Covaleskie, John 114
Crick, Bernard 112

De la Fatigue (Chrétien) 51
Deleuze, Gilles 54–7
Department of Defense Dependents Schools (DoDDS) 75, 77
depression 59n3, 60n5
Dewey, John 29, 81, 96
documentation folders 8–9, **9**
DoDDS *see* Department of Defense Dependents Schools
dynamic state, human flourishing 123–4

early childhood education: constitution 5–7; framework of 3; institutions 8; practices of observation 6–7; responsibility 3
Ecclestone, Kathryn 105, 107, 108, 111
educational morphology 85
educational theory, implications for 126–7
educational world 5
Either-Ors 96, 97
Elements of a Post-Liberal Theory of Education (Bowers) 29
Emersonian perfectionism 103
empathy and sympathy 62–4
epistemic closure 64

INDEX

epistemic empathy 70n3; in childrearing and education 65–7; idea of 64–5; limitations 68–70; and modelling 67–8
ethnographic research 6
eudaimonia 118–20, 128n1
Exhausted, The (Deleuze) 54
exhaustion: positive power of 54–7; potentiality and 53–4; tiredness and 50–2, 57–9
Experience and Education (Dewey) 96

fair-mindedness 65–6, 69
family heritage 40–2
family history 46
family memory: gratitude, innovation, and responsibility 46; intergenerational dynamics 39–40; overview of 36–8; parents' memory 44–5; reflection 42–4; research project 47n2; reviviscence 42–3; transition to parenthood 40–2; transmission 37–9, 42–3
family tree 41
fast learning process 84–5; future generation 88–9; gathering information 91–2; material invention 85–6; natural order 86; school experience 89–90; suspension, profanation and attention 87–8; taming/reinventing school 92–4; time of delay 87
fatigue society 49
fatigue university 49–59
Feinberg, Walter 78–9
Ferrara, Alessandro 115

Germany, early education in 3
Goodman, Paul 114

Hauerwas, Stanley 25
Hebenstreit-Müller, Sabine 6
Hirsch, E.D. 24
Hirst, Paul 28
human flourishing 118–19; in Aristotle's philosophy 119–21; educational theory, implications for 126–7; human potential, actualisation of 122–4; 'intrinsically worthwhile' 122; in Kant's philosophy 124–6; overview of 121–2
Humboldt, Wilhelm von 11

ICT *see* information and communication technologies
individualization, *Bildung* regime of 10–11
information and communication technologies (ICT) 93
INPE Conference Special Issue 1–2
intensive parenting 46
intergenerational relationships 38–40
Isocrates' gift of time 91

Japanese public schools 75
Jones, Harrison 112
Jubilee Centre for Character and Values 107

Kant's philosophy, human flourishing in 124–6
King, Martin Luther 111
Knightly Virtues, The 113, 115n2
Koch, Sandra 8, 10, 14n4, 14n11
Krenek, Ernst 98
Kristjánsson, Kristján 113–14

language education 77–8, 80
learning environment 92–3
Liberal Education 33
liberalism 31–4
Liberalism and Social Action or of Democracy and Education (Dewey) 29
Liberal Rationalism 26
liberal theology 25, 27
Lickona, Thomas 106
'life as a whole' concept 123

Masschelein, Jan 4, 10–12, 20–1
McCormack, Gavan 77
McLaughlin, Terry 26–8
memory transmission 37–9, 42–3
Mendus, Susan 109
Merrick, Michael 33
mindfulness 64–5, 70n5
modern school system 80
Mohn, Bina Elisabeth 6–7, **7, 8,** 14n7
Montessori, Maria 73–4, 79, 82
Moses, Stéphane 89
Murai, Minoru 79–81
Music of Changes (Cage) 100
music theory and meaning-making 100–2

Nagel, Thomas 61–2
Nebe, Gesine 8, 10, 14n11
Need for a Recovery of Philosophy, The (Dewey) 24
New Humanities of liberal education 31
Nietzsche, Friedrich 4, 51–2
Norimatsu, Satoko Oka 77

objective goods, human flourishing 124
observation, practice of **7, 8**
Okinawa (Japan), Amerasians in *see* Amerasians in Okinawa
open-mindedness 65–6, 69
'our children are not our children' 88
Oxford Dictionary of English 51, 94n3

parent–child relationship 39, 45
parenthood, transition to 40–2

INDEX

parents' diaries 42, 45
parents' memory 44–5
Parks, Rosa 113
peace education: absence for children 74–7; educational and political context 78–81; educational issues faced by Amerasians 73–4; language education 77–8; Montessori's model of 73–4, 79, 82
Penn Resiliency Program 111
philosophy of education 1, 17–21, 23, 27; analysis 18; definition 18; objective man 19
Pitch of Philosophy, A (Cavell) 102
political disappearance: absence in character education 111–14; imagination of 114–15; and moral philosophy 108–11
political philosophy 109
Positive Education Summit 107
post-humanism 18
postliberal education 23–7; testing 27–31; theology 24–6
Post-Liberalism: Studies in Political Thought (Gray) 30
potentiality and exhaustion 53–4
practice theory 5
problematisation of relationships 39
Psychic Life Of Power, The (Butler) 5

racism and sexism 76
rational-autonomy strain in liberal theory 27
reenactive empathy 64
reflection and family memory 42–4
responsibility principle 46

return of religion 25
reviviscence 42–3
Richmond, Oliver 31
Ricken, Norbert 4, 10–12, 20–1

Schatzki, Theodore R. 4, 5
Schiller, Friedrich 11
school pedagogy 91
Senses of Walden, The (Cavell) 101
social practices 5; activities and arrangement in 5; analysis of 12; theories of 5
Spieker, Ben 108
Standish, Paul 77–8
Stein, Edith 63
Steutel, Jan 108
Stiegler, Bernard 86
sympathy, empathy and 62–4

Theory of *Halbbildung* 11
Thompson, Christiane 17–21
Thoreau, Henry D. 100–2
tiredness and exhaustion 50–2, 57–9, 59n4
Todd, Sharon 1–2
transmission and family memory 42–3

UK Resilience Programme 111

valuing relations 40

Warburg, Aby 60n5
White, Patricia 113
Williams, Bernard 109
Wittgenstein, Ludwig 17, 21, 26